CW00482694

# DESEGREGATION
## IN
## BOSTON AND BUFFALO

SUNY Series in Afro-American Studies
John Howard and Robert C. Smith, Editors

# DESEGREGATION
## IN
## BOSTON AND BUFFALO

## The Influence of Local Leaders

## STEVEN J. L. TAYLOR

*State University of New York Press*

Published by
State University of New York Press, Albany

For Information, address State University of New York Press, State University Plaza, Albany, N.Y., 12246

Production by Diane Ganeles
Marketing by Anne Valentine

Library of Congress Cataloging-in-Publication Data

Taylor, Steven J. L., 1958-
   Desegregation in Boston and Buffalo : the influence of local
leaders / Steven J. L. Taylor
      p.  cm.—(SUNY series in Afro-American studies)
   Includes bibliographical references and index.
   ISBN 0-7914-3919-4 (hc : alk. paper). —ISBN (invalid)
0-7914-3920-4 (pbk. : alk. paper)
   1. School integration—Massachusetts—Boston—History.   2. School
integration—New York (State)—Buffalo—History.   3. Busing for
school integration—Massachusetts—Boston—History.   4. Busing for
school integration—New York (State)—Buffalo—History.   5. Boston
(Mass.)—Politics and government.   6. Buffalo (N.Y.)—Politics and
government.   I. Title.   II. Series.
LC214.23.B67T396   1998
379.2'63'0974461—dc21                                        97-50230
                                                                  CIP

10  9  8  7  6  5  4  3  2  1

# Contents

# Tables

# Figures

# Acknowledgments

There are literally hundreds of persons who are directly responsible for my completing this project. I do not have the space and time to mention all of them, but I am most appreciative of the assistance that they have provided me. I must, however, name those professors at the University of Minnesota who guided me through every step of my research. From the Department of Political Science, I received the priceless assistance of Virginia Gray, William Flanigan, and August Nimtz; I was also tremendously assisted by Ronald Aminzade of the Department of Sociology and John Wright of the Department of Afro-American Studies. I am also most grateful to Gary Orfield of Harvard University. The assistance of these six professors combined helped me through one of the most challenging endeavors in my life. I am also grateful to the School of Public Affairs at American University for providing me with funding in the final stages of the writing of this book.

My research was made possible by the 65 community leaders from Boston, Massachusetts and Buffalo, New York, who provided me with interviews. Their anecdotes, lessons, and insight were essential for both this project and future research projects that I intend to undertake. A special thanks goes out to those unsung heroes and *she*roes in both cities, such as Maurice Gillen in Boston and Yvonne Hargrave in Buffalo.

My ultimate gratitude goes to my Lord and Savior Jesus Christ for giving me the health, strength, and emotional and spiritual endurance to complete this project. By guiding me to its completion, He has demonstrated the truth of the biblical verse that says, "With God, all things are possible." (Matthew 19:26)

# CHAPTER ONE

◻

# Introduction

## Race as a Central Issue in U.S. Politics

At the beginning of the twentieth century, African-American sociologist W. E. B. DuBois wrote that "The problem of the twentieth century is the problem of the color-line,—the relation of the darker to the lighter races of men in Asia and Africa, in America and the islands of the sea."[1]

DuBois' prediction came true in the U.S. during the second half of the twentieth century. The ascension of the race issue to national prominence came during the 1950s and 1960s when African-Americans won court and legislative battles against segregation in education, public accommodations, and housing. It was the first of these areas, education, that was perhaps the most controversial. In the 1954 *Brown vs. Board of Education of Topeka* decision, the U.S. Supreme Court unanimously ruled that segregation in public education was in violation of the fourteenth amendment of the U.S. Constitution, and thus illegal. This ruling invalidated laws in the southern and border states which required blacks and whites to attend separate schools. For the first 15 years after the *Brown* decision, action against desegregation in public education was largely confined to those states that had mandated separate schools, the southern and border states. In these states it was easiest to prove that there had been intentional segregation of the schools. In the 1970s, however, cases arose challenging non-southern school districts for intentionally segregating their public schools, even in the absence of laws mandating segregation. In many cases where the districts were found liable, busing was ordered as a remedy for past intentional segregation. This generated a great deal of opposition, and injected race into the political debate in localities where the issue had previously been sublimated.

Of those political issues with a strong racial content, very few have inflamed the public more than school desegregation, particularly when it is attempted in the form of busing. For many individuals, advocacy of busing represents an "extremism" of the civil rights movement. Persons who had no opposition to the desegregation of the armed forces, to the elimination of barriers in the use of public facilities, and who supported some aspects of the *Brown decision* have drawn the line when desegregation mandates the transportation of students from one neighborhood to another. Even many dedicated liberals view "forced busing" as beyond acceptable limits of integration.

The controversy over mandatory busing was so strong that for a time it became a major issue in national elections. Alabama Governor George Wallace made it a central issue in the 1972 and 1976 Democratic primaries, while one-time presidential front-runner Senator Henry M. Jackson (D-Wash) joined the anti-busing bandwagon in 1976. Since the late 1970s and 1980s busing shared the distinction with abortion, a balanced budget, and the American flag as the subjects of proposed amendments to the U.S. Constitution. The fact that there was an impetus to constitutionally ban forced busing attests to its salience as a political issue. This salience is due to the racial component of the controversy over busing. The increasing polarization over racial issues renders unpopular decisions to desegregate public schools, particularly when the methods to desegregate go beyond what many consider the boundaries of acceptability.

Orders mandating busing, as well as those imposing affirmative action remedies, are measures where courts have moved beyond mandating that municipalities merely cease discriminatory practices in the present. Here municipalities are required to address *past* discrimination. When such remedies are imposed, localities without a history of laws mandating segregation, and where racial issues had not previously dominated political discussion, suddenly become the battleground of disputes over political issues closely related to race. This study looks at two localities where court-ordered busing and the mere threat of busing presented tough challenges to the local political leadership, and how the different actions of the local leadership led to very different outcomes when school desegregation was ordered by the federal courts.

When examining court-ordered desegregation of public schools in the United States, the most infamous cases are those of the southern city of Little Rock, Arkansas and the northeastern city of Boston,

Massachusetts. It is the latter case that is a major focus in this study. Boston's experience with school desegregation can be regarded as a "worst-case" scenario. Violence plagued some of Boston's public high schools from the very first day of the implementation of the desegregation order in September 1974. As the school year progressed, the violence reached crisis proportions, necessitating the involvement of state law enforcement officials. The violence took the form of stonings of buses, several stabbings, and racial brawls in a few of the high schools. There was also racial violence outside of the school in some of the neighborhoods affected by the court order. The violence was at such a level that the Boston situation received worldwide press coverage, and the city was developing a national reputation for racial intolerance. Moreover, Boston had to cope with the costs of increased law enforcement and a temporary acceleration of white flight from the city.

While Boston was going through its desegregation crisis, a federal court ordered the desegregation of the public schools of the nearby city of Buffalo, New York. Buffalo is the other focus of this study. Buffalo did not encounter the problems that Boston encountered, and those few scholars who are familiar with this city's case might regard it as a "best case" scenario. The first phase of Buffalo's desegregation program began in 1976. Unlike Boston, in Buffalo there were no reported incidents of violence. In 1977 the second phase saw the introduction of specialized "magnet schools" in the black neighborhoods of Buffalo, which resulted in the voluntary movement of many white students to inner-city schools that were previously predominantly black. A third phase, implemented in 1980 and 1981, involved the forced busing of large numbers of white students into black neighborhoods. Again there were no reported incidents of violence, nor was there an acceleration of white flight from the public schools, as had been the case in Boston.

This study explores the factors that would lead to either success or failure when a controversial measure such as school desegregation is implemented, with a primary focus on the actions of the local leadership. It is a comparative study that looks at two cities, Boston and Buffalo, which share many similarities in matters related to school desegregation.

## Similarities Between Boston and Buffalo

Boston and Buffalo are similar on seven key dimensions that are relevant to the issue of school desegregation. These are (1) geographic location, (2) size of the city, (3) partisanship, (4) religion and ethnicity, (5) black proportion of the total population, (6) segregation of housing patterns, and (7) the development of the school desegregation cases. As for geographic location, both cities are located in the Northeast, in neighboring states, and they are less than 500 miles apart from each other. They are also both mid-sized cities. In the 1970 U.S. Census (the last before the cities began desegregating their schools), Buffalo's population was 458,000, and Boston's was 628,000.[2]

Demographically speaking there are many similarities between the two cities. Both cities were overwhelmingly Democratic in both voter registration and elected representation. The Democratic superiority in the two cities is directly related to their ethnodemographic similarities. Both Buffalo and Boston have large white ethnic populations and Roman Catholic majorities. South Boston shares similarities with South Buffalo.[3] Both are working class Irish communities with their share of very old housing. Buffalo's predominantly Italian West Side community is similar in many ways to Boston's North End and East Boston. Buffalo, however, has a much higher proportion of East Europeans, mainly Poles, but this ethnic community shares many of the same demographic characteristics as the other ethnic groups.

There are similarities in the black populations of the two cities. Prior to World War II the black populations in both cities were relatively small, and they were based in small neighborhoods in close proximity to the central business districts. In Boston the center of the black community was in the centrally located South End, while in Buffalo it was in the Ellicott District of downtown. After the War the black communities in the two cities branched out further. In Boston the black community stretched into Roxbury during the 1940s through the 1950s, then southward into North Dorchester during the late 1960s, then throughout the 1970s it extended further south into Mattapan. In Buffalo it extended north into the Masten District in the late 1940s through the early 1960s, then eastward into the Fillmore District in the late 1960s through the mid-1970s, then north into the University District from the late 1970s on. In both cities, as the black population expanded, it remained rigidly segregated. By the time the school desegregation cases went to court, Boston's black population was 16 percent of the total, and Buffalo's non-white population was 21 percent of the total. In the public schools, whites were 54 percent of Boston's students, and 61 percent of Buffalo's students.[4] The increase in the number of blacks over the decades did little to decrease the racial segregation of the housing patterns. These segregated housing patterns led to segregated schools, particularly in the elementary and intermediate levels.

In both Boston and Buffalo the perception during the 1960s and early 1970s was that the state governments could impose remedies to satisfy the black parents in their struggle against city governments. Both Massachusetts and New York were reputed to be liberal states whose governments were not hostile toward civil rights. These states' governors during the late 1960s and early 1970s were liberal Republican patricians who had expressed some support for civil rights. Moreover, the state legislatures were considered to be liberal.

Despite the liberalism of the state governments, however, they did not grant relief to those who were advocating the desegregation of the urban public school systems. Only token measures were adopted by both states, measures the states later attempted to rescind. In 1965 the Massachusetts state legislature passed the "Racial Imbalance Act," which mandated that the school districts of Boston, Springfield, and Cambridge make attempts to address the issue of racial imbalance. This law exempted the suburban school districts and placed the burden solely on the three large urban districts, those with the largest number of blacks. Nine years later the legislature reversed itself and struck down the Act. This latter move was vetoed by Governor Frank Sargent, who favored his own plan of circumventing the Act.

Simultaneously the Buffalo school system was given mild directives by the state government to address the problem of racial imbalance. In 1965 the city was ordered to begin taking steps to desegregate the schools, but desegregation moved at such a slow pace that in 1972 the New York State Commissioner of Education ordered the Buffalo Board of Education to implement a desegregation plan that would include busing. The state legislature responded by passing a bill outlawing busing for the purpose of achieving school desegregation.

In both cities it became apparent that the only recourse available to the black community was the federal courts, whose judges were appointed for life and thus spared from political retribution by hostile white voters. The federal district courts ruled in favor of the plaintiffs in both cities and mandated busing as a means to ensure school desegregation. While these decisions may have been satisfactory to the plaintiffs, the constituents represented by the defendants saw this as a further erosion of their democratic rights. The remedy mandated by the courts was quite in line with the U.S. Constitution, but it was not perceived as legitimate by opponents because it was not supported by persons who were elected into office. What made desegregation unpalatable to many was that in both cities busing was mandated as a means to remedy racial imbalance. This is a measure that would break the insularity of the ethnic enclaves. The courts' argument that busing would serve to combat discrimination in the public schools is not an argument that was well received by white ethnics. Many in the working class ethnic communities were indifferent because they did not believe that African-Americans were severely discriminated against or that there was a need for federal remediation. Most of the affected ethnic neighborhoods were poor neighborhoods with many residents who were unlikely to see themselves as being better off than blacks. They too historically suffered from discrimination, and many in these communities were not unfamiliar with poverty. Because of their lack of interaction with blacks, they were totally unaware of the fact that their children's schools, underfacilitated as they were, were in better condition than the schools in the black community.

## Differences Between Boston and Buffalo

Despite their many similarities, there are some fundamental differences between Boston and Buffalo, differences that I believe did contribute to dissimilar outcomes when school desegregation was implemented. One difference is the ethnic histories of the two cities. Boston's largest ethnic group is Irish-Americans, and they historically encountered a great deal of ethnic and religious discrimination in their efforts to advance economically and politically in Massachusetts. Buffalo also has a large population of Irish-Americans, and of other white ethnic groups which share the Catholicism of the Irish-Americans. But in Buffalo, neither the Irish, nor the Poles, nor the Italians were subjected to the same level of discrimination as their Catholic counterparts in Boston. As a result, in Boston there was a much higher level of resentment against the elite power structure, and school desegregation was regarded as an assault by this power structure.

Closely related to the inter-ethnic struggles in Massachusetts is the division between Boston and the rest of the state, a division very noticeable in the Massachusetts legislature. Many of the actions taken by "outstate" legislators were designed against Boston, often out of disdain for the ethnic politicians who dominated the city. This heightened many Bostonians' resentment against directives given by outsiders, including directives to desegregate the schools. In New York State, on the other hand, Buffalo is part of "outstate," or "Upstate" as it is labeled by many New Yorkers. (Buffalonians prefer to call their region of the state "Western New York," not "Upstate".) Buffalo is not often the focus of legislation by hostile anti-urban legislators, hence there is less cause for resentment against desegregation. Those few legislative disputes between Buffalo and the rest of New York State are rarely, if ever, the result of inter-ethnic tensions. The difference between Boston and Buffalo in regard to their relation to the rest of their respective states is a difference that is closely related to the inter-ethnic tensions within Massachusetts.

Though both cities' desegregation cases were remarkably similar, the cases had some key differences that led to dissimilar outcomes. Both cases were filed in federal courts in 1972, but in Boston the decision was rendered in 1974, two years before Buffalo. The two-year difference provided Buffalo with a chronological advantage over Boston, and allowed officials in that city to capitalize on Boston's experiences, while giving them time to develop strategies to avoid some of the problems that Boston encountered in 1974.

Another difference in the two cities' court cases is the structure of the judges' decisions. In Boston the decision was phased in over a two-year period, with forced busing of both white and black students being required from the outset. The first phase of the plan required the desegregation of schools in grades 1 through 12, covering all sections of the city except for Charlestown and East Boston. Those two areas were exempted in the first phase, and kindergarteners were to be exempted indefinitely. With the other areas of the city, white communities were paired with sections of the inner city, and selected students were to be exchanged. Phase II, implemented in 1975, extended desegregation to Charlestown, while East Boston was indefinitely exempted from mandatory student reassignments. Instead there were magnet school programs placed in East Boston to attract students from the inner city.

In Buffalo the decision was phased in over a six-year period, with most of the forced busing of white students being deferred until the sixth year of desegregation. The first phase involved the closing of schools in black and white communities, and the reassignment of students. There were also boundary changes which required the mandatory transfer of a small number of black and white students. Phase II, implemented in 1977, involved the closing down of selected predominantly black neighborhood schools and reestablishing them as magnet schools with specialized curricula designed to attract students from throughout the city. Meanwhile many of the displaced students in the inner city were reassigned to predominantly white schools. Phase III, implemented in 1980 and 1981, involved the first large-scale forced busing of white students. In selected predominantly white schools, grades pre-kindergarten through two were removed, the schools redesigned as "Academies" housing students from grades three to eight, while the younger children were bused to designated "Early Childhood Centers" in the inner-city. Meanwhile in the inner-city schools designated as Early Childhood Centers, all grades above the second were removed, and the children bused to the paired Academies in the predominantly white neighborhoods. Phase III, the final phase of the Buffalo Plan, was fully implemented in 1981, five years after the initial phase.

The extended length of the implementation in Buffalo is one area in which the two municipalities are fundamentally different in regard to desegregation, a difference that had some impact upon the way the masses reacted to the decisions. This does not, however, in any way negate my assertion that the two are very similar cases. The reason why Buffalo's plan was more gradual than Boston's was because the members of the Buffalo Board of Education agreed to cooperate with the federal court, and were able to convince the judge to allow them to delay the facet of the plan that required massive forced busing of white students. Conversely in Boston the School Committee refused to cooperate with the courts or to develop a plan desegregating the schools. Therefore the federal court developed its own plan, one that was more controversial than a phased-in plan such as Buffalo's. This still supports my general position that the elites were responsible for the differences. The different actions of the elites on the two cities' school boards led to the different desegregation plans.

There is one very obvious political difference between Boston and Buffalo of the 1970s, a difference that is obvious to any observer. In Buffalo there were black elected officials on the municipal level, whereas in Boston there were none on that level. In this book I discuss how the presence of municipal black elected officials played a key role in ensuring a more peaceful transition in Buffalo.

Between Boston and Buffalo there are differences in geographic location, economic structure, size, and neighborhood identification, but I do not see these as being significant enough to prevent one from considering the two cities very similar in regard to factors relating to school desegregation. The fundamental differences in this regard are those concerning inter-ethnic relations, year of the court decision, and racial characteristics of elected officials. These are differences that form the basis for this study.

## Interviews of Community Leaders

The qualitative data for this study is gathered through interviews of influential persons in the black and white communities of Boston and Buffalo. For respondents I selected local leaders who had some connection with the school desegregation cases in Boston or Buffalo. The cast of informants includes elected officials, appointed government officials, judicial officers, community activists, and representatives of neighborhood organizations. All of these are persons who were familiar with the intricacies of the desegregation decisions in their respective cities. The following table provides a geographic and racial breakdown of the informants:

**Table 1.1**
**Racial And Demographic Background of Informants**

|  | Boston Informants | Buffalo Informants | TOTAL |
|---|---|---|---|
| White Informants | 18 | 21 | 39 |
| Black Informants | 12 | 14 | 26 |
| TOTAL | 30 | 35 | 65 |

There was a total of 65 informants, 30 of whom were from Boston, and 35 from Buffalo. Of the 30 from Boston, 18 were white and 12 were black, and of the 35 in Buffalo, 21 were white and 14 were black. Fifty-nine of the interviews were conducted in person, while six were conducted over the telephone. The 59 face-to-face interviews were conducted during five trips to each city (and one to New York City) that were made over a seventeen-month period from December 1993 to May 1995. All but two of the interviews were taped, and later transcribed. The transcripts range from four pages (a seventeen-minute interview) to 25 pages (a two-hour interview). The mode was 12 pages (45 minutes on tape).

Of the 65 informants, 37 were past or current elected officials, five of whom held offices in state government, while 32 held office in municipal government. Five of the informants held appointed office, four on the municipal level and one on the federal level. Three were officials in federal courts. The remaining 20 informants were private citizens who were nonetheless highly visible in their respective communities. Three were religious leaders, eleven were civil rights activists and attorneys, four were antibusing activists, and one was a tenant activist. Among the elected officials were individuals who had been unelected community activists during the court cases, and among the 20 informants identified as community leaders were heads of organizations and agencies.

### Definitions of Unique Terms

In order to provide clarification for readers, it is important to explain the meanings of several key terms that are occasionally used throughout this thesis. Massachusetts itself is officially designated as a **commonwealth,** not a state. It is one of four "states" that are so designated. The reason why I will persistently use the term commonwealth in this thesis is because the meaning of the term provides insight into the ethnic character of Massachusetts. The Massachusetts Bay Colony was founded by Puritans as a Christian settlement. It had a theocratic government whose purpose was to uphold godly principles. The term commonwealth reflects the moralistic disposition of the founders, who believed that their system of government would be to the benefit of all of the inhabitants. This contrasted with the vision of government held by later immigrants, namely those arriving from Ireland.

Massachusetts also has unique names for government institutions. The legislature of the commonwealth, including the senate and house of representatives, is officially designated as the **Great and General Court,** commonly referred to as the "General Court." In references to Massachusetts the terms legislature and General Court will be interchangeably used. Another unique term describing Massachusetts governmental institutions is **School Committee.** This is synonymous with the terms "board of education" and "school board," which are used in localities in other states. Another local peculiarity is the tendency of Bostonians to refer to schools with the use of the definite article. For example, Solomon Lewenberg Middle School is referred to as "the Lewenberg," while Jeremiah Burke High School is affectionately called, "the Jerry."

There are also some terms denoting ethnic groups that must be defined. The terms **"Yankees"** or **"Brahmins"** refer to the white Anglo-Saxon Protestant descendants of the Puritan settlers. In this context these terms are used to distinguish New England W.A.S.P.s from those W.A.S.P.s who settled in other regions of the country. This term also has class implications. Yankees and Brahmins are persons with a high social standing, either due to the prominent roles their families have played in politics, or due to the financial security of their families, or, most often, due to both. New England Brahmin families became established early because they were the individuals who were responsible for the founding of their municipalities. In Boston they proudly labeled their city as "The hub of the universe," and to this day the term **"the Hub"** is commonly used by Bostonian writers when referring to their city. Though Buffalo is not in New England, New England Yankees settled there and established the city as a municipality. Therefore the term is sometimes used to refer to Anglo-Saxon Protestants in that city.

Some neighborhoods within the Hub are commonly referred to by nicknames rather than their official names. South Boston is often called "Southie," East Boston is known as "Eastie," Charlestown is called "The Town," and some refer to West Roxbury as "Westie." Throughout this book these nicknames are occasionally used by both the writer and by some of the respondents.

# CHAPTER TWO

◻

# Inter-ethnic Struggles in Boston and Buffalo

By the time that Boston and Buffalo's cases reached the attention of the federal courts, school segregation and its resolution was portrayed as a conflict between the black and white communities, and the decisions to remedy segregation reflected the portrayal of the conflict as black versus white. A historical analysis, however, makes it quite clear that the conflicts surrounding the desegregation of the schools are closely related to previous conflicts between different ethnic groups within the white communities of both cities, particularly in Boston.

In the 1970s African Americans in both Boston and Buffalo were the latest of populous ethnic/racial groups attempting to receive recognition and political representation. This chapter looks at the struggles that each of the more populous groups went through in their efforts to gain the political representation that their numbers might dictate they should receive in a democratic setting. These inter-ethnic struggles transformed the political character of the cities as Anglo-Saxon settlers and their descendants were displaced by later immigrants in the scramble for political control. In Buffalo the changes were gradual, but in Boston the changes took less time, and were more dramatic.

## Political Struggles Among Boston's Ethnic Groups

Few American cities could have been as different from one another as Boston of 1974 was from Boston of one century earlier. Nineteenth century Boston was a city that was both economically and politically dominated by descendants of Puritan settlers from

England. Though the Puritans were known for their religious intolerance, their descendants, the influential "Yankees," had built up the city's reputation as a bastion of progressive ideas. During the antebellum period Boston was a hotbed of abolitionist sentiment. Moreover, it was the site of one of the largest communities of free blacks in the United States.

The Boston of the 1970s was vastly different. The Yankees had lost much of their visible political influence, having been displaced by Catholic descendants of Irish immigrants. The city's reputation for racial liberalism was rapidly vanishing as Boston was joining Birmingham and Little Rock on the list of racially explosive American cities. In less than a century Boston had undergone a tremendous political transformation, largely the result of ethnic settlement patterns.

The influence of Puritanism however persisted, even after the founding of the United States and the constitutional guarantee of separation between church and state. Massachusetts remained classified as a "commonwealth," not as a state. Daniel Elazar defines the commonwealth conception of government as being one "in which the whole people have an undivided interest—in which the citizens cooperate in an effort to create and maintain the best government in order to implement certain shared moral principles."[1] The Puritans' original vision was that of establishing a holy commonwealth based upon Christian ideals. Their descendants retained some of these ideals after the Commonwealth of Massachusetts became one of the United States. Though the U.S. Constitution forbade them from maintaining a "holy commonwealth," they held fast to the belief that government should promote and uphold moral principles. For this reason Elazar describes the Yankees' political culture as *moralistic*.

Because of the Yankees' belief that government should serve to achieve moral aims, Massachusetts was the seat of revolutionary activity. The Massachusetts patriots, descendants of Puritans, professed a deep commitment to the principles of democracy, freedom, and liberty. The Revolutionary War was purportedly fought to bring into power a new government that would uphold and defend these principles. This was directly in line with the moralistic view of government which had a profound impact upon the politics of Massachusetts.

The settlement in Massachusetts by large numbers of immigrants was another factor that greatly affected the politics in the Commonwealth. The first large wave of immigrants to settle in Boston came from Ireland, escaping political persecution at the hands of English colonizers and starvation brought about by the

Potato Famine. In his work *Boston's Immigrants,* Oscar Handlin notes that before the mid-1840s the Irish in Boston were not viewed as a threat, and there was a general tolerance toward them.[2] But as the famine drove more of them to Boston, the level of tolerance decreased. The Irish soon found themselves the victims of intense persecution by the Yankee majority. Yankees discriminated against the Irish on both ethnic and religious grounds, particularly the latter. Handlin said that there was a fear that the Irish were sent by the Pope in an effort to Catholicize the United States.[3] But even before the famine, these fears were demonstrated, such as in 1834 when arsonists set fire to a convent in Charlestown, a city adjoining Boston, which would later become annexed into the city.

Charlestown would also become one of Boston's three large Irish ghettoes. The other two were Roxbury and South Boston, affectionately called "Southie." According to J. Anthony Lukas, each of these sections was noted by the counties in Ireland from which the inhabitants originated. Roxbury was heavily populated by immigrants from Galway and South Boston by persons from County Cork. Charlestown was an extension of the small Irish ghetto in the North End, just across the Charles River in Boston proper. The North Enders originally came from Counties Louth and Meath in Northeastern Ireland. Most of the Irish North Enders eventually moved into other parts of the city, first into Charlestown, where they established a community.[4]

Life was quite difficult for residents of Boston's Irish ghettoes. These displaced peasants were now situated in a rapidly industrializing city for whose economy their skills were ill-suited. During the 1840s and 1850s the Irish were on the bottom of Boston's socioeconomic ladder, even slightly below the city's African-American community. The Irish were crowded into slum areas that were plagued with a high rate of infant mortality, tuberculosis, unemployment, and crime. The numbers of immigrants swelled too quickly for them to be absorbed into employment in the fledgling textile industry, hence many of the men had difficulty securing steady jobs. The dire conditions were exacerbated by the high level of prejudice against the Irish. Many native-born Americans were frightened by the dramatic increase in the Irish population of Boston. They were repulsed by the poverty in the Irish ghettoes and by the Catholic religion practiced by the residents. One response of the native population was to prevent Irish immigrants and their descendants from gaining employment in many of Boston's business establishments. Signs saying "Irish Need Not Apply" became commonplace in the Hub.

The Yankees also endeavored to exclude the Irish from Massachusetts political activities. This was an effort doomed to failure due to the rapid growth in the size of the Irish population, a gain of 166,000 between 1820 and 1860.[5] While they were still the dominant political group, the Yankees tried to make entry into politics difficult for the Irish community as a whole. An organization known as the "Order of the Star Spangled Banner" was formed to combat the perceived influence of Catholic immigrants. The order was part of a national movement called the "Know Nothing Party." Though the Know Nothings were not very successful nationally, they were highly successful in Massachusetts for a brief period of time. In 1854 the Know Nothings swept the elections, winning 389 of 393 seats in the State House of Representatives, all 41 Senate seats, the Governor's Office, and the mayoralty of Boston.[6] Once in office they acted on their anti-immigrant platform, enacting a law that a person must live in the U.S. for 21 years before he could vote, imposing a tax on immigrants, and the establishment of a "nunnery committee" to investigate convents.[7]

Despite the above, the Know Nothings had a reputation for being progressive and reform-minded in other areas. Their Yankee moralism was made evident by their support of causes such as temperance, abolition, and women's rights. This progressivism put the Know Nothings further at odds with the Irish Catholic community. That community's leading spokesman, Archbishop John Bernard Fitzpatrick, opposed the Protestant-led Temperance Movement, and he refused to condemn slavery.[8] This reflected a strong anti-abolitionist sentiment within Boston's Irish community. They feared that abolition would lead to a mass exodus of ex-slaves to Boston and to the replacement of Irish workers with former slaves who would work for less remuneration.

The antislavery Know Nothings were former Whigs who would eventually affiliate with the Republican Party. Both the Whig and Republican Parties had the support of industrialists, a class that would benefit from the influx of a large number of low paid workers into Massachusetts.

Slavery was a major issue that helped formulate the modern party system in U.S. politics. The Republican Party was an outgrowth of the "Free Soil Party" that opposed the extension of slavery into the territories. The Democratic Party, on the other hand, was more tolerant of the "peculiar institution." In Massachusetts the partisan divisions reflected ethnic divisions. The Yankees in Massachusetts and the rest of New England made that region the core of Republicanism.

The GOP adopted Yankee moralist planks in regard to slavery, temperance, immigration, and other issues. The Irish Catholics, on the other hand, affiliated with the Democratic party, making it a biconfessional party in Massachusetts and other states with large immigrant populations.

Elazar describes the political culture that Irish Americans come from as being **individualistic.** Individualists have a utilitarian view of politics. In other words, politics is to be used as a means for individuals to advance themselves; it is not seen as a way to improve society as a whole. Elazar states that "political life within an individualistic political culture is based on a system of mutual obligations rooted in personal relationships."[9] This conception of politics allows a strong role for ward bosses who hand out favors to constituents, with the expectation that the constituents will return the favors. Elazar believes that persons in an individualistic political culture see little benefit in political reform, and are somewhat tolerant of corruption among public officials. This is anathema to moralists who fight for civil service reforms and who see the patronage system as an invitation to corruption.

Individualists understand politicians having a desire to economically improve themselves. What they do not understand is moralists' use of politics to crusade for social causes. This is why persons from individualistic backgrounds, such as Irish Americans, did not support abolition, even if they themselves were not personally benefitting from the institution of slavery. They saw the fight against slavery as an issue that should be kept out of national politics, hence they did not support efforts to force the government to end or curtail slavery.

The end of the Civil War may have brought some resolution of the issue of slavery, but it brought only a temporary cessation of the conflict between the Yankees and the Irish in Boston. Oscar Handlin states that for a brief period following the war there was a lessening of oppression against the Irish.[10] During this period two Irish-born mayors were elected with Yankee backing. This short-lived tolerance came about because both the Yankees and the Irish supported the Union and opposed the British-backed Confederacy. The contributions of Irish-Americans to the Union effort are legendary; they were overrepresented among the ranks of Union soldiers. Boston sent two regiments to fight in an Irish brigade. After the war the Yankees rewarded the Irish with a relaxation of discrimination. But by 1880, according to Handlin, the postwar tolerance was giving way to "a long period of bitterness."[11]

In the last two decades of the nineteenth century there was a re-emergence of the battles between the Yankees and the Irish. These battles were primarily fought in the political arena, where the Yankees were trying to defend their position against a growing and highly mobilized Irish-American population. The Irish were organized by ward bosses and a Democratic City Committee, which operated as a loosely structured political machine. The most notable bosses included Martin Lomasney of the West End, Patrick Kennedy of East Boston, and John Francis Fitzgerald ("Honey Fitz") of the North End. Unlike the two former mayors of Irish descent, the Irishmen supported by the machine were antagonistic toward the Yankees. In 1905 the party bosses reaped success by electing Honey Fitz as Mayor. Fitzgerald was the first American-born Irish Mayor of Boston, and the first who came to power by capitalizing on opposition to the Yankee establishment.

The Yankees, however, did not count themselves out. They used their domination of the state government to impose control over the city. This they did by implementing "progressive reforms" to curtail the power of people like Fitzgerald, Lomasney, and Kennedy. In 1903 the General Court made Boston's aldermanic elections at-large rather than by district, and replaced the party caucus with the state-sponsored primary. Then in 1909 the city revised its charter again. Party nominations were abolished, and the 87 member bicameral City Council was replaced by a single chamber with nine members, all elected at-large.[12] These revisions took away partisanship and dealt a blow to party leaders, such as those who placed Honey Fitz into office. It also led to the demise of the Democratic Party machine. But the irony was that Fitzgerald was not succeeded by a Yankee or a conciliatory Catholic. Rather the reforms brought into office an Irish Catholic pol from Roxbury, who, though at odds with the machine, was even more at odds with the Yankee power structure. James Michael Curley, first elected in 1914, was to dominate the Boston political scene for the next 35 years, much of which was marked by his personal wars against the "Brahmin bluebloods."

Curley's tactics flew in the face of Yankee reformers. He served four non-consecutive terms as mayor between the years of 1914 and 1949. While in office, he used the city treasury to fund public works projects and to expand the number of city jobs, many of which went to his political allies. John Stack stated that "By 1920 the Irish had transformed the city's bureaucracy into an elaborate political fiefdom. The police and fire departments, water and public works, and the school department all had strong Irish representation. . . . An extensive patronage system hailed the ascendancy of Irish politics."[13] Curley also secured the return to district representation on the City Council. In 1924 the nine-member Council was replaced by a 22-member body, with each member representing one of the city's 22 wards. The nine-member Council was re-instated in 1951, the year after Curley left office.[14]

Curley's alleged corruption and profligate government spending angered the Yankee "reformers." They launched vigorous efforts to drive Curley out of office. These efforts were under the auspices of the "Good Government Association," which Curley critically labeled as the "goo-goos." But the goo-goos and other so-called reformers could not halt the Irish takeover of Boston City Hall. By the time Curley left office, no other ethnic group had a realistic chance of capturing the mayoralty, while very few non-Irish gained seats on the Boston School Committee or City Council. Stack described the School Committee as "an Irish Bastion of Power." He also notes that of 110 city councilmen elected from 1924-1949, 84 were Irish, 12 were Jews, 9 Yankees, 4 Italians, and 1 black.[15]

While the Irish dominated the municipal government, the Yankees retreated to the government of the commonwealth and used the state's supremacy over the city to restrict the power of the Irish-controlled city. The General Court passed legislation that reduced the number of municipal elected officials, replaced district representation with at-large representation, gave the governor the power to appoint Boston's police commissioner and licensing board, and established Boston's tax limit. The General Court also assumed control over the Boston Financial Commission.[16] These legislative bills were known as the "Boston Bills" because they were measures applying only to Boston, exempting the remainder of the state.

Eventually, however, the Irish became a formidable force in the state government. When the Republicans were still in control of both legislative houses of the General Court, Irish Catholic Democrats did manage to win statewide offices on occasion. Most notable during this period were the election of David I. Walsh as governor and U.S. Senator, and the election of Curley himself as Governor. But Curley and other Massachusetts Democratic governors during his era were faced with Republican legislatures. The Democrats had never been in control of either house of the General Court.

In the national Democratic landslide of 1948, at the end of Curley's career, Irish Catholics finally established a firm foothold in the state government. In that year the governorship was captured by Democrat Paul Dever, and for the first time in history, the state legislature fell under Democratic control. The House Democrats chose as their Speaker Thomas P. "Tip" O'Neill, Jr., from the Irish working class district of North Cambridge. That year the Commonwealth's large Catholic population was also able to exercise its political muscle by passing a referendum outlawing the sale of contraceptive devices in Massachusetts. Nineteen forty-eight marked the rise of Irish Americans to the level of equal partners with the Yankees in state government.

The Irish community was also coming into its own economically. As they advanced politically throughout the twentieth century, the Irish middle class continued to grow. There were thriving Irish-American middle-class communities in the southwestern section of the city, the annexed areas of Hyde Park, Roslindale, and West Roxbury. This third section, "Westie," was more suburban in appearance than it was urban. These three areas were in the highest numbered wards in Boston (Wards 18–22), hence they are referred to as the "High Wards."

Meanwhile, at the turn of the century, the Irish in Boston had been joined by another group of Catholic immigrants: the Italians. Mainly from Southern Italy and Sicily, large numbers of Italian immigrants began to reach U.S. shores in the 1880s, settling in urban areas such as New York, Newark, New Haven, Providence, Buffalo, and Boston. In Boston they settled in the West End, the North End, and East Boston, displacing the Irish in those sections.

Despite the common religion and shared experience as impoverished immigrants, the Irish did not welcome the Italian immigrants with open arms. In addition to physical attacks against Italians in the North End, the Irish were reluctant to allow the Italians to gain a foothold in the labor unions, the church hierarchy, and the municipal government. This gave Italians a disdain toward the Irish-controlled Democratic Party, hence many registered as Republicans.

The trend of Italians supporting Republicans began to change in the late 1920s and early 1930s. Ironically it was the candidacy of an Irishman, Al Smith, that lured Italian Americans to the Democratic Party. The pro-Democratic national realignment of the 1930s was preceded in the 1928 election by smaller subsections of the national electorate. Clubb, Flanigan, and Zingale refer to this as an "Al Smith Uprising that preceded the Roosevelt Revolution of the early 1930s."[17]

It can be argued that prior to the national realignment toward the Democrats in the 1930s, there was a regional realignment in the

Northeast during the 1928 election. Though Smith lost in a landslide defeat, he was able to carry some areas that had never previously gone Democratic, specifically in the GOP stronghold of New England. In 1928 Massachusetts and neighboring Rhode Island were the only states outside of the South to vote for Smith. Samuel Lubbell looked at the twelve largest cities in the U.S., including Boston, and found that in 1928 there was a shift from the G.O.P. to the Democrats in the presidential election. Lubbell states that it was the religious issue that brought these cities into the Democratic column. Smith carried 122 counties that had previously been Republican. Seventy-seven (77) of these counties were predominantly Catholic, and 57 remained staunchly Democratic in the next five presidential races.[18] Smith's candidacy began the stirrings of a national realignment that would culminate during the next decade with Franklin Roosevelt and his New Deal.

V. O. Key looked at the 1928 election in New England. One city he focused on was Somerville, Massachusetts. Somerville is a heavily Catholic city with a large number of immigrants and descendants of immigrants, mainly from Italy and Ireland. It borders Boston's Charlestown. In 1928 there was a dramatic rise in the percent voting Democratic, and that level did not drop off in subsequent elections. In looking at other cities and towns in Massachusetts, Key found that the most urbanized and most Catholic towns showed a realignment toward the Democrats beginning in 1928. But in those towns that were heavily Protestant, there was a decline in Democratic support in 1928.[19]

This realignment in Boston was undoubtedly the result of shifting allegiances of Italian voters. The Irish voters had been solidly Democratic before 1928, and most non-Catholic voters remained Republican in that election. This leaves only one major ethnic group, the Italians, to account for the shift toward the Democrats. The New Deal of the 1930s cemented the ties of the non-Irish ethnic groups to the Democratic Party. Despite some drop-off of support during the Second World War, Boston's Italians have remained heavily Democratic since 1928.

Affiliating with the majority Democratic Party, however, did not give Italians greater representation in municipal elected office. The at-large system for electing municipal officials prevented the election of Italians from the North and West Ends and East Boston. The irony is that a "reform" designed to limit the number of Irish officeholders worked to the Irish community's advantage once they became the dominant ethnic group. As was stated earlier, the City Council and

School Committee had very few members who were not Irish. Though Italians became the second largest ethnic group in Boston, it was not until 1993 that an Italian American was elected as mayor.

The other white ethnic group that established a sizable community in Boston was the Jews. Throughout the nineteenth century there were German Jews in Boston, but their numbers were not large. The 1880s, however, marked the beginning of a large influx of Russian Jews to Boston. John F. Stack notes that the Brahmins were initially less hostile to Jews than they were to the Irish when they were the new immigrants.[20] One possible reason was that many of the Jews did not have a peasant background, and there were some who arrived with skills suited for an urban setting. Though these skills may not have been an economic advantage in pre-industrial czarist Russia, in the more developed U.S. this facilitated the upward mobility of some Jews in urban areas such as Boston.

Despite the xenophobic tendencies of many Yankees, Jewish immigrants to Boston did not encounter as high a level of hostility from them that the Famine Irish encountered. Initially the Jews were concentrated in the slum areas of the North and West Ends, among persons of other nationalities. But as their numbers increased, they established a colony, an urban *shtetl* in the section of Roxbury and North Dorchester along Blue Hill Avenue. In 1944 novelist Wallace Stegner, Ph.D. described the area as "perhaps the most solidly Jewish neighborhood in the United States, with only 2 per cent of Gentiles in it's population."[21]

The cultural distinctiveness of the community resulted in its occasional siege by anti-Semitic mobs. By the 1940s Boston was regarded as the most anti-Semitic city in the U.S. Within the Irish community there was a reverence for Father Charles Coughlin, the radio priest who was considered to be an anti-Semitic demagogue. Coughlin had many supporters in the Hub, prompting Mayor Curley to boast that Boston was the "Strongest Coughlinite city in America."[22]

Boston's anti-Semitism was demonstrated, not only by support for Father Coughlin, but also by physical attacks against Jews along Blue Hill Avenue, attacks which increased in intensity during World War II. The blame was placed upon Irish boys from South Boston, Roxbury and Hyde Park.[23] These anti-Semitic activities gained national attention in the mid-1940s.

Tensions between Boston's Irish and Jewish communities had existed prior to Coughlin or the attacks on Blue Hill Avenue, and like the Italians, Jews initially shunned the Irish-controlled Democratic party. Many Jews tended to be liberal in outlook, but it was a reform-minded liberalism that was more in line with the Republican Party at that time, particularly the progressive wing of the G.O.P. But during the New Deal, when the Democratic Party began adopting some tenets of Progressivism, Jewish voters also shifted their allegiance to the Democratic Party. This helped bring about the realignment of that era. After the Democrats embraced much of the progressive agenda, particularly its economic agenda, many former progressive Republican voters switched to the Democratic Party. Jewish voters throughout the U.S. were a part of that switch. What hastened the realignment of Jewish voters was World War II and the Democrats' strong stance against the Axis powers, this at a time when isolationism was still welcome in some Republican circles.

As Boston's Jewish community expanded southward into the section called Mattapan, Roxbury became increasingly black. The growing black community was expanding from its base in the South End/Lower Roxbury area. Though the South End was the base of the Hub's black community, it was not the site of the original black community in Boston.

Boston has one of the oldest black communities outside of the South; it began as a small neighborhood of blacks who were free prior to the Civil War. Massachusetts outlawed slavery in 1790, thus paving the way for blacks in that state to establish a settlement. They originally lived in the North End along the waterfront, but eventually moved to the West End, just north of Beacon Hill, where their wealthy employers resided. When the Famine Irish began to arrive in Boston in the 1840s, for a brief time they occupied a lower position than the city's small black population.

Because of the moralism of the dominant Yankees, Boston was regarded as a racially tolerant city. Some prominent whites in the city expressed strong abolitionist sentiments, and this made it an attractive place for former slaves from the South to settle in. The alleged racial tolerance of Bostonians was reflected in legislation, if not in actual practice. The slave trade was proscribed in Massachusetts in 1788, and by 1790 slavery had been abolished in the state.[24] But even prior to that the city had a community of free blacks, who were granted voting rights in 1788. John Daniels reports that throughout most of the period from 1776 to 1895 there was a black member on the Common Council, and there were two from 1893–1895. These members were elected from the West End. In the 1895 election, three blacks were sent to the Common Council: two from the West End, and one from the South End.[25] Other legislative reforms during the antebellum period were the repeal of anti-miscegenation laws, and the

1855 milestone passed by the Know Nothings: the outlawing of segregation in public schools.

After the Civil War, blacks became somewhat of a political force in Boston. In the 1866 election two blacks from the West End were elected to the state House of Representatives, the first blacks elected to any state legislature in the U.S. Both were affiliated with the Republican Party. While the Irish, the city's largest minority group, affiliated with the Democratic Party, blacks were almost unanimous in their support for the Yankee-dominated Republican Party.

Boston's African-American community's good political fortune ended as the nineteenth century came to a close. Two factors led to a loss of representation in the state legislature. The first was a legislative redistricting in 1895 that split up the West End ghetto. A second was the renovation of the West End, a prelude to urban renewal. The renovation policy was to replace wooden dwellings with brick dwellings. As a result blacks were displaced, and most moved to the South End, site of a growing black community whose numbers were being increased by the influx of migrants from the South. The last black person elected to the General Court for many years to come was William L. Reed, whose final successful race was in 1896.[26] Then the 1909 municipal charter change that abolished the ward-based Common Council ended black representation on the municipal level. The last of that era's black city councilman, J. Henderson Allston, left office in 1909.[27] A 1905 charter change transformed the School Committee from a district-based committee into a five-person body that was elected at-large. The eventual result of this change was that in 1913 the Boston School Committee also lost its last black representative of that era, Dr. Samuel E. Courtenay.[28] The municipal "reforms" of the Progressive Era decimated what black political leadership there was in Boston.

During the eighteenth century, what existed of Boston's free black community was in the North End; during the nineteenth century it was in the West End, and by the twentieth century it was in the South End. The South End was the seat of the black community at the start of the Great Migration of southern blacks to the North. Though Boston was not a major destination of the migrants, it did witness some growth in its black population. The South End ghetto began expanding into Roxbury. By the 1940s the black community was large enough to regain some of the political clout it had lost at the turn of the century. In 1946 a black Republican named Laurence Banks was elected as a State Representative from the South End. He served for one term before being defeated by a white Democrat in the 1948 election.[29]     *Copyrighted Material*

Meanwhile the black community in Boston was undergoing a shift in allegiance from the Republican Party to the Democratic Party, somewhat later than the black realignment in other major cities. The leader of black Democrats in the South End was Silas "Shag" Taylor, the owner of a pharmacy. Taylor was a close ally of Mayor Curley. In 1958 Taylor helped to secure the victory of Boston's first black Democratic office-holder, Lincoln Pope. Pope was elected to the State House of Representatives. This began an era of continuous black representation in the General Court. It would take another generation and a charter change before blacks would be continuously represented on the Boston City Council and School Committee. Figure 2.1 is a map of Boston showing the various communities within and outside of the city.

### Political Struggles Among Buffalo's Ethnic Groups

Buffalo and Boston share demographic similarities that date back to the eighteenth century. Like Boston, Buffalo was first settled by Protestant New Englanders. In the 1830 census the city was overwhelmingly Protestant, with ninety percent born in the U.S. David Gerber said that when Buffalo was incorporated as a municipality in 1832 (just ten years after Boston's incorporation), "The powers given the Common Council to regulate even minute aspects of daily life were founded upon pre-laissez faire concepts of commonwealth and positive government."[30] As in Boston, the Yankees in Buffalo demonstrated a moralistic conception of government.

This moralism, however, conflicted with the economic realities of Buffalo. As a major port, the terminus of the Erie Canal, Buffalo was the site of expanding commerce, which conflicted with the view of a "commonwealth" government regulating business. Gerber says that eventually the values of Protestant churches were subordinated to commitment to the development of industry in this rapidly growing city. Gerber presents Buffalo's Yankees as being a group that placed more emphasis on industrial growth than on moralistic aims. This differentiated them from their New England relatives. They did, however, share the New Englanders' support of the Whig Party.

As in Boston, immigration made Buffalo a two-party city. The flood of immigrants to the U.S. greatly affected Buffalo. The first group was from Germany. There had been Germans living in Buffalo since its incorporation, and they made up the bulk of Buffalo's small Catholic population. But they were subjected to the same level of

**Figure 2.1**
**The Neighborhoods of Boston**

discrimination as Boston's Catholics. The Germans settled on the near East Side and established the first Catholic parishes of the city. They also formed the core of support for the Democratic Party. But despite their religious and political differences from the Yankees, they were accepted and had an easier time assimilating than Boston's Irish. This is undoubtedly because there was not a strong difference in economic class between Buffalo's Germans and Yan-kees. Germans came to the city as artisans, capitalists, and skilled workers. This facilitated their assimilation into the region's economy.

The next immigrant group, the Irish, did not have as easy a time assimilating into the economy of Buffalo. In the late 1840s and 1850s large numbers of Irish political and economic refugees began settling along the north bank of the Buffalo River, very near to the Lake Erie waterfront. This is an area that became known by its political desig-nation, the "First Ward." In the early twentieth century the Irish community expanded across the Buffalo River into "South Buffalo." South Buffalo became the center of Buffalo's Irish-American com-munity, just as South Boston became the center of Boston's Irish-American community. Unlike the Germans, the Irish did not arrive in Buffalo with the skills that would help them succeed in an urban industrial setting. When they settled in Buffalo, they tended to work as unskilled laborers, as did their counterparts in Boston.

The Irish joined the Germans in building up the Catholic Dio-cese of Western New York and the local Democratic Party. However, the Germans began abandoning the latter and realigning with the Whigs. Local Whigs made intense efforts to lure the Germans into their party, but they made no such efforts among the Irish.

While there was not the same level of discrimination as in Boston, Buffalo was by no means free of anti-immigrant sentiment. The Yankees were frightened by the rising immigrant population. By 1855 over 60 percent of Buffalo's 74,214 residents were foreign-born, 31,000 from Germany, and 18,000 from Ireland, and most were Catholic. Even among the Germans, sixty percent were Catholic.[31] The large and growing number of immigrants spurred on a nativist backlash in Buffalo, as it did in Boston. Moreover, public institutions were resistant toward accommodating the Catholic population. Mark Goldman, author of two books on Buffalo, writes that

> "Buffalo's public schools, where children read the King James Ver-sion of the Bible, and read nativistic textbooks, were overtly anti-Catholic. . . . Similarly, Catholic children were excluded from the Buffalo Orphan Asylum; Catholic women were not permitted at the Home for Indigent Women, and the Catholic mass (sic) could not be said at the Erie County Poor House, despite the fact that the over-whelming number of inmates were Catholic."[32]

The anti-Catholic and anti-immigrant forces mobilized politi-cally. In 1849 they organized a Buffalo chapter of the Order of the Star Spangled Banner, and in 1854 founded Lodge 107 of the Know

Nothings. That year the Know Nothings boasted 1,478 members.[33] The political arm of the movement, the American Party, captured 47 percent of the vote in the 1854 New York State gubernatorial election, falling short of its victory in neighboring Massachusetts.[34]

One of the prominent Buffalonians who joined the Know Nothings was former U.S. President Millard Fillmore, whose mother and father came from Massachusetts and Vermont respectively. Upon the urging of Massachusetts Whig Edward Everett, Fillmore joined one of the Know Nothing lodges in January 1855. The following year he was the American Party's candidate for President. Fillmore's candidacy, however, demonstrated the failure of nativism in Buffalo. Though Fillmore was a Buffalonian, his titular leadership of the nativist movement did little to make the movement as strong in Buffalo as it was in Boston. In 1856 he captured only 26.5 percent of the vote in his hometown.[35] This marked the decline of the Know Nothing movement nationally, before it ever reached much of a peak in the hometown of its presidential candidate.

In addition to its failure to catch fire in Buffalo, another difference between that city's Know Nothing movement and that in Boston was its lack of a progressive political agenda in Buffalo. While Know Nothings in Boston advocated women's rights and abolition of slavery, I have found no records indicating that such issues were high on their agenda in Buffalo. As a matter of fact, Millard Fillmore abhorred abolitionism and signed into law the 1850 Fugitive Slave Law, which decreed that the North was no longer a safe haven for escaped slaves. After the law went into effect, Buffalo became a major stop on the Underground Railroad. This was due to its border location. Even so, Buffalo never became the hotbed of abolitionist activity that Boston was thought to be. For example, in an 1860 referendum on black suffrage, 77.6 percent of Buffalonians rejected the idea.[36]

One factor that may account for the different immigrant experience in the two cities was the presence of a large German community in Buffalo, and the acceptance of this immigrant group. Though the majority of German immigrants were Catholic, a sizable number were Protestants. Nativists favorably compared German immigrants to the Irish and appealed to Germans to join forces with them. Gerber reported that 100 German immigrants joined the local American Protective Association, a nativist organization.[37] These nativist overtures to the Germans reflected similar earlier efforts by the Whigs to lure Germans away from the Democratic Party. The Whigs' efforts were somewhat successful; German support for Buffalo's Democracy was declining.

It was during the 1860s that the Republican Party had become the party of choice for the majority of voters in Buffalo's German community. Clubb, Flanigan, and Zingale state that the demise of the Whig Party and the appearance of the Republican Party led to a change in political alignments.[38] In the 1860 elections there was a shift to the Republican Party, but it was not an "across the board" change. Clubb, Flanigan, and Zingale would identify the 1860 election as a "differential change," because while some units increased their support for one party, others began to support the other party. While the 1860 election solidified southern support for the Democrats, it also saw some groups shift to the Republicans. Buffalo's Germans took part in this differential realignment favoring the G.O.P. This was a departure from decades of support for the Democratic Party.

After the demise of the Whigs and the advent of the Republican Party, the German community was becoming so heavily Republican that by 1859 Franklin Allberger, a German American, received the GOP nomination for mayor, and went on to win the general election. Allberger's election was a result of a fusion between Republicans and former Know Nothings. This realignment left the Democratic Party overwhelmingly Irish. But because the Irish were not a majority in Buffalo, and because the Germans were the predominant ethnic group, Buffalo became a Republican enclave.[39] Buffalo also came to be identified as a German town; many of the city's industrialists and a long string of mayors were of German descent.

In the 1870s, as Buffalo was growing into a major industrial city, there began a new influx of immigrants to the city, these being from the East European nation of Poland. Historian Walter Borowiec wrote that they encountered the "Hostility of other, early immigrant groups, particularly Germans."[40] The Poles settled on the far East Side of Buffalo, adjacent to the German community. The area became known as "Polonia." By 1890 there were some 22,000 Poles in Buffalo, and by 1900 they had surpassed the Germans as the dominant group on the East Side.

Despite the Poles' superiority in numbers, the Germans were in a much more secure position in Buffalo. The Germans had become the dominant group both economically and politically. Polish men worked in factories owned by German-American industrialists, while German legislators represented the Poles on the East Side. The aforementioned hostility of earlier immigrant groups slowed down the Poles' entry into Buffalo's politics. The local Republican Party was dominated by Germans, while the Democratic Party was controlled by an Irish machine that was reluctant to cede power to another ethnic group. It was not until the 1890s that Poles began making inroads in politics. In 1891 Jacob Rozan was elected to the Erie County Board of Supervisors, becoming the first Polish elected official from Buffalo. The following year Jacob Jasiek was elected an alderman, the first Polish elected official on the municipal level. In 1904 a Pole from Buffalo was elected to the New York State Assembly. These three officials were Democrats. The first Polish Republican elected in Buffalo was Francis Gorski, who was elected to an at-large seat on the Common Council. Gorski's successful candidacy demonstrates the bipartisanship of Buffalo's Polish community at that time.

These gains eventually came to a rapid halt as a result of a 1906 charter change passed by "reformers." The charter revision mandated an at-large city commission. This is similar to a charter change passed three years later by Boston's Yankee reformers as they tried to reverse the gains of immigrants and their descendants. Another change that came at that time was a state assembly district gerrymandering that split up Buffalo's Polonia. The effect of these measures was that from 1916 to 1927 there were no Poles elected from Buffalo on the municipal and state levels.

The reformers in Buffalo had been very active since the 1880s. As in Boston these were Yankees with New England roots. Some of them were Democrats, and most notable among them was Mayor Grover Cleveland, the son of a New England-born minister. Cleveland was elected as Mayor in 1881, as Governor in 1882, and in 1884 he went on to become elected as President of the United States. As mayor and governor, Cleveland initiated a series of reforms that limited the political influence of immigrant groups in Buffalo. When he was mayor he selected cabinet members without the consultation of the aldermen, and as governor he made appointments based on merit rather than patronage. In 1889 a group of his allies, the Citizen's Association, proposed the city charter that provided for the at-large election of aldermen. The charter also proposed that the city commissioners be appointed by the mayor. These reforms were bitterly opposed by the Democratic machine, which was led by the Sheehan Brothers, a pair of South Buffalo Irishmen.[41]

The Democrats were able to wrest one concession, and that was to retain a small degree of ward representation, but this was eliminated in 1914 when a slim majority of voters approved a referendum to abolish the Common Council, the Board of Aldermen, the mayoralty, and all other existing city officers, departments, and courts.[42] This was in response to alleged corruption of municipal officials and strikes that had turned violent.

Though the W.A.S.P. reformers were quite active in Buffalo at the turn of the century, they were not as successful as their Boston counterparts in slowing the political progress of the Catholic population. At this time Buffalo's immigrants and their descendants were realizing a level of political success that was unheard of in Massachusetts. By the end of the 1800s the Irish had control of the Buffalo Streets Department, the Corporation Counsel's Office, and the Department of Public Works. The local Democratic boss, William Sheehan, was the Lt. Governor, having been elected in 1891.[43]

One reason why the reform movement in Buffalo was not as strong as it was in Boston may have been that fewer of Buffalo's Yankees were interested in the idea of a "commonwealth." Unlike the Yankees who remained in New England, those in Buffalo did not bring about the dominance of a moralistic political culture. Brenda Kurtz Shelton said that many of the Yankees who moved west to Buffalo came after the Erie Canal was built, and with the aim of making money. They were businessmen first and foremost, with little desire to improve society. Those who were reformers in the 1890s were a minority among the "old families."[44] Furthermore, these Western New York propagators of the social Gospel were in an alliance with the Catholic archbishop, Stephen Ryan. Ryan's successor, James E. Quigley, was also liked by the Protestant community.[45]

The Catholic-Protestant cooperation of the era was also evident in the secular arena, where there was a cooperation between the local Democratic and Republican parties. In the 1896 presidential election Boss Sheehan was one of many prominent Buffalo Democrats who supported William McKinley over William Jennings Bryan.[46] This was in line with a national trend of that year. Clubb, Flanigan, and Zingale identify the 1896 election as a realigning election that favored Republicans. It was a differential realignment in which Republicans made gains in the North, East and parts of the Midwest, while the South and West became more Democratic.[47] Boss Sheehan's endorsement of the Republican candidate reflected a regional trend that year. During this time there were also significant overtures made by the G.O.P. to the Democrats' Catholic constituency. By the turn of the century Buffalo's population of foreigners was too large for rational politicians, including Republicans, to campaign against immigrants. Therefore local Republicans denied any association with the anti-immigrant American Protective Association, and both parties courted the labor vote.[48]

While it is true that reformers supported charter changes that would lead to some disenfranchisement of immigrant peoples,

Shelton notes that some aspects of charter reform had bipartisan support.[49] Moreover, Boss Sheehan was able to moderate the original reform proposals that were proposed by the Citizen's Association, Buffalo's version of the Good Government Association. There even appeared to be bipartisan cooperation over the issue of immigration. Shelton reports that local organized labor advocated restrictions on immigration, which seems ironic given that so many union members were of immigrant stock.[50] But a closer review of the situation eliminates the appearance of irony. By this time the older immigrant groups—Irish and Germans—were no longer considered as "immigrants." With these two groups controlling the politics of Buffalo, any support of restrictions on immigration cannot be construed as restrictions against the Irish or Germans, but against later immigrant groups.

The group whose numbers were rapidly increasing at this time were the Poles, who came to Buffalo to work in its growing industrial plants. The Polish community's increasing size, however, did not evoke a great deal of fear and backlash because the prosperous 1890s had created a demand for more industrial workers, a demand satisfied by Polish men.

While the Polish immigrants were seen as filling an economic need, Italian immigrants were regarded far less favorably. The Italian immigration to Buffalo began in the early 1880s, when large numbers of peasants from southern Italy and Sicily started settling in various sections of the city. There were several different Italian communities in Buffalo, each distinguished by the area of Italy the residents came from. On the lower East Side were streets with immigrants from Calabria and Campania, and on the outer East Side were streets with people from Abruzzi and Campobasso. The Sicilians settled on the lower West Side, near the Niagara River.[51] It was this latter neighborhood that became the primary Italian community in Buffalo, referred to as "Little Italy."

While the Poles sought and found employment in Buffalo's factories, the Italians found employment in jobs that kept them out of doors. They were often employed as longshoremen, construction workers, railroad construction workers, hod carriers, bricklayers, etc. Those in public employment were hired as street cleaners and garbage collectors.[52] Two factors steered Italians into these outdoor occupations. The first was that their agricultural background led many to prefer working outdoors. A second factor was job discrimination wherein Italians were regarded as less capable than Polish men were of working in factories.[53] Because the jobs they were relegated to were seasonal, Italians were at the bottom of the economic ladder in Buffalo. They had fled poverty in Italy, hence they arrived with few means at their disposal to improve their lot. Moreover, like their Irish counterparts of four decades earlier, they had few skills that would promote their rapid advancement in an industrial setting. The discrimination against Italians was so severe in Buffalo that, according to one report, in 1910 they were more segregated than the city's small black population.[54] Italians were crowded into the most densely populated tenements in Buffalo. Until the arrival of large numbers of blacks during the Depression, Italians were perceived to be the ethnic group that posed the greatest threat. Persons of northern European stock feared their "swarthy" looks, and believed that Italians had criminal propensities. These stereotypes were also accepted by the Irish, who had been similarly characterized forty years earlier. Though they shared the Catholic religion, Italians were not well accepted by some of the Irish. Italian families who moved beyond the confines of Little Italy were subjected to violent reprisals, often at the hands of Irish Americans.

The anti-Italian sentiment reached a violent climax in 1907 when a riot broke out during a parade held by Italian unionists. The Italian marchers ventured out of Little Italy, and the result was a violent encounter between Italians and non-Italians.[55]

When they were the newest immigrant group, Buffalo's Italians encountered similar experiences as the Irish in both Buffalo and Boston. The Poles, however, were more accepted, probably because of the sector in which many were employed. The economically dominant persons of the city benefitted from Poles, who worked primarily in industry, and who came with some skills necessary to survive in an industrial setting. The Irish and Italians, on the other hand, came largely from rural settings, and they lacked the skills that would make their labor as beneficial to the economic notables. Therefore the most influential people perceived these groups as more of a threat than as economic contributors to society. This is why their entry into the economic and political mainstream was so difficult when they were new immigrants.

The disputes between Italians and Irish did indeed have political ramifications. Because of the Irish dominance of the local Democratic Party, Italians, for the most part, affiliated with the G.O.P., as they did in Boston. Also as in Boston, it was the candidacy of Al Smith that lured Buffalo's Italians into the Democratic Party. Smith's candidacy also converted Buffalo's Polonia from a bipartisan community into an overwhelmingly Democratic community.[56]

Though the party remained under the control of an Irish-led machine (the Erie County Democratic Committee), it has been as Democrats that Poles and Italians have become potent political forces in Buffalo. They were assisted by a charter change in 1927 that reversed some of the "reforms" of the previous decade (just three years after a similar reversal in Boston).[57] As Democrats both Poles and Italians had to struggle with the Irish for fair representation within the Democratic Party. Though Poles vastly outnumbered Irish in Buffalo, they were not able to nominate a Polish Democrat for the city's mayoralty. This led to an intra-party division between Poles and Irish. Taking advantage of this split among the Democrats, in 1949 the Republican Party supported a Pole, Joseph Mruk, in the G.O.P. mayoral primary. Not to be outdone, the Erie County Democratic Chairman, William Mahoney, backed Stephen Pankow, who had been born in the Ukraine but raised in Poland. Pankow lost in the primary to John Hillary, an Irish American who subsequently ran an anti-Polish campaign against Mruk, the G.O.P. nominee.[58] The Republican strategy of nominating Mruk had the intended effect of splitting the Democratic Party. The majority of Polish voters defected from the Democratic Party to vote for Mruk, thus giving him the mayoralty.

The city charter prevented Mruk from succeeding himself, so the G.O.P. had to select a different nominee in 1953. The organization backed and nominated a German (Becker). Meanwhile Pankow won the Democratic nomination, and eventually the mayoralty.[59]

Since Pankow could not succeed himself in 1957, the Democratic machine backed an Italian American, Frank Sedita. Sedita won the nomination and was opposed in the general election by Chester Kowal, a Polish Republican. Again the Poles supported the G.O.P., but Sedita won by a 60-vote margin, thus becoming the city's first Italian-American mayor.[60] A 1959 charter revision allowed Sedita to succeed himself. Though he was defeated by Kowal in 1961, he was returned to office in 1965 and re-elected in 1969. Upon his retirement in 1973 Buffalo received its first Polish-American Democratic mayor, Stanley Makowski.

The Irish maintained control over Erie County Democratic politics, but were unable to hold the mayoralty of Buffalo for an extended period of time. Finally in 1977 James Griffin, an independent South Buffalo Democrat, was elected mayor on the Conservative Party line. He held that office until 1993, longer than any other mayor of Buffalo.

By 1980 five of the six largest ethnic/racial groups had held control of Buffalo City Hall at one time or another. City Hall has been in the hands of Anglo-Saxon, German, Polish, Italian, and Irish mayors. The large group yet to capture the mayoralty is African Americans.

As was the case in Boston, Buffalo had an antebellum black community, but it was much smaller than Boston's West End ghetto. Blacks began settling in Buffalo in the 1820s, before the influx of any other ethnic group, save for Native Americans and Yankees.[61] After the Fugitive Slave Law was passed, Buffalo's proximity to Canada made it a major stop on the Underground Railroad. There was abolitionist activity in Buffalo, but not on the scale of Boston.

Blacks in Buffalo first settled in a lower East Side community referred to as "Vine Alley," not far from the neighborhood of wealthy whites who employed them, just as the West End ghetto was near to the wealthy Beacon Hill section of Boston. Blacks were later joined by Germans, who also settled on the East side. The black community remained very small during antebellum days, hovering in the range of 700 residents.[62] This community faced both official and unofficial discrimination. For example, until 1872 blacks were required to attend separate schools,[63] and to sit in the balcony of the Eagle Street Theater which was in their own community.[64] Some of the most blatant acts of prejudice took place during the Civil War when there occurred a draft riot, whose participants were mainly from the city's Irish community.

The civic elites blamed the rioting on a "mutual jealousy and dislike between the Celtish and African races."[65] This interpretation, however, ignored the root causes of the dislikes, which were as much economic as racial. Many Irish workers were angry after waterfront managers had used black strikebreakers to replace Irish dockworkers who were demanding decent wages and working conditions. This action by the waterfront executives fomented friction between the two communities. Moreover, well-to-do citizens of Buffalo were able to avoid the Civil War draft by paying others to take their places. This put the burden on the Irish community to supply the regiments with men to fight in the South in a war whose outcome could lead to an increase in the supply of strikebreakers.

After the Civil War the black community remained relatively small, but it retained cultural institutions, including Baptist and Methodist churches. The community did not experience significant growth until the First World War, when the boom of the munitions industry lured many southern blacks to Buffalo. The following is the black population of Buffalo according to decennial census results:[66]

**Table 2.1**
**Black Population in Buffalo: 1880–1920**

| Year | Number of Blacks | Total Population | Percent Black |
|------|------------------|------------------|---------------|
| 1880 | 857              | 155,134          | 0.55          |
| 1890 | 1,118            | 255,664          | 0.44          |
| 1900 | 1,698            | 352,387          | 0.48          |
| 1910 | 1,773            | 423,715          | 0.42          |
| 1920 | 4,511            | 506,775          | 0.89          |

Those blacks who migrated to Buffalo during the war and the decade following it settled in Vine Alley and nearby areas such as in the city's small community of East European Jews. Buffalo's Jewish community was much smaller than that of Boston, but did maintain a small urban *shtetl* on the lower East Side. This *shtetl* quickly disappeared as the black community expanded during the decade following World War I. Many Jews moved into the German-American Masten District of the upper East Side, which became the nucleus of the very small Jewish community that was only two percent of the city's population in 1950.[67] Nevertheless, most of the Jews and other whites in Masten left during the 1950s as the growing black community expanded northward.

The migration of blacks to Buffalo was encouraged by the economic elites. In an ethnographic study conducted in the 1920s, respondents interviewed by Niles Carpenter tended to identify 1916 as the year that race relations began to worsen in Buffalo. That year "a group of Southern negroes was brought to Buffalo during a strike of longshoremen for strikebreaking.[68] Afterwards, during the industrial boom of the 1920s, employers actively recruited southern blacks to work in the city's factories.

The black community continued to expand from its origins in Vine Alley. Even so, until the Depression there was not one black elected official in Buffalo. Finally in 1934 a Republican named Sherman L. Walker became the first black elected official in Buffalo. Walker was elected to the Erie County Board of Supervisors, where he served for 13 years before being succeeded by a Democrat named Leeland Jones. In 1949 Jones was elected to the Common Council, becoming Buffalo's first black elected official on the municipal level. Blacks have been continuously represented in the county legislature since 1934, and on the Common Council since 1949. Then in the early 1960s a black physician, Dr. Lydia Wright, was appointed to the Buffalo Board of Education. There has been continuous black representation on that body for more than 30 years.

While Boston was experiencing a long drought in black elected officials, blacks in Buffalo were consistently represented in the county legislature, Common Council, and Board of Education. When the black population grew to include the upper East Side, blacks took over a second seat on the Common Council. Then in 1965 a Democrat named Delmar Mitchell made history in being elected to an at-large seat on the Common Council. Mitchell was the first African American to win a citywide seat in Buffalo. He eventually was elected as City Council president, a position that requires a popular citywide election. Blacks have retained at least one at-large seat on the Common Council for the past 30 years. Contrariwise, in Boston blacks have not been able to win at-large City Council seats, with the exception of the 1967, 1969, and 1981 elections. Even when there were nine at-large seats available, blacks were unable to win one. This is drastically different from Buffalo, where there are only three at-large seats and the council presidency, for a total of four. Since the 1960s blacks have held at least one of these seats, at least two since the 1970s, and sometimes they have held three of the four at-large seats, including the presidency of the Common Council. Nevertheless, no one from the African-American community has been able to capture the mayoralty, despite winning the Democratic nomination in 1977 and 1985.

## A Comparison of Boston and Buffalo's Inter-ethnic Struggles

Both Buffalo and Boston were settled by Protestant New Englanders with moralistic inclinations. But this moralism was mitigated in Buffalo by the entrepreneurial spirit of that city's Yankee settlers. They were lured westward by the industrial boom brought on by the construction of the Erie Canal. This departure from moralism may have served to lessen the intensity of cultural conflict between the Yankees and later immigrants. Another difference between Buffalo and Boston was that Buffalo had large numbers of Germans among its early settlers. Members of this predominately Catholic ethnic group became leading citizens of Buffalo. This

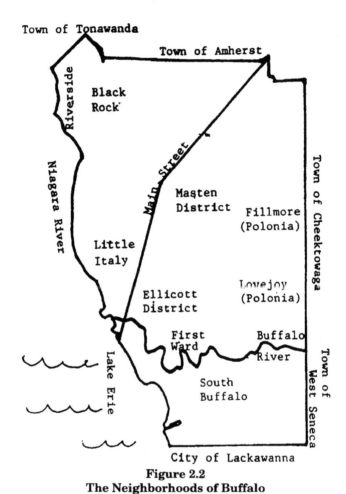

**Figure 2.2**
**The Neighborhoods of Buffalo**

contributed to more harmonious relations between Catholics and
Protestants in Buffalo.

As this chapter explains, however, Buffalo's Yankees did not completely abandon the moralism of their New England patriarchs. The
turn-of-the-century reformers were nearly as active in Buffalo as they
were in Boston. In both cities they strengthened the power of the mayors at the expense of the neighborhood-based city councils, then they

took away district representation on the city councils and replaced it with at-large representation. A key difference is that in Buffalo these changes did not lead to the demise of the Democratic machine, nor were they as far-reaching as in Boston. In Buffalo a 1929 charter revision brought back district representation, and brought and increased the representation of ethnics on the City Council. In Boston, the changes destroyed the fractious Democratic political machine, which was based on neighborhoods and ward politics. With the centralization of politics, the ward bosses had less relevance on the political scene, hence their machine ceased to exist. When ward representation was returned in 1924 (albeit on a smaller scale than before the reforms), it was too late to rescue Boston's old machine.

The irony was that the ultimate effect of the turn-of-the-century reforms in Boston was the Irish domination of the municipal government. Because of their large proportion of the city's population, the Irish were eventually able to displace the Yankees and control both the Mayor's office, the City Council, and the School Committee. The first mayor to rise to power in Boston without the help of the declining machine was James Michael Curley, who solidified the Irish domination over the municipal government.

Buffalo's Irish-American community never had the numbers to dominate the municipal government. Though they controlled the Democratic political machine (which persisted despite the short-lived "reforms"), they were forced to share power with other ethnic groups, such as Poles and Italians. Therefore the Democratic coalition in that city consisted of ethnic groups who did not share the history of battling against the moralists, groups who had given a great deal of support to the Republican Party until 1928. This led to more cooperation in Buffalo than there was in Curley-era Boston. The Irish community in Buffalo has more of a history than Boston's Irish community of involvement in the politics of coalition and concession to other ethnic groups.

The Erie County Democratic Committee, Buffalo's machine, eventually brought African Americans into the Democratic coalition, and into the city government. The machine backed black candidates for the City Council and county legislature, while Democratic mayors appointed blacks to the Board of Education. In Boston there was no such structure to bring blacks into municipal government. The result was that by the time the school desegregation issue rose to the forefront, Buffalo had an integrated roster of municipal elected officials, while in Boston it was all white. In Boston the local government was dominated by persons whose ancestors had been severely persecuted by Yankees. One of the aims of this study is to determine if the political elites in Boston viewed school desegregation as a revival of this persecution of the residents of the city's communities. But despite having some level of inclusion in Democratic Party politics, blacks in Buffalo were no less physically segregated than those in Boston. It was this high level of housing segregation in both cities that made *de facto* segregation and *de jure* segregation easy to disguise.

# CHAPTER THREE

◻

## The Politics of School Segregation

In both Boston and Buffalo, the plaintiffs in the black communities alleged that the segregation of their cities' schools was the result of deliberate practices of the municipal governments. Therefore they sought relief, first from the state governments, then from the federal district courts. In both cities the defendant municipal governments claimed that any racial identifiability of the schools was the result of segregated housing patterns over which they had no control. They asserted that they had been involved in no deliberate attempts to segregate the schools. These assertions were rejected by the federal courts in both cases. This chapter looks at the court cases in both cities and at the different practices that led to both the Boston School Committee and the Buffalo Board of Education being found guilty of practicing *de jure* segregation, in violation of the 1954 *Brown vs. Board of Education of Topeka* decision of the U.S. Supreme Court.

This chapter describes the student assignment policies of both school boards. The information provided comes from the court cases, the U.S. Civil Rights Commission, and from interviews of persons who were closely involved with the cases.

### The Boston School Committee's Response to the Racial Imbalance Act

The "housing patterns" defense was less applicable in the Commonwealth of Massachusetts than in other states. In 1965 the General Court had passed a law, the *Racial Imbalance Act* (RIA), that proscribed school committees from allowing racial imbalance in their public schools, regardless of the housing patterns. Under the terms of the legislation, any school that had a minority enrollment exceeding fifty percent was considered imbalanced and subject to review. This law mainly applied to three municipalities: Boston, Cambridge, and Springfield, the cities with sizable minority populations. Hence it was opposed by many white urban legislators. Nevertheless, as historically has been the case with other state laws designed to affect Boston, the non-urban majority in the General Court passed the RIA, and it was signed into law by the Governor.

Prior to the passage of the RIA, members of Boston's black community had been challenging the racial imbalance in the city's schools. Members of the local NAACP went before the Boston School Committee in 1963 and asked that it address the issue of *de facto* segregation. The Committee vehemently denied that there was any type of segregation in the Boston public schools. Frustrated by the Committee's intransigence, the activists launched a school boycott, a picket of the School Committee's headquarters, and a sit-in at the offices of the members. This was the start of the battle to desegregate the Boston public schools.

After the passage of the RIA in 1965, the Massachusetts Board of Education, a state body, filed suit against the Boston School Committee for the latter's violation of the RIA. The case went to trial in 1967 before the Supreme Judicial Court (SJC) of Massachusetts. The SJC held that the RIA was constitutional, and the city was ordered to comply. Throughout the next six years, however, the city failed to develop a plan that would truly alleviate the problem of racial imbalance. The remedies that the city devised did not meet the standards of the state Board of Education.

The School Committee came up with a four-stage plan. The first stage incorporated new school construction, support of an Open Enrollment Program, and support of two privately sponsored integration programs: Operation Exodus and the Metropolitan Council for Educational Opportunity (METCO). With the Open Enrollment Program, students were allowed to enroll in schools in any section of the city, provided that there were available seats, and that the students supplied their own transportation. Capitalizing on this rule, a group of parents organized Operation Exodus, which transported black students to schools outside of the black community. METCO was founded in 1966 to bus black students to welcoming suburban school districts.

Though the Boston School Committee's "Stage One" plan voiced support for Exodus and METCO, the Committee refused to provide any funding for them.[1] There also was testimony during the trial that School Department employees had a history of attempting to prevent Exodus students from registering in predominately white schools.

According to the court report, "At some of the transferee schools, the students encountered locked doors, physical segregation in separate classrooms, auditoriums and corridors and placement in the rear of classrooms. Anticipating the arrival of black students, administrators of some transferee schools had desks unbolted from the floor and removed from classrooms."[2]

In a 1965 hearing before the U.S. Civil Rights Commission, the Director of Operation Exodus, Mrs. Ellen Jackson, made the following statement:

> There were many subtleties used to harass us. . . . I would say that the School Committee was not at all helpful. In the first part of our program of 1965, it was a ticklish thing known as the yellow transfer card. It was something that was supposed to be necessary for a child to have in order to transfer from one school to another. Ironically enough, we didn't know anything about the yellow transfer cards until the morning of the first day of school when the past chairman of the School Committee decided to take a very risky trip into Roxbury and tell us that we had to have the yellow slips. It was a very inconsistent ruling too, because when our parents entered the new school, some of them were able to have their children seated without yellow transfer cards. Some of them were not and the treatment some of our children received was really atrocious. This is just the word to use. . . . Some of the children were physically segregated in the classrooms by being pushed into the back part of the room. Some of the children were kept in the auditorium all day, in the hallways all day. Some of the school doors were actually barred and locked so our children could not get in. . . . When the more tangible affronts stopped, there were more subtle ones such as: "This child is a behavior problem and we can't keep him here." or "This child is late, so we can't keep him here." Very, very inadequate reasons were given as to why often the child could not stay in the school.[3]

Six years after the start of Operation Exodus, it appeared that black students were still being steered away from taking part in the Open Enrollment Program. In testimony before the Massachusetts Committee Against Discrimination in 1971, it was found that (a) parents and students were misled or provided little information about available seats in other schools; (b) principals, guidance counselors, and administrators discouraged black students from applying for the Open Enrollment Program; (c) personal interviews were used to determine the race of Open Enrollment applicants and to discourage black applicants from applying; and (d) there was an arbitrary selection of Open Enrollment applicants. Judge Garrity concluded that the School Committee's support for Open Enrollment was solely to provide white students with an escape from schools in which their numbers were declining.[4] One former chairman of the Committee stated that without open enrollment, white students at racially changing schools would be "pretty much chained to their seats. They wouldn't be allowed to move."[5]

Stage Two, which began in 1968, involved more school construction. Stage Three (1969) modified the open enrollment to allow students to transfer only if their transfer would decrease racial imbalance. The School Committee, however, allowed exceptions that effectively eviscerated the "controlled transfer plan." One exception was grandfathering students who had previously illegally enrolled in an out-of-district school. This even applied to younger siblings who had not yet enrolled in the out-of-district school.[6] Another exception applied to multi-school elementary districts. Here a student could leave his/her neighborhood school if the receiving school was still in the same "district."[7] A third exception was the "group exception" voted by the Committee. In one case, 14 white students were allowed to avoid attending the Lewenberg Junior High School because of a "high crime rate in the neighborhood."[8] A fourth exception was an all-encompassing "hardship transfer." These were often granted on "explicit racial grounds."[9]

The fourth stage (1971) mandated a report on METCO and Exodus, a report on new schools, a progress report on the construction program, and included a lengthy proposal for metropolitan solutions. Another aspect of Stage Four was the adoption of a plan for the districting of the Lee Elementary School, which was about to open, and which was first proposed as a school that would be racially balanced.

## Elementary School Districting

The Lee School provoked a bitter controversy. When the school was first proposed in 1967, the selected site was in an area at the dividing edge between the black and white communities in the Dorchester section of Boston. By the time the school was completed in 1971, the neighborhood had somewhat changed; the area immediately surrounding the Lee was black, but the neighborhood surrounding it was racially mixed. When the school opened in 1971, the School Committee allowed white students to opt out of their neighborhood school (the Lee School) and attend either the Fifield or O'Hearn Schools, which were overwhelmingly white and in white neighborhoods. A number of black students of the Lee's district illegally registered into the school, but the Committee chose to allow them to remain. Therefore, though the Lee School was in a racially mixed district, it opened as an overwhelmingly black school because the Committee abandoned its policy of "neighborhood schools." A former School Committee member whom I interviewed explained why the Fifield and O'Hearn options were provided:

> By the time [the Lee School opened] the . . . school was well into the black community. And a lot of the whites were looking for ways out so that they didn't have to go to the school. And we gave them . . . an option, "Go to this brand new Lee School, or go to this school . . . where there'd be more white kids in it. . . ." And most of the white people opted for the other way. See, the reason that you did it, well the reason that you did it is that you knew that they'd either not go to the school, or they'd leave the city.

Another instance wherein the Committee abandoned the "neighborhood schools" policy was with the Weld School in the overwhelmingly white Roslindale section of Boston. Though the Weld was in a white neighborhood, the students who lived there were not zoned to attend there. The school, located in a 98 percent white district, opened in 1970 with an enrollment that was 94 percent non-white. According to court records, the school was purportedly opened to relieve overcrowding in the 90 percent black Bradford-Walcott district. "Approximately 130 non-white students and 11 white students were selected mostly by lot and assigned to the Weld. . . . Nearly all of the 57 first and second grade black pupils might have been assigned, with no greater inconvenience, to vacant seats in predominantly white schools in the Sumner and Longfellow districts. Parents of the black students were given no choice about their children being bused distances of from one and a half to two miles."[10] In other words, the School Committee abandoned its policy of neighborhood schools and adopted a policy of forced busing to transport black students to the Weld School, past nearer schools that were predominately white. In addition, those students living in the vicinity of the Weld were not assigned to their "neighborhood school" during the school's two years of existence.

## Secondary School Districting

Boston's elementary schools, such as the Lee and Weld schools, had district lines that were either drawn, though not always adhered to. With the intermediate and high schools, there were no district lines, rather there were elementary schools designated as "feeder schools" for intermediate and high schools. Judge Garrity ruled that the manipulation of feeder patterns was a means by which the School Committee managed to segregate the intermediate and high schools. The court cited several instances where this was done. In the Mattapan section, the Lewenberg Junior High had become predominately black. Therefore grammar school students in white neighborhoods in the Lewenberg's district were presented with the option of attending the Irving or Rogers schools, which were predominately white. At the predominantly white Thompson School, students finishing grade 8 were given the option of attending Wilson Junior High rather than the Lewenberg upon reaching grade 9.

In the predominately white Cleveland School District, there was a problem with overcrowding. Students there in grade 9 were sent either to Russell Junior High or South Boston High School, both white schools that were overcrowded. In doing so the School Committee exacerbated the overcrowding problem to avoid sending the students to black schools with available seats, namely King Junior High, Girls High, or Jeremiah Burke High. Assistant Superintendent Griffith admitted that this move was to accommodate white parents.[11]

The overcrowding at South Boston High School was dealt with through the construction of portable temporary classrooms on the school grounds. Rather than send students to schools in nearby (but predominantly black) Roxbury, they overenrolled South Boston high (0 percent black) by 676 students in 1971–72, while Girls High (92 percent black) was underenrolled by 532 places.[12] The court found that the overutilized schools tended to be predominantly white, while the underutilized schools tended to be predominantly black. The overflow at white schools was accommodated through the use of portables.

The irony surrounding portables is that in June 1965 the School Committee decided against their use because they were "educationally unsound," but reversed itself three months later and placed portables in South Boston. Then in June 1966 the Committee rejected the use of portables for the purpose of racial balance. Nine months later, in March 1967, the Committee reversed itself again and approved the use of 38 portables to relieve overcrowding in white areas. In 1968, 1969, and 1971 the Committee rejected the state Board of Education's recommendation to use portables in the racial imbalance plans for those years.[13] One former School Committee member whom I interviewed had the following to say about the decision to construct portables:

I don't think that there was a deliberate attempt to keep the black kids out. It was a deliberate attempt to let the white kids go to their own neighborhood school, which couldn't physically accommodate them.

The intricacies of feeder patterns that were adopted in 1968 greatly contributed to the segregation of Boston's high schools. According to the regulations, graduates of intermediate schools that ended with grade 8 (middle schools) went to high schools that were from grades 9–12, while graduates of intermediate schools that ended with grade 9 (junior high schools) were sent to high schools that were from grades 10–12. The junior highs tended to be in white neighborhoods, and the middle schools in black neighborhoods, thus increasing the racial imbalance in the receiving high schools. The two predominately black junior high schools that were in existence were converted to middle schools.

The Holland School, for example, opened in 1972 as a predominately white elementary school ending in grade 6. Therefore its graduates were fed into a junior high, the overcrowded Cleveland, and later to South Boston High, which was also overcrowded. The nearest intermediate school to the Holland was the King, which was predominately black, but the Holland's graduates were not assigned to the King because the Holland opened as a K-6 school. Had the Holland opened as a K-5 school, its graduates would have been assigned to their neighborhood middle school, the King, where there were available spaces. The Associate Director of Boston's Educational Planning Center testified that parents of students at the Holland were adverse toward the idea of their children going to King Middle School.[14]

The Court notes that after the feeder patterns were adopted, the racial composition of some high schools "changed . . . virtually overnight."[15] At Boston English High School, in 1967–68 the student body was only 18.5% black, but in 1968–69 the entering class was 56.5% black. The following year it was 76% black and 18.5% other-minority. During the 1967–68 school year there were 1600 white students at English, but in September 1969 the number of white students enrolling there was 15.[16] A similar transformation occurred at the Jeremiah Burke High School, which also became overwhelmingly black. In both these cases the feeder patterns adopted in the late 1960s contributed in no small way to the transformation.

The Court notes two instances areas where the School Committee chose not to follow its own feeder patterns. In East Boston the high school, East Boston High (100 percent white), was a grade 9–12 school, yet the local junior high, the Barnes, was a 7–9 school. Under the feeder patterns, students graduating from the Barnes should have been required to go to the nearest 10-12 school. However, they were instead sent to East Boston High, which was underutilized because many students in its district did not go there for grade 9. Likewise at the Barnes, grade 9 was underutilized.[17] In another part of the city was the Michelangelo School, a heavily white school that fed into English. Once English became a black school, the students were given the option of going to all-white Charlestown High instead.[18]

After it became obvious that the Four Stage Plan of the Boston School Committee did nothing to remedy the problem of racial imbalance, the state Board of Education drew up its own plan, one that would provide for some mandatory busing. The Boston School Committee challenged this in the Supreme Judicial Court, again losing. In October 1973 the SJC ordered the Boston School Committee to prepare to implement the Board of Education's plan.

Meanwhile the case was working its way through the federal courts. In 1972 black plaintiffs filed a case against the Boston School Committee, alleging that the latter had practiced *de jure* segregation of its schools, in violation of the 1954 U.S. Supreme Court's *Brown* decision. On June 21, 1974, Judge W. Arthur Garrity of the U.S. District Court of Massachusetts ruled that the Boston School Committee had indeed intentionally maintained a dual-school system. He ordered immediate implementation of the plan of the state Board of Education.

### Alleged Manipulation of District Boundaries

The Boston School Committee's perpetual defense was that any racial identifiability of the public schools was solely the result of housing patterns over which they had no control. Despite these assertions, during the federal trial it was discovered that the Committee had manipulated school boundaries so that the schools' enrollments would reflect the segregated housing patterns. In an appeal of the *Morgan vs. Hennigan* decision, it was revealed that there was a north-south dividing line extending from immediately south of South Boston southward through Roxbury and into Dorchester. This line divided the black school districts from the white school districts. The predominately white schools were located some distance east of the dividing line, which, according to the court, meant that more racial balance could result if the line was moved eastward. Had the Committee moved the lines, more white students would have been assigned to schools closer to their homes, even though the schools would have been more racially balanced. The court also discovered that "there were several multi-school elementary districts that were segregated according to race within the district, with rare exceptions."[19] These practices were in violation of the "neighborhood school" principle. Schools were not located in the center of their districts but "near the edges of irregular districts, requiring some students to attend a relatively distant school when there is another school within one or two blocks."[20]

## Housing Discrimination in Boston

It appeared that the School Committee took advantage of the housing patterns to create segregated schools, then blamed the racial isolation solely on housing patterns. These housing patterns were often the result of official discrimination. The Boston Housing Authority maintained segregated projects that were built with both federal and state funds. In testimony before the Civil Rights Commission in 1965, it was revealed that at that time there were 25 public housing developments in Boston, of which in 17 of them less than five percent of the families were black, with six developments having no black families. Four of the developments were more than 90 percent black. Only 3.5 percent of the 3,681 units housed black families.

The racial imbalance in public housing was due to an official policy of segregation. This was made evident in the federally assisted Mission Hill Development. In 1965 the Mission Hill Housing Development was 0.1 percent non-white, whereas the Mission Hill Extension, which was directly across the street was 87 percent non-white. In the state-aided BHA projects there was a similar pattern of segregation. Of the state-aided developments, the Camden Street Housing project was set aside for blacks, who occupied 98.6 percent of the units. In the other nine state-assisted projects, the black percentage ranged from 0.1 percent to 5.8 percent.[21]

The Boston School Committee had a policy of building very small elementary schools, many of which were located in the immediate vicinity of the public housing developments and which mainly served the students from those developments. The schools constructed beside the white developments were from 94 to 99.9 percent white.

Similarly, those schools placed beside black housing projects also reflected the racial composition of the developments.[22] The court ruled that the construction of very small schools was for the specific purpose of creating racially homogenous districts surrounding the schools. Larger elementary schools were constructed after 1966 when the state refused to approve funds going to schools that would be racially segregated.[23]

The segregation of public housing was part of a policy developed in 1938 by the Federal Housing Administration. The FHA's Underwriting Manual advises housing administrators to avoid the "infiltration of inharmonious racial or nationality groups." It further advised a "prohibition of the occupancy of properties except by the race for which they are intended."[24] FHA discrimination continued in Boston into the 1970s. In 1971 a consortium of Boston Banks formed the Boston Banks Urban Renewal Group (BBURG) to grant FHA mortgages to blacks. BBURG's policy was to grant mortgages only within a specific geographical area of the city and launch a block-by-block expansion of the black community.[25] BBURG did not provide FHA mortgages to blacks seeking homes outside of this restricted area, thus perpetuating the segregation of housing.

BBURG's lending policies expedited a long-expected southward expansion of the black ghetto into Mattapan which was then a Jewish enclave. Judge Garrity cites a 1962 report that "predicted with 95% accuracy the size of the black population and those neighborhoods in Boston which would become predominantly black by 1970."[26] The report was based on a study commissioned by the School Committee itself. Garrity ruled that the Committee's school construction projects between 1953 and 1972 were based upon predictions of the racial composition of the neighborhoods, and were located so that the schools would be racially homogenous.[27]

### Discrimination in Examination and Vocational Schools

In the appellate court, mention was made of how the districting decisions affected the racial composition of the examination schools, which were supposed to be immune to districting policies. The court reports that "there were districting changes affecting certain fifth and sixth grade classes that were 'tracks' to the three examination schools. White students ultimately comprised more than 80 percent of these classes."[28]

It was quite apparent that the black schools did not adequately prepare students for entrance into the three grades 7-12 examination schools, Boston Technical High, Girls Latin Academy, and Boys Latin School. The rate of blacks passing the entrance examination for these schools was far lower than the rate for whites. This may have been partly due to the fact that, as was reported to the Civil Rights Commission, in some of the black elementary schools, students were not required to perform the same amount of work as students in white schools.[29] A report by the Massachusetts State Advisory Committee to the U.S. Civil Rights Commission shows that in the black schools the students read at a lower grade level and scored lower on intelligence tests. This difference increased as the students moved up in grades. Consequently fewer students from black schools were able to secure admission into the examination schools.

One black informant spoke of how these disparities existed in a particular school back in the 1950s:

> . . . . And [a white acquaintance] was talking about her kid and science and stuff like that. And she had a kid who was in the same grade as my kid. So I said to my daughter, "Do you have any science in school?" And she said, "Naw!" She didn't look as if she even knew what science was. So I went up to school and I spoke to the teacher, and I told of my friend, the same story. And she said, "Oh no. It's the same curriculum all over the city. They may be doing it at one time, and we're doing it another time." Well in about two or three weeks [my daughter] had this science project. So I said "Gee, that's nice." And she said, "Well I don't see why I've got to be the only one [in the class] with a science project."

Because of such disparities in the curriculum, black students had difficulty securing admission into the examination schools. It was also obvious that black faculty were not able to find positions teaching in these schools. Between the years of 1967 and 1972 the three examination schools had only one black faculty member per school.[30] This is far worse than the dismal record of the school system as a whole.

Judge Garrity also noted that there was discrimination in the vocational programs, discrimination directly related to the segregation of the district high schools. Six district high schools offered part-time cooperative vocational programs, and in five of these schools the enrollment in the vocational programs was overwhelmingly white. The sixth had been predominately white until the early 1970s. At these

six schools the students were provided with on-the-job training in po
sitions that offered monetary compensation. It was also discovered that
these schools recruited prospective cooperative-industrial students
only from the predominantly white junior high schools. The predominantly black schools that offered vocational training did not provide the
option of on-the-job training, nor did the School Committee attempt to
secure such a program at the predominately black schools.

## Discrimination in Hiring and Promotion

During the trial it was found that, as in the examination schools,
there was a paucity of black teachers in the vocational programs at
the district high schools. There were no black teachers in the vocational programs at South Boston, Charlestown, and East Boston
High Schools, and there was no evidence indicating that there were
any at the other district high programs.[31]

Judge Garrity ruled that employment discrimination was sys-
tem-wide and led to segregation among professional staff. According
to the court records, in the 1972–73 school year, 244 of the 356 black
teachers in the Boston Public School System were assigned to the
System's 59 predominantly black schools. This isolation of the black
teachers in black schools increased from 1967 to 1972. The following
are the percentages of black teachers assigned to schools with black
majorities:[32]

**Table 3.1**
**Concentration of Black**
**Schoolteachers in Boston**

| Year | Percent of Black Teachers in Predominately Black Schools |
|------|---------------------------------------------------------|
| 1967–68 | 67% |
| 1968–69 | 68% |
| 1969–70 | 70% |
| 1970–71 | 72% |
| 1971–72 | 74% |

It was also revealed that 81 of Boston's 201 schools had never had a
black teacher, while 35 schools had only had one in any year since
1967–68. Also, in 1972–73 all five black headmasters were at schools
with black majorities, and all 14 black assistant principals were at
predominantly black schools.[33]

Those blacks who were teachers were subject to discrimination. Two minority recruiters were used to identify the race of the black prospective substitute teachers. More than one-third of the black teachers were provisional, with no rights to transfer to other schools. The black schools had a higher percentage of provisional teachers. It was discovered that the higher the black percentage of the student body, the greater the number of provisional teachers, and the lesser the teachers' number of years of experience. Teachers with the most seniority were given opportunities to transfer, and these transfers were rarely to predominantly black schools. In the years 1971 and 1972, there were 39 transfer requests from black to white schools, but none the other way. Since the granting of the requests was based on seniority, very few black teachers had the option of transferring to the most desired schools. This is due to the fact that as late as the early 1960s only one percent of the teachers were black,[34] hence few had seniority by the 1970s. This accounts for the nonexistence of black teachers in white schools, and the lack of experienced teachers in black schools.

By the 1972–73 school year the situation had slightly improved over the 1960s. When the case was filed, blacks accounted for 5.4 percent of the permanent teachers (231 of 4,243) and 3.5 percent of the professional staff. Though this was an improvement, these numbers still reflected a disparity between the city's black population and the number of black teachers and professional staff. At this time blacks constituted 33 percent of the system's students, and 16 percent of the population of Boston.[35]

Many of the black teachers were weeded out by a local examination, the "Boston Teacher's Examination," which was never formally validated. Once this examination became controversial, the Committee substituted it with the Educational Testing Service's National Teacher Examination. One criticism at the trial was that the Committee relied exclusively on the NTE to weed out teachers, even though the ETS guidelines warn against it being used as a criteria to invalidate applicants.[36]

## The Buffalo Board of Education's Response to the State Order to Desegregate

In 1962 the leadership of the Buffalo branch of the NAACP came forward with a written statement criticizing the racial segregation of the Buffalo Public Schools and asking the Board of Education to begin to develop a remedy. This is precisely how the process began in

Boston less than one year later. Also as in Boston, the city officials refused to address the situation, so it was left up to the state. In 1963 New York State Commissioner of Education James Allen requested all local boards of education to report which schools had minority enrollments of greater than 50 percent. This was in line with a 1960 Board of Regents policy statement urging the desegregation of the public schools in New York State.

In 1965 a group of citizens in Buffalo appealed to the state to intervene again, after having been rebuffed by the city when trying to remedy the racial imbalance in the schools. They alleged that (1) the schools were racially imbalanced, and (2) students in the black community were receiving an inferior quality of instruction. This was validated in a report submitted to the U.S. Civil Rights Commission two years earlier. That report documented overcrowding in classrooms in the black community, which led to the students being denied participation in special progress classes for gifted students. There was also segregation of special progress classes, with black students being sent to one school and whites being sent to another. The report also states that the physical plant, library resources, and course content were inferior at the black schools.[37]

When the case went before the State of New York Department of Education, Commissioner Allen held that the Buffalo schools were indeed imbalanced, and he ordered the Board of Education to adopt a policy to racially balance the public schools. The Board responded by submitting a plan that was deemed ineffective by Allen. They were again ordered to submit a desegregation plan. In April 1967 the Board sent proposals to the Commissioner, which called for the following:

1. The hiring of a Commissioner of Integration

2. The development of middle schools that would be integrated

3. No forced busing of white students.[38]

### Actions of the Common Council and Mayor

In January 1968 the Board began a program called Quality Integrated Education (QIE), which would involve voluntary busing of black students to schools in peripheral areas of the city. The QIE program was limited by the lack of available seats in the schools in the peripheral areas. To remedy this, in May of 1968 the Board voted to construct portable classrooms in the peripheral schools. Less than one week later the Common Council began the process of passing an ordinance that would require that any additions to a school building be built of the same material as the school building itself. This, in effect, banned the use of portables. The ordinance was vetoed by the Mayor, but he was overridden. The Board then filed suit in state court against the city and Common Council and had the ordinance invalidated. This delayed construction of portables for one year.[39]

The Buffalo Common Council became further involved in the fight to halt the desegregation of the schools. When a new junior high was under construction, the Board voted to convert it to a middle school, thus placing one more grade into the integrated structure. But when the bond issue for final funding was submitted to the Common Council, the Council turned it down. The Council also refused to fund a Board proposal to set up a citywide system of grades 4-8 multi-district integrated middle schools, replacing the junior highs, and ensuring integration from grade 4. In 1971 the Common Council refused to negotiate a lease or purchase of an out-of-use Catholic high school in South Buffalo. During the trial it was discovered that the Council wanted assurances that the school would remain as white as it had been when it was run by the Diocese of Buffalo.

During the federal trial in 1976, the Board of Education cited these actions of the Council as evidence that the Board had intended to desegregate the schools but was prevented from doing so by the Buffalo Common Council. But the facts brought out in the trial show that the Board was no more committed than the Council was to desegregating the public schools. In January 1972 New York State Education Commissioner Ewald Nyquist ordered the Buffalo Board of Education to come up with a desegregation plan by April 1, 1972. Instead the Board voted (4-3) to inform Nyquist that they were unable to come up with a plan.

An action of the Mayor of Buffalo made it even less likely that the Board would act to desegregate the public schools. Soon after Nyquist ordered the Board to submit a plan, Mayor Frank Sedita appointed to the Board of Education Carol Williams, a foe of busing. Sedita had written in a letter that the appointment was based upon Mrs. Williams' opposition to cross-busing.[40] I interviewed several persons who were on the City Council during the Williams confirmation hearings. One of them had this to say:

> The whole thing was, "we're appointing you because you, are you in favor of busing, or not in favor?" We didn't look at what the other qualifications were. It was, "Were you for or against busing?" and [not] "What you're gonna do with education."

## School Districting Procedures

Judge John Curtin refused to let the Board off of the hook and escape blame for perpetuating school segregation in Buffalo. He cited a lengthy list of Board actions that were designed to expand or preserve segregation. These actions were nearly identical to those practiced by the Boston School Committee. The student assignment processes were very similar in the two cities. Buffalo also made use of feeder patterns in elementary schools, which were used to determine which secondary schools students would attend. As in Boston the Board manipulated these patterns to perpetuate segregation.

A case very similar to the Lee School was the districting for Buffalo's Woodlawn Junior High School. In 1958 the Board decided to construct a new junior high school to alleviate overcrowding in some of the grammar schools. The site chosen was on Woodlawn Avenue, in the black East Side, but very close to Main Street, which separated the black community from the white community. Like the Lee, Woodlawn was constructed at the edge of the black community. This school was designed to house students from grades 7–9 after they had finished at K-6 elementary schools. While the school was under construction, the black community was promised that it would be racially integrated, which meant its district would cross Main Street, the dividing line between the black and white communities. In 1963 Superintendent of Schools Joseph Manch declared that, "The zone will cross Main Street if I have anything to say about it."[41] In 1964, however, several months before the school was to open, Dr. Manch stated that, "It is not now feasible, I believe, to draw the district lines for Woodlawn in such a way as to achieve a racial balance that would be meaningful or stable. I don't think there is any middle ground anymore."[42] Manch cited opposition from white parents west of Main Street as one reason.

When the final districting plan was drawn for Woodlawn, it did include an area west of Main Street, incorporating a white community. But a large portion of this area was made into an "optional zone," allowing students to attend other schools, just as white students districted to the Lee School were allowed to attend the Fifield or O'Hearn schools in Dorchester. In Buffalo the option allowed the students to transfer to School 56 (K-8) then to Lafayette High School in grade 9 rather than to Woodlawn.[43] In the area west of Main Street that was not optional, students were able to go to the Board and receive transfers keeping them away from Woodlawn. Among the reasons for transfers was "fear of black children." Some transfer forms had no reason listed at all.[44] When Woodlawn opened in 1964 it was 99 percent black and remained so for the next twelve years, despite its location close to the white community west of Main Street. Judge Curtin cited the disparity between the racial composition of the surrounding area and that of the school as evidence of intentional segregation of Woodlawn Junior High School.

The Buffalo Board of Education also made discriminatory use of feeder patterns. Like the Weld School in Roslindale, there were two predominantly black schools in white neighborhoods on the West Side of Buffalo. These were schools 16 and 17 (both K-6), while the white schools in the same vicinity were schools 30 and 56. Before Woodlawn Junior High opened up, school 16 was predominately, though not overwhelmingly black. But after that school was designated as a feeder school for Woodlawn, white students began transferring to school 30, which fed into 56 for grades 7 and 8. As a result, the white population at school 16 declined from 39 percent in 1962 to 9 percent in 1968.[45] This change did not reflect a racial change in the district. The neighborhood surrounding school 16 was predominantly white in 1962, and it remained so in 1968. In what one witness described as "anomalous," the school had been predominantly black since the early 1960s.

School 17 is another West Side school that was "anomalous." Though 17 was just inside of a white neighborhood, it was nearly all-black. This situation existed because there were predominantly white areas in school 17's district that were designated as optional areas. Students in these areas could attend schools 56, 54, or 74, the first two being predominantly white schools on the west side of Main Street.

Optional areas existed in sections other than the Woodlawn district. Further downtown, on the outer East Side, School 31 was a predominantly black school whose zone included a white section. Students in that particular white neighborhood were provided with the option of attending School 40, which was predominantly white. In 1965 the Board moved the optional area into the district of School 57, which was also predominantly white.[46]

The shift of School 57's boundary is an example of the manipulation of district lines for segregative purposes. The court cited a situation where this was done on the West Side. Schools 34 and 4 were within blocks of one another, with School 34 considered as an annex of 4. The School Board had situated the boundaries such that these two schools, in the same district, were both racially imbalanced, but in opposite manners. In 1973 School 4 was 73.2 percent minority, while School 34 was 86.6 percent majority.[47] This is very similar to the situation in Boston where there were multi-school elementary districts in which the schools were segregated according to race. In the Buffalo situation, school 4 was so underutilized that all of the students in its annex (School 34) could have been accommodated there with no problems. But when the Board did attempt to shut down this antiquated edifice and send the students to School 4, the residents protested. The Board relented and maintained a rundown, severely underutilized, substandard building. Judge Curtin ruled, however, that "the Board cannot maintain a segregated facility in order to placate the local community."[48]

## Segregation of High Schools

During the trial it was revealed that the Buffalo Board of Education had a long history of discriminatory use of feeder patterns. This resulted in segregation on the high school level. It has been alleged that the Board's actions made East High School Buffalo's black high school. East is situated on the border between the Masten District and the historically predominantly Polish Fillmore District. Prior to 1953 East was overwhelmingly white, with a large number of students of German descent (from the Masten District) and Polish descent (from the Fillmore District). The two schools with the highest concentration of blacks were Fosdick-Masten and Hutchinson High Schools, which were both closed in 1953 (the former being transformed into a vocational school). Most of the black students from those schools were sent to East High, giving that school a large number of black students for the first time in its history, thus making it the only academic high school with a large concentration of blacks. The actions of the Board during the subsequent years contributed to the racial imbalance of East High. By 1966 three-fifths of Buffalo's black high school students attended East High.[49]

In 1954 the easternmost section of the East High district (which was predominantly Polish) was made an optional area, where residents no longer had to attend East. That year the Board also extended East's district further south so that black students from the Ellicott district would be required to attend East rather than South Park High School in the Irish community of South Buffalo. The Board also changed the all-white Lovejoy area from East's district to the district of Kensington High School. In 1957 a predominantly black area where students were assigned to Grover Cleveland, Bennett, or Lafayette High, was made a part of East's district, thus adding to the racial imbalance of East. Also that year all-white School 43 was designated as a feeder school for South Park rather than East, even though it was just as close to East.[50]

Even after all of these adjustments, East High School's actual District remained heavily white with many persons of Polish descent. This was due to the location of the school. The court records indicate that by 1970, though East's district was 40 percent white, the school itself was 99 percent black. This disparity was due to a policy called "foreign language transfers." Each of Buffalo's academic high schools was required to offer Spanish, French, and Latin. The so-called "special languages," such as Polish, Italian, Hebrew, and Russian, were offered only at designated high schools. Up to 1960 each of the seven academic high schools offered at least one special language. At East the language offered was Polish, which was appropriate due to the location of the school near Polonia. In 1960, however, the year East's black proportion climbed past fifty percent, Polish was removed from the school, thus making it the only academic high school that offered no special languages. The Polish language course was transferred to South Park High School, which is located in the Irish-American community of South Buffalo. From that point on, white students wishing to transfer from East could request to take Polish and be granted a transfer to South Park High School. In 1971, for example, South Park High School had 143 out-of-district students, mostly from East, studying Polish and Russian. The records also show that in 1970 176 foreign language transfers were given to students from East.[51] One of the persons I interviewed alleged that though there were large numbers of foreign language transfers granted, the students were not required to remain in a language class once they had transferred. This was not brought out in the trial. In the 1978 appellate case, however, it was noted that sometimes "different standards for obtaining 'language transfers' were applied to black and white students."[52]

In 1972, after the racial impact of the foreign language transfers was made known, the Board ordered East High School to offer a full range of foreign languages and cease offering language transfers. By this time, however, it was too late to reverse the pattern of imbalance. White students found other means to avoid attending a school that had been nearly 100 percent black in 1971. In October 1972 there were still 197 white students from the East High district studying languages at South Park High School.[53] That year 1.7 percent of the students enrolled at East were white (up from 0.2 percent the previous year), but had it not been for the language transfers, East's student body would have been 13.6 percent white.[54]

During the federal trial the plaintiffs alleged that the Board also attempted to segregate the vocational and technical high schools. A former President of the Board admitted that "the policies of admissions to vocational and technical schools were being operated, to the Board's knowledge, in a manner which was discriminatory against black applicants."[55] Prior to 1972 the criteria for admissions were elementary school grades, a personal interview and sometimes (*always* in the case of Hutchinson Technical) an admission test. Somehow the procedure led to blacks being steered away from McKinley, Seneca, and Hutch-Tech (which respectively were 83, 82.5, and 85.1 percent white in 1971) and toward Burgard, Emerson, or Fosdick-Masten (which were 41.7, 45.2, and 94 percent minority respectively).[56] The admission procedure was revised in 1972, as was Hutch-Tech's entrance examination. Of these vocational schools, the physical plant of Fosdick-Masten was in the worst condition, and was the only one not close to full enrollment. The Board planned to move it into the new East Side High School building, but these plans ended when the Common Council eliminated the new building from its 1974–75 budget.

The elimination of the new East Side High School was another issue that led to the city being found guilty. A site for the new school had already been purchased for $4.6 million. It was to replace two black schools, Fosdick-Masten Vocational High School and East High, and relieve overcrowding at overwhelmingly white South Park High School, in South Buffalo.[57] Bringing students from South Park would have made the school a desegregated facility. A last-minute reversal prevented this from becoming a reality. One former member of the Board of Education had this to say about the decision not to proceed with the construction of the new East High School:

> I was there on the Board when that vote was taken to not build a new East High School, which was supposed to be built in a neutral kind of zone that would have integrated a large high school. And then East High School, which was over in the East Side of Buffalo, which was all black at that time. But then that was the Board, after even the money had been appropriated by the city for that. So they made a deliberate decision because there was that scare that black children coming in and white children: they were gonna have all these problems, and so forth. They made a decision not to construct. That's after all the planning had been done, all the monies had been appropriated, and so forth. So those were deliberate acts to maintain the status quo and to keep things as they were.

## Housing Discrimination in Buffalo

Despite all of the above evidence, the defendants in Buffalo maintained that they were not responsible for the segregation of the city's public schools. They used the same defense used in Boston, which was that segregation was the result of housing patterns, of which they had no control over. But as in Boston, the plaintiffs alleged that the housing discrimination in Buffalo was caused by official actions of the municipal government. In the trial it was proven that the City of Buffalo helped create segregated housing patterns both through its public housing policies and its urban renewal policies.

Public housing in Buffalo is administered by the Buffalo Municipal Housing Authority (BMHA). The BMHA was formed in the 1930s to manage FHA-funded housing. As in Boston, the City of Buffalo adhered to the FHA guidelines against integrated housing.[58] During the trial the plaintiffs submitted newspaper articles advertising one of the developments as being "specifically designated for negroes,"[59] while white residential projects were constructed in the suburbs and peripheral areas of the city. One witness testified that the BMHA maintained discriminatory policies at least until 1970.[60]

The court records show statistics from 1966 that showed that of the 13 public housing developments in the city of Buffalo, only four could be considered integrated. The three developments on the near East side (the black ghetto) were either 99 or 100 percent black, whereas six in more peripheral locations were less than seven percent black. In the four developments that could be considered as integrated, the black proportions ranged from 13 to 58 percent. But even among these integrated projects there was clear evidence of discrimination. The Commodore Perry Projects in the First Ward were 19 percent black in 1966, but the Commodore Perry Extension, which was right across the street, was 58 percent black.[61] Much of this continued segregation of the developments was due to the fact that the BMHA allowed managers of individual developments to use an informal waiting list procedure that "enabled white applicants to avoid the identifiably black projects."[62] Overall this appears to be very similar to the pattern in the projects administered by the Boston Housing Authority.

During the trial it was also found that the City of Buffalo's urban renewal and relocation policies helped segregate blacks into the central city. During the 1950s the city launched an urban renewal program in the Ellicott District. The city purchased large areas of the District along with the homes, razed the homes, and relocated nearly all of the displaced black families into the Masten District. This confined the black population to the non-razed areas of the Ellicott District and to the adjacent Masten District.[63]

Judge Curtin cited the public housing segregation and the relocation of displaced blacks to the Masten District as evidence that the city had helped produce the segregated housing patterns that led to segregated schools. Therefore the city could not hide behind the defense that the segregated schools were the result of segregated housing over which they had no control.

## Discrimination in Hiring and Promotion

A final similarity with the Boston case was that in Buffalo the plaintiffs also alleged that the School Board's discriminatory policies had concentrated black teachers and administrators in black schools. It was revealed during the trial that in 1970 there were fifteen elementary schools that were 85–100 percent white that had no black teachers, while 63.3 percent of Buffalo's black elementary school teachers were assigned to 15 schools that were predominantly black. By 1973 the situation had not significantly improved; there was not one black teacher in nine elementary schools that were 85–100 percent white, and 57.6 percent of the non-white elementary school teachers were assigned to fourteen predominantly black schools. In 1970 41.6 percent of the faculty at the three predominantly minority special schools were non-white, while only 5.6 percent of the teachers in the other three special schools were non-white. In 1973 28 percent of the teachers in the predominantly minority special schools were non-white, while only 3.1 percent of the teachers at the four other special schools were non-white.

At the intermediate level the situation was similar. In 1970 the two all-black junior highs, Woodlawn and Clinton, had minority teacher percentages of 25.9 and 10.9 percent respectively, while in the predominately white middle and junior highs there were very few non-white staff. By 1973 the non-white faculty percentage at Woodlawn and Clinton averaged 28.7 percent, yet it averaged 8 percent at the other four intermediate schools.

In 1970 39 percent of the minority academic high school teachers were sent to East, comprising 21.4 percent of the faculty there, while at six other academic high schools the percentage of non-white teachers ranged from 3.7 to 12.9 percent. By 1973 the situation had worsened. That year 47.2 percent of the minority academic high school teachers were assigned to East, comprising 32 percent of the faculty there, while at the other six academic high schools the percentage of minority faculty ranged from 2.1 to 9.7 percent.

The situation at the vocational-technical schools mirrored that of the academic high schools. In 1970 Fosdick-Masten High (which was nearly all-black) had a non-white teacher percentage of 16.7 percent, while none of the other vocational technical schools had minority percentages exceeding 2.5 percent. In 1973 Fosdick-Masten's minority faculty ratio was 23 percent, while at the five other vocational high schools the percentage of minority faculty members ranged from 1.6 to 6 percent.

Minority principals and assistant principals were also concentrated in predominantly black schools. In 1970 there were only four minority principals and seven minority assistant principals. Each of these eleven individuals was assigned to a school that was over 98 percent black. In 1973 there were 14 non-white principals, 13 of whom were assigned to schools that were predominantly non-white.[64]

What existed in Buffalo is a mirror image of Boston during the same period of time: a small number of black teachers, far from representing their percentage of the city or school district population, and an even smaller percentage of black principals and assistant principals. In both cities most of the black teachers and nearly all of the black principals and assistant principals were sent to predominantly black schools. As a result, many of the predominantly white schools had no black teachers at all. In both cities' court cases the judges cited this as evidence that there was indeed discrimination in hiring and promotion, just as there was in districting.

### Differences Between the Boston and Buffalo Cases

A very notable difference between the two cities was the higher level of involvement of the Buffalo City Council and the mayor in public school matters than what was seen in Boston. This was evident in the portable classrooms controversy where the Council passed an ordinance banning their use. In Boston there was far less Council intervention in School Department matters. The Boston School Committee had a greater deal of independence than the Buffalo Board of Education. Until 1974 members of the Buffalo Board of Education were appointed by the mayor and subject to confirmation by the Common Council. In Boston the members ran for their seats. Another fundamental difference is that the Boston School Committee has some fiscal independence from the Council and the mayor. The city charter guarantees the School Committee an annual budget of the same amount of money as the previous year's school budget. Any allocation above the previous year's budget must come from the Council. In Buffalo every dollar must be approved by the Council and signed by the mayor. One former elected official had this to say about why he did not get more involved with the Boston public schools:

> I thought the school system was a loser for me. I never, never talk about something you have no control [over] as a public official. Helpless.

The actions of the Buffalo Common Council and mayor demonstrated that they did not feel helpless in intervening with the schools over desegregation. The Common Council turned down funding for the construction of portables, for the conversion to a 4-4-4 grading system, for the new East Side High School, and refused to negotiate a lease for the building that Bishop Ryan was housed in. All of these efforts would have facilitated the desegregation process, but the Council stymied them. The mayor also got involved in the controversy by appointing to the Board a member because of her opposition to busing.

In Boston the above actions were done by the School Committee, not the Council. In comparison to the Common Council, the Buffalo Board of Education appeared more moderate on the issue of desegregation, despite their general opposition. All of the council-vetoed spending items that would have helped to decrease racial imbalance were measures passed by the Board of Education in response to pressures from the State Department of Education. While the Boston School Committee refused to provide any funding for Operation Exodus or METCO, the Buffalo Board of Education did fund the Quality Integrated Education (QIE) program that provided for one-way busing of black students who chose to attend schools in peripheral areas where there were available seats. The construction of the portables was a means to make available those seats. It is doubtful that such measures would have been approved by the Boston School Committee.

The moderation of the Buffalo Board was due to the fact that they were not elected, and were not as worried about punishment at the polls. One person I interviewed, a member of the elected Board, described the appointed members as "professionals" who "didn't have political ambitions." Such was not the case with the members of the

Boston School Committee. Many of the members of the Committee went on to higher elective office, and many others campaigned for higher office, but lost. For some members, the School Committee was a mere stepping stone to the City Council, the General Court, the Mayor's Office, or other full-time elective positions. Therefore it was essential that they avoid being castigated as sitting on the wrong side of the fence on a volatile issue like school desegregation.

While the Boston School Committee played the role as the protector of "neighborhood schools," in Buffalo that role was played by the Common Council. The Council had direct control over the school budget and was required to confirm the prospective members of the Board of Education. When the appointed Board of Education did not feel the need to carry the torch for the "neighborhood school" advocates, the elected Council carried it. During the late 1960s and early 1970s members of the Council kept the School Board in check and made certain that they did not bend to the forces pushing for school desegregation, particularly if it involved busing. The fact that the Council members were required to face the voters made them less moderate on school integration than the School Board, whose members did not have to stand for election. Some advocates of neighborhood schools recognized the reluctance of the appointed School Board to challenge the state. Their answer to this was to push for a change in the charter to provide for an elected School Board. Neighborhood school advocates were responsible for the charter change in 1974 for an elected Board of Education in Buffalo.

While the Board was non-elected, there was not a strong push from that body to challenge the state Commissioner of Education. Contrariwise in Boston the School Committee was at the forefront in challenging the Racial Imbalance Law and the orders of the Supreme Judicial Court and the Federal District Court.

# CHAPTER FOUR

◻

# The Responses of the Local Community Leadership

In both cities the majority of the recognized leaders in the white communities strongly opposed plans to desegregate the public schools, particularly if the plans included busing. The school boards refused to obey state directives to develop desegregation plans. As a result, both school boards were taken to court. In Boston, where there was state legislation mandating school desegregation, litigation began in state court, but there was a pending case in the federal district court, which was first filed in 1972. The Buffalo case was also filed in federal district court in 1972.

In late 1973 the Supreme Judicial Court of Massachusetts ruled against the Boston School Committee, and ordered it to implement a plan for desegregation. The Committee refused to file a plan. In June 1974 the city lost in federal court as well, and again refused to file a plan to desegregate the schools. Because the School Committee refused to cooperate, the courts developed the student assignment plan in Boston. The plan included busing and was soundly denounced by local leaders of the white communities. When the first phase of the plan went into effect in 1974, there was a great deal of violence in reaction to it. The city of Boston was forced to request the assistance of the state law enforcement personnel to assist in the maintenance of order.

The violence that met the first phase led to the moderation of the responses of some of busing's opponents. Though they did not soften their opposition, many advocated calm. In anticipation of Phase II, leaders in Charlestown worked to minimize the violence in their community when school would open. They met with some success in that there was considerably less violence than the first year.

Meanwhile in Buffalo, the leaders took note of what was happening in Boston. Cognizant of the possibility of this also happening in Buffalo, opponents in Buffalo decided to cooperate with the courts and to advocate calm from the very beginning. When the federal courts ordered the desegregation of the Buffalo Public Schools in 1976, the Board of Education worked to develop a student assignment plan that preserved the concept of the neighborhood school and minimized busing during the first two phases. Opponents as well as proponents of the order advocated obeying the court decision. When desegregation began in 1976, the scene was quite peaceful. In 1981 Phase III in Buffalo expanded forced busing to include large numbers of white students. Again opponents and proponents advocated obedience of the order. When this expanded cross-district busing plan was implemented in 1981, there were no racial incidents reported at the schools. This chapter explores the leaders' role as a possible factor for the markedly different reactions in two cities that are otherwise markedly similar.

## The Case in Boston

The *Morgan vs. Hennigan* case had its origins in the courts of the Commonwealth of Massachusetts. Prior to the decision, the Boston School Committee filed suit against the Commonwealth of Massachusetts Board of Education for withholding funds to the Boston Public Schools. Funds were withheld because the Committee refused to develop a desegregation plan that was acceptable to the Board. The Board adopted another plan, one that would require cross-district busing, which the School Committee rejected as failing to take into account the safety of the school children of Boston. On October 29, 1973, the Supreme Judicial Court (SJC) of Massachusetts (the highest court in the Commonwealth) ruled that the Committee "failed to show that the Board's plan did not properly take into account the safety of children traveling to and from school and that the plan was not invalid on theory that it provided for districts which were overly large and gerrymandered."[1] Justice Reardon of the SJC noted that the Board's plan mandated a gradual implementation of desegregation, giving the School Committee an opportunity to provide its input, something the Committee had thus far refused to do. Reardon admonished the Committee to "seize this opportunity and, by contributing its knowledge, experience and good faith, ensure the improvement of the plan and its implementation."[2] Rather than follow the Court's suggestion, the Committee awaited the decision pending in federal court. The following spring (1974) the SJC ruled that the Board's plan be implemented beginning in September. The federal court decision was rendered on June 21, 1974, but it was not to the Committee's liking. Judge W. Arthur Garrity of the U.S. District Court of Massachusetts ruled that the Boston School Committee was guilty of maintaining a dual school system, in violation of the Fourteenth Amendment of the U.S. Constitution, as interpreted by the Supreme Court in the 1954 *Brown vs. Board of Education* decision. The Committee was ordered to implement the Board of Education's plan to desegregate the schools, which, as stated earlier, required cross-district busing as a remedy. An individual who was closely connected with the case had this to say about following the Board's plan:

> The 1974 implementation order is just adopted wholesale from the state court. It was the state Supreme Judicial Court. In the spring of '74, had ordered in place and implemented, beginning September, a desegregation plan that had been worked out in the State Court, as a result of hearings conducted by a Harvard professor. And that was the plan that (was) put into effect. (It was) hoped, and indeed mistakenly expected, that the federal court single judge, taking as the federal order, a plan that had been ordered into effect by the highest court in the state, the Supreme Judicial Court of Massachusetts, after lengthy hearings in the superior court, Supreme [Judicial] Court, "here's a plan that's gone through all sorts of analyses and tests, and I think that's what we'll use." . . . Judge Garrity would be sort of piggybacking, to an extent, on the prestige of the seven justices of the Supreme Judicial Court of Massachusetts. It helped . . . to some extent, but it didn't prevent the turmoil that did ensue.

Phase I of the desegregation plan, which came to be castigated as one developed by outsiders from the federal court, was in actuality a plan that was first developed under the orders of a state court, and developed by the state Board of Education. It was the hope of the federal court that the prestige of the Supreme Judicial Court of Massachusetts would help convince municipal officials to accept the desegregation plan. It soon became apparent, however, that the Boston School Committee was not swayed by the prestige of either the SJC or the Commonwealth's Board of Education. The Committee rejected the state's plan, yet did not provide an alternative plan.

The federal court maintained the tactic of using local individuals in developing a desegregation plan. Judge Garrity commissioned a panel of local "Masters" to help develop the year-long phased in implementation. The final result was the division of Boston into eight community districts, seven of which sliced Boston up into a pie, with each slice containing an inner-city community and a peripheral community. During the first phase of the plan, all of the predominantly white districts save for East Boston and Charlestown were affected by the order. The second phase, which was implemented in September 1975, included Charlestown, and it mandated the development of "magnet schools" with specialized curricula that might encourage voluntary desegregation. Table 4.1 shows the districts, followed on the next page by a map that shows the paired districts:[3]

## Table 4.1
### Paired Districts in Boston's Desegregation Plan

| Name of District | Black Communities Included | White Communities Included |
|---|---|---|
| Brighton-Mission Hill | Mission Hill | Alston/Brighton |
| Jamaica Plain | Part of Roxbury | Jamaica Plain |
| West Roxbury | Part of Mattapan | West Roxbury and Roslindale |
| Hyde Park | Part of Mattapan | Hyde Park |
| Dorchester | North Dorchester | Dorchester, particularly east of Washington Ave. |
| South Boston | Part of Roxbury | South Boston |
| Madison Park | South End | Charlestown |
| East Boston | None | East Boston |

In developing the magnet school program, the court-appointed masters paired twenty colleges and universities with particular schools in the efforts to develop innovative and attractive programs. Moreover the State Board of Education allocated $900,000 to begin planning for magnet schools, while the state Secretary of Education recommended the allocation of additional funds for this effort. Also, the U.S. Office of Education of the Department of Health, Education, and Welfare designated Boston as a highest priority for obtaining federal dollars under the Emergency School Aid Act.[4] Once the magnet schools were in full swing, there were 27 in the Boston system.

**Figure 4.1**
**Paired Districts in Boston's Desegregation Plan**

## Reactions of Boston's White Leadership Prior to Phase I

When one thinks of Boston's antibusing movement, quite often the first person whose name comes to mind is Louise Day Hicks, who gained a national reputation for her leadership of Boston's antibusing movement. Mrs. Hicks, a lawyer from South Boston, was from a well-known family in her community, her father having served as a judge in Boston. In 1961 she ran for her first elective office: a seat on

Boston's five-person School Committee. In 1961 Mrs. Hicks was allied with the political camp of President John F. Kennedy. She did not at that time have a reputation as a racial conservative. In her victorious race in 1961, she received a large share of the black vote in Boston. When the Boston NAACP first mounted a challenge against desegregation, one of its leading members, Paul Parks, suggested that they meet with Mrs. Hicks, whom he considered as a friend to the black community. She initially appeared to be receptive to their concerns, and indicated that she would address them before the School Committee. But as members of the black community became less moderate in their demands, Mrs. Hicks' moderation also waned. She refused to acknowledge that there was any segregation—*de facto* or *de jure*—in the Boston Public Schools. Mrs. Hicks rose to the position of Chairwoman of the Committee and thenceforth staunchly defended it against accusations from the black community.

In 1967, after having served three terms on the School Committee, Mrs. Hicks ran for mayor, hoping to succeed the retiring Mayor John Collins. She was the first-place finisher in the September primary, with Secretary of State Kevin H. White coming in second. In her victory speech, Mrs. Hicks defended the neighborhood school principle, and harshly criticized the Racial Imbalance Act. She made the statement, "You know where I stand,"[5] which became her rallying cry in the struggle to preserve the neighborhood school principle.

In a close election, Hicks was defeated by White, but in 1969 she won election to the Boston City Council. One year later, Hicks ran for the congressional seat of retiring House Speaker John McCormack, another South Bostonian. Hicks won that seat, and in 1971 entered a rematch against White for the mayoralty. Hicks was defeated again, this time by a substantial margin. The following year she won the Democratic primary for re-election to her congressional seat, but she lost in the general election to another South Bostonian, John Joseph Moakley, a Democrat who ran as an independent after losing to Hicks in the primary.

In 1973 Hicks again ran for a seat on the City Council, this time winning. She took office in January 1974, only months after the School Committee had lost its case in the SJC, and months before it lost in the federal district court. Mrs. Hicks was on the Council during a propitious moment for one whose major issue was opposition to busing.

When Judge Garrity's order was rendered, Mrs. Hicks immediately moved to the forefront of Boston's political scene. She and another councilor Albert "Dapper" O'Neil were quick to condemn the decision and to ally themselves with the neighborhood groups forming in opposition. The two were closely affiliated with the organization "Restore Our Alienated Rights," more commonly known by its acronym of ROAR. ROAR held marches and demonstrations on City Hall, downtown, and throughout the ethnic enclaves where resistance was strongest to Garrity's order. Hicks was present at many of these rallies as a featured speaker. Meanwhile back in City Hall, she and O'Neil were also involved in the effort to block the implementation of Garrity's order. The two led an effort to refuse to appropriate money for the mandated desegregation effort. They professed to have no worry about being cited for contempt.

As September neared, and violence appeared inevitable, there was a last-minute effort by many to enlist the help of elected officials to prevent violence. School Committee Chairman John Kerrigan, another staunch opponent of the order, televised a statement on September 1 imploring Bostonians to refrain from violence. Hicks refused to do the same, stating that violence was inevitable. On September 9, a prelude to this predicted violence occurred downtown outside of the federal building. Senator Edward M. Kennedy was confronted by antibusing protesters who were holding a rally outside of the building. They began throwing objects at him and smashed a glass door after the Senator had entered the building.

The statement that Hicks did make for the public was a "Declaration of Clarification," signed by herself, State Senator William Bulger and State Representative William Flaherty, both of South Boston. The following is an excerpt from the Declaration:

> It is against our children's best interest to send them to school in crime-infested Roxbury. That is the issue. All of the rest is only a distraction. . . . There are at least one hundred black people walking around in the black community who have killed white people during the past two years. . . . Any well informed white suburban woman does not pass through that community alone, not even by automobile.[6]

## Elected Leaders React to the Implementation of Phase I in Boston

It was not until the eve of the opening of school that Mrs. Hicks issued a plea for calm, but this went unheeded by some of her constituents. Despite this late plea, the opening of school at South Boston High saw black students confronted by angry demonstrators, many of whom hurled rocks, bottles, and other objects at the school buses from Roxbury. There were also missiles thrown at buses of black students being transported to Hyde Park and Roslindale High Schools in the High Wards. At different points during the initial implementation of desegregation, both South Boston High and Hyde Park High were closed due to racial violence, violence which had led to the stabbings of students in both schools. The most highly publicized of these events occurred on December 11, 1974, when a white student was stabbed at South Boston High School. Word quickly spread, and members of the community joined white students in surrounding the school and preventing the black students from boarding the buses that wou..d transport them home. Hicks went to the school, along with Senator Bulger, but only Hicks would address the crowd. She pleaded with them to disperse and to let the black students board the buses and return to Roxbury. The angry crowd ignored her pleas. The black students were able to leave only after the crowd was tricked by the use of decoy buses, and the police led them out the back of the school and onto other buses that took them to Roxbury.

The pleas from Mrs. Hicks represented to some a moderation of the antibusing leader. Though she remained adamantly opposed to cross-district busing, she began demonstrating more moderation than other leaders in the movement. Some within ROAR began to speculate that she had made a deal with her old nemesis, Kevin White, who was running for re-election in 1975. After the election, in which White won a third term, many of Mrs. Hicks supporters were hired by the White administration. In the late 1970s Mrs. Hicks herself, after leaving the Council, was appointed to the city's Retirement Board by Mayor White. A person who had served in a high position in the White administration described that appointment as a "peacemaking effort."

After Hicks had left the School Committee in 1967, that body's leading voice against busing was John Kerrigan, who eventually became chairman of the Committee. The conflict between the School Committee and the Commonwealth Board of Education had intensified during Mrs. Hicks' final year on the Committee. In 1966 the Committee had voted to defy the Racial Imbalance Act, and went to court challenging the Act. The SJC ruled in 1967 that the Act met the requirements of the state constitution and admonished the Committee to comply with the Act rather than challenge it. Compliance, however, was not forthcoming. For this reason, the Massachusetts Board of Education took the initiative of drafting a desegregation plan, which was challenged in the SJC by the School Committee.

Again the Committee lost and was ordered to immediately comply with the RIA.

In January 1974, under Kerrigan's leadership, the School Committee came up with a plan that was not in compliance with the Board of Education and the SJC. In the spring of that year the SJC ordered the Committee to adopt the state plan, which included busing, but the majority of the Committee had no intention of adopting such a plan. In July 1974, one month after the federal district court placed the same order on the Committee, the Committee voted not to file any desegregation plan. Neither the Committee's majority nor the Superintendent would challenge Kerrigan's defiance of the court order. Superintendent William Leary, who was regarded as a pawn of Chairman Kerrigan, is quoted as referring to him as "my chairman."[7]

The deference of the Superintendent to the Chairman was perhaps a key reason for the refusal of the Committee to obey the court. Kirby, Harris, Crain, and Rossell state that in most cases when a school board actively works to desegregate, it is the superintendent who has provided the leadership.[8] In Boston it was thought that the reverse was the case, that Superintendent Leary, and his successor Marion Fahey were more likely to look to the Committee before making decisions. This may have to do with the fact that the Committee is the body with the sole responsibility of hiring the superintendent. Neither the mayor, nor the city council, nor community groups have any say in the selection of the superintendent of schools.

Kirby, et. al. believe that, even with a school board that opposes desegregation, if a superintendent supports it, a program can be developed. In Boston, however, the structure for the hiring of superintendents made it unlikely that a superintendent would oppose the School Committee. Certainly Superintendent Leary did not part ways with the Committee, which left it in the hands of the federal court to develop a desegregation plan.

Morton Inger and Robert T. Stout looked at eight non-southern communities that desegregated prior to 1966, and they found that the school districts that had the most difficulty integrating were those where superintendents did not act decisively to do so, whereas those with supportive superintendents were more easily desegregated.[9] Inger and Stout cited Boston and Buffalo as examples of districts with difficulty desegregating in the 1960s.[10] This is because of lack of support from the superintendents.

In looking at districts that successfully desegregated, Inger and Stout found that the public will accept a desegregation plan if it believes that the idea has come from a legitimate body, such as the school board.[11] They do not accord such legitimacy to the civil rights community nor to the courts. By refusing to develop a desegregation plan, Superintendent Leary and the Boston School Committee denied desegregation the legitimacy needed for acceptance by the public. One informant, a very vociferous opponent of forced busing, faults the old School Committee for leaving desegregation in the hands of the federal court. The following are some of the comments this informant made regarding actions that should have been taken by those in power at the time:

> I definitely think the fact that the federal courts did this for us without any participation input was devastating. I think people thought they could toy with the federal court. . . .
>
> And obviously there were folks that had legitimate concerns about the equity and issues of resources. And those in leadership positions should have taken those concerns seriously and been leaders and tackled the problem and dealt with it. Not left it for strangers to make decisions. . . . I think that we missed the boat. We should have been able to try to deal with this on our own. And certainly I would assume that people in power knew that people were unhappy. And there should have been discussions and consensus-building on how we could bring everyone to the table and address those concerns without having to get it to the level that it got to. . . .
>
> I think that if the school board or the mayor had been involved in, more involved in, there probably would've been a great big—I don't think people would've liked it any better. I just think the outcome might've been better.

It is interesting that this informant stated that "strangers" were involved in the drawing up of the desegregation plan. Much of Judge Garrity's student assignment plan was based on recommendations given to him by court-appointed "masters" who were from Boston. One of the masters was Edward McCormack, a former Boston city councilor and state Attorney General who was from a very prominent South Boston family that included John McCormack, the late Speaker of the U.S. House of Representatives. The masters were hardly "strangers" to Boston.

One would also be hard pressed to label Judge W. Arthur Garrity as a stranger to Boston. Garrity was born in Worcester, Massachusetts, just 45 miles east of Boston, and had lived in Boston since graduating from Harvard Law School in 1944. Prior to that he attended Holy Cross College, a Jesuit institution in Worcester. Like many of the opponents of busing, Garrity had been raised in a devout

Irish-Catholic family. His great-grandfather had emigrated from Ireland in the mid-19th century and settled in Charlestown. The Garritys eventually settled in Worcester where they became part of that city's middle-class Irish community.

W. Arthur Garrity left Worcester in 1941 to attend Harvard, then in 1944 he settled in Boston. In 1952 he married the former Barbara Ann Mullins and settled in suburban Wellesley, where he lives to this day. Garrity also became a member of the Clover Club, an organization of Bostonians of Irish descent. Despite all of this his detractors have accused him of having completely lost touch with his fellow Irish-Americans.[12] They cite his Wellesley address as evidence. These opponents of busing refused to accord Garrity, the court, and its appointed masters the legitimacy that the more familiar School Committee and its Superintendent were given.

The opponents of desegregation framed the order to bus as one that came from the Federal District Court. None of the interviewees who opposed the plan mentioned the fact that it was actually developed by the State Board of Education, and that its implementation was ordered by the SJC. Nor did the interviewees blame Eddie McCormack and the local masters for the plan. Blame was placed solely on Judge W. Arthur Garrity. Garrity served as an easy target. Before the decision he was relatively unknown in Boston and lived in affluent Wellesley. By labeling the plan as that of Judge Garrity, the antibusing leaders were able to further deprive desegregation of its legitimacy. This would have been more difficult to do if the plan had been blamed on more familiar and more local institutions such as the SJC, the state Board of Education, or McCormack and the other masters.

In the fall of 1974, after Phase I had begun, the School Committee continued to refuse to obey court orders to come up with a second phase that would complete the implementation process. In December Judge Garrity held that three members, Kerrigan, Paul Ellison, and John McDonough, were in contempt of court. In an effort to remove themselves from the burden of the contempt holding, the Committee came up with a plan in January 1975. It too met neither state nor federal court requirements, but it was enough for Judge Garrity to remove the contempt citations against the three.

As Phase II approached the School Committee softened its tone somewhat. Though the members did not participate in developing a plan for Phase II, they were less strident. Nineteen seventy-five was an election year, but some of the noted busing opponents seemed to be trying to avoid contributing to the chaos that was currently being witnessed with Phase I. During the campaign, McDonough joined moderates Kathleen Sullivan and Paul Tierney in urging the obedience of Garrity's order. Even Ellison, who was a staunch opponent, did not make busing a major issue in his re-election campaign. These members seemed to be backing away from the intransigence that many felt had contributed to the problems during Phase I. In searching through articles from the *Boston Globe,* I noticed that by the end of the campaign, in November, there were no reports of School Committee candidates making antibusing statements.

There was less moderation with Kerrigan, who in 1975 was running for a seat on the City Council. During the campaign, he made note of the racial violence in Louisville, Kentucky, which was undergoing a court order to desegregate. At a ROAR rally during his campaign, Kerrigan is alleged to have said, "Louisville is resisting. . . . But remember this, Louisville is Boston's farm club. So let's show this to the world."[13] Kerrigan was poised to win a seat on the City Council and join antibusing zealots Louise Day Hicks and Dapper O'Neil.

The involvement of city councilors on this issue was a departure from custom. Because of the relative independence of the School Committee, members of the Council, as well as the mayor, tended to stay out of educational matters. But busing became such a volatile issue that councilors felt it was necessary to break with custom. In the wake of the decisions of the SJC and the Federal District Court, the Council voted 8-0 to place a non-binding referendum on busing in the next city election. The Council also voted to refuse to finance the costly desegregation plans. To show their support for the fight against the decision, four councilors, Hicks, O'Neil, Christopher Ianella, and Patrick McDonough, each displayed an initial of ROAR in the windows of their adjoining offices, spelling out the word. The Council also allowed ROAR to meet in its chambers. It was inevitable that during the 1975 city council races busing would be the major issue, with most candidates stressing their opposition to the court decision. One member of the City Council told me, "I don't remember one white politician who wasn't" publicly opposed to the decision.

That statement held true for many members of the General Court as well. The most visible on this issue were Raymond Flynn, William Bulger, and Michael Flaherty, all from South Boston. Flynn was perhaps the most moderate of the group, having refused to endorse the "Declaration of Clarification" that was signed by his fellow South Bostonians, Hicks, Flaherty, and Bulger. In August 1975, when many of his neighbors were about to confront civil rights demonstrators at Southie's Carson's Beach, Flynn held a "Southie Pride Day" to divert angry South Bostonians away from the Beach. Nevertheless before the opening of Phase I, Flynn had advocated a boycott of the public schools in protest of Garrity's decision. As time went on, Flynn came to be identified with the Massachusetts Coalition Against Forced Busing (MCAFB), which was less confrontational than ROAR.

Moderation is not a word that can be used to describe Senator Bulger's actions during this era. Not only did he sign the "Declaration," but he also publicly warned against neutrality on this issue. At an antibusing rally in October 1975, the Senator is reported to have proclaimed that, "We are here to tell you that if you are not with us, you are against us, and if you are against us, we will fight you."[14] In February 1976 Bulger addressed a group of antibusing men, where he is said to have told them to "Resist. . . . Fight, no matter what form the fight takes."[15]

## The Involvement of the Kevin White Administration

Boston Mayor Kevin White joined the municipal and state legislators in abandoning the traditional *laissez faire* policy toward the public schools. Though White opposed busing as early as 1967 when he first ran for mayor, he maintained a distance from public school-related issues. This was because of the lack of control that a mayor in Boston has over the School Committee and its budget. The school desegregation controversy, however, threatened to become a public safety issue, which forced Mayor White to become involved. During the summer of 1974, after Garrity's decision, White went through various white communities in Boston holding meetings. These meetings, however, were kept private, and the public was left unaware of any pronouncements that the mayor might have made against violence.

Mayor White did, however, make it clear that he disagreed with the order. Some of his supporters in the black community were disappointed. A desire among activists in that community was for the Mayor to make public speeches stressing his commitment to nonviolence, rather than his opposition to the order. One activist had this to say about some televised announcements the Mayor made asking for calm when school opened:

> When the desegregation order came out, Kevin, the mayor, Kevin White set up a series of TV promos. And these sports figures would get on the TV. They'd say, "Now listen, we can do this. We've got a tough fight ahead of us, but we can do it."

What are they talking about? Nobody got on and said, "Well listen, these are just kids. Young people should learn to get—" It was all a very negative promotion, that, "This is gonna be tough, but we can do it. You know, if we just put our heads to it, and put our hearts, we can do it. It's not a bad—" It was the most negative promotion that I've ever heard. And so, the thing didn't have a chance is what I'm trying to say. Nobody who was anybody in the politically—you know a lot of the church members and so forth—but nobody who really had the clout came out and said, "This shouldn't happen."

The televised speech that the mayor did make was one that gave encouragement to the opponents of busing. In reference to the threat of white parents to boycott the public schools, White said, "It is their decision to make."[16] The mayor neglected to inform these parents that keeping their children out of school was against the law.

After the start of Phase I, Mayor White made it increasingly clear that he was strongly opposed to the order, and he alienated himself further from the black community. When violence plagued South Boston and Hyde Park High Schools, Mayor White issued a statement that the safety of the schoolchildren was not the city's responsibility, rather it was that of the federal government for ordering Phase I. He publicly stated that if he did not receive more federal aid to protect the school-children, he would not, "publicly support on my own volition the implementation of the second phase of the plan."[17]

Throughout Phase I Mayor White's actions indicated that he sided more closely with his old nemesis Hicks than with his former supporters in the black community. In September 1974 he refused to approve money for overtime payment of implementation staff.[18] He publicly supported the appeal of the decision, and he allowed the School Committee to appoint its own counsel, rather than using the city's corporation counsel. White assured his constituents that the case would be appealed all the way to the U.S. Supreme Court. In December he announced that "The State [desegregation] plan is unworkable and unfair," and that citywide busing should not be imposed "until the problems in Phase I have been resolved."[19]

On the eve of Phase II Mayor White, who was campaigning for a third term, was scheduled to provide greetings at a prayer meeting led by Dr. Benjamin Mays, the African-American Superintendent of the Atlanta Public Schools, and a mentor of Dr. Martin Luther King, Jr. A number of local dignitaries, including Cardinal Medeiros, were present. White failed to show up. That fall he did manage to appear at the South Boston Information Center, as a guest of Rep. Flaherty.

White was positively received at the antibusing storefront. In January 1976 the re-elected mayor said that the city was going broke because of desegregation, and he threatened early closings and teacher layoffs to save money. Later he also threatened the cutback of 615 city jobs. An order from Judge Garrity forced White to come up with the $13 million needed to keep the schools open.[20] It is also important to note that throughout the first year of Phase II, women from Charlestown were involved in peaceful "mothers' marches" against forced busing, while the mayor's coordinator in that neighborhood was a supporter of the marches.

D. Garth Taylor believes that the power and prestige of Mayor White's office was sufficient to make an impact upon the implementation, but White chose instead to serve as a "coordinator of opposition." Taylor writes that a mayor has at his disposal the "ability to influence the public because of their respect for him, for his office, and because of their support for him in the past."[21] This was particularly true of Kevin White. According to polling data from the summer of 1975, 26 percent named Mayor White as the first or second choice of public leaders who could have the most influence on how parents responded to the Phase II plan. This is compared to 24 percent for Marian Fahey, the new Superintendent, 27 percent for School Committee Chairman John McDonough, and 16 percent for Judge Garrity. It was also found that 48 percent of the respondents in a Boston neighborhood survey stated that they had a "great deal" or "some" respect for the mayor. This compares with 49 percent for Humberto Cardinal Medeiros and 23 percent for Judge Garrity, but far less than the 73 percent for John Kerrigan.[22] The significant gap between BSC member Kerrigan and the Judge, and between the Mayor and the Judge explains the public's reluctance to accord legitimacy to a plan developed by the Court without the input of the School Committee.

Instead of using his prestige and power to assist in the implementation of Phase I, White encouraged the protesters by telling them that participating in boycotts of school would be up to their individual conscience, and he went on leading them to believe that their opposition would succeed in overturning Judge Garrity's order. By publicly siding with the opponents of Garrity's order, the mayor was able to salvage his re-election in 1975. In that race he narrowly defeated state senator Joseph Timilty, who was more closely allied with ROAR.

Christine Rossell also faults Mayor White for refusing to provide legitimacy to the court order. She believes that he could have done so by public statements urging obedience, and by co-opting resistant groups and mediating disputes.[23] Rossell speaks of the *political bro ker model* wherein the mayor bargains with groups like ROAR and uses his patronage to neutralize opponents. This criticism of White was shared by one of the informants, a former elected official on the state level. The informant spoke of patronage and said, "He had some tools. I don't think he used those tools."

This view was disputed by a high-ranking official from the White Administration. In an interview this former official reminded me of the independence of the Boston School Committee, which made it difficult for the Mayor to co-opt the opponents of the plan. The informant said, "We didn't control the School Department. . . . That was the bad thing. We couldn't control the judge and didn't have one vote in the School Committee. They were all singularly elected."

Not having worked at City Hall, Rossell and the former state elected official assumed that the White Administration could easily co-opt ROAR members with jobs and neutralize their opposition. This, however, was difficult in an environment where the School Department was autonomous from the Mayor's Office. In Buffalo opponents were co-opted and hired by the school department, but the Boston School Department was too opposed to Garrity's order to work to neutralize opponents. Had the BSC developed a desegregation plan, they could have hired opponents to work with specific aspects of the plan. The hirees would have felt a sense of ownership of the plan and thus would have been less likely to oppose it. This is the strategy that was adopted in Buffalo. In Boston, however, the Mayor only had non-school jobs at his disposal. Had he hired opponents in these positions that had no relevance to school policy, he would have had a difficult time justifying the need for them to keep silent on the school desegregation plan. Moreover, without their involvement in such a plan, they would not have felt the need to defend the plan. Though Mayor White had many non-school patronage jobs at his disposal, this was of little help in the school desegregation controversy.

The events that occurred in Boston served as some confirmation of Kirby et. al.'s statement that the masses will publicly oppose segregation when the following conditions are present:[24]

1. The mayor is inactive
2. The mayor is conservative
3. There is more conflict within the school board
4. The superintendent is less active.

Each of the above conditions was met in Boston. Before the implementation of the order became a law enforcement crisis, Mayor White had a hands-off policy toward the public school system. Afterwards, he sided with the opponents of the order, which caused him to meet the second condition. The Boston School Committee could not unite over a school desegregation plan. Only Sullivan and Tierney supported compliance with the courts, and superintendents Leary and Fahey did not pursue an aggressive agenda. They were considered to be pawns of the School Committee that appointed them.

Eventually, however, White followed the course of other leaders who opposed the order: he moderated his stance and tried to calm the tensions. On April 24, 1976 the mayor led a "Prayer Procession for Peace," a march that began near the State House and proceeded to City Hall. Among those leading the column with White were U.S. Senators Kennedy and Brooke and Governor Michael Dukakis. The local NAACP also participated in the march. Though the march was not designed to support the court order, sponsoring and participating in it was a significant gesture from an Irish mayor who normally would not even march in St. Patrick's Day Parades.[25] In the summer of 1976 White finally made a speech telling the public that no amount of demonstrating could reverse the court's decision, and that school desegregation and busing would continue. Charles V. Willie (one of the court-appointed masters) and Susan Greenblatt believe that by finally taking a public stand in favor of enforcing the law, Mayor White and other officials in Boston "brought a long history of turbulence to an end."[26]

## The Role of the Boston Media

The informant who expressed displeasure with the negative media announcements that Mayor White had in place before the order was one of several who were also displeased with the media in general. Despite being disappointed with Mayor White, this person had even stronger criticisms against the local media:

> I was described in one newspaper article as a welfare mother. Never was a welfare mother. They never checked. I don't know, maybe I looked like a welfare mother, I don't know. (*Boston Globe* editor) Tom Winship (recently) said, "I wish we had done better during that period."

Another informant who early on was active in the desegregation
struggle had the following to say about the role the media played:

> There was no win. I mean the media, in the white community the
> media listened, hyped, did sound bytes, both electronic and written
> media, that there was no control of in terms of the minority com-
> munity. Or at least a balanced view being given and written about
> or talked about again through the media by either the members of
> the black community and the leadership.

An opponent of the court order, a lifelong South Bostonian, was
also critical of the media's coverage of the negative events happening during Phase I. This individual had the following to say about the
media's portrayal of the residents of South Boston:

> The national media would come in and talk to folks that probably
> weren't that well educated themselves and would paint a picture
> with a very broad brush that this person represented the entire
> community, when that was not necessarily true. They certainly
> showed our ugliest side. They should have, I think, more sensitivity
> should have been used, trying to understand the feelings people
> were dealing with, and their sense of loss of control.

A former official with the South Boston Information Center also castigated the media for concentrating only on the negative incidents:

> They focused more on the violence that was going on in South
> Boston. And there were some ugly incidents. But nobody was, no-
> body was seriously hurt. A couple of buses were stoned in South
> Boston in full view of the press. The press pretty much was sta-
> tioned outside of South Boston High School and in the South Boston
> neighborhood for several years. They set up shop outside South
> Boston High School. There was an area that I think was cordoned
> off for the press. And they hung out there for several years. So any
> time an ugly incident happened in South Boston, it would be on the
> 6 o'clock news.

Christine Rossell looked at *Boston Globe* articles from this period and concluded that, contrary to what many might think, the
*Globe* did not support desegregation. Moreover, she stated, the *Globe*
was bent on emphasizing negative incidents surrounding the implementation. In a study of ten cities, Rossell found that Boston had the
"highest score (average and total) emphasizing conflict or negative

outcomes in the first six months of the pre-desegregation year (before substantial protests had taken place)." In agreement with one of the informants cited above, Rossell said that the *Globe* went to great lengths to interview antibusing leaders and to publicize conflicts regarding the implementation. The effect was that the public had an inflated view of the costs of desegregation, and was more likely to oppose it.[27]

## Organizations on Both Sides of the Struggle in Boston

The local media was one of several established institutions in the white community which was reluctant to support the decision to desegregate. Some of the local labor organizations took public stands against busing. The Boston Teacher's Union (BTU), an affiliate of Albert Shanker's American Federation of Teachers, vehemently opposed the decision. Angry with the order for parity in hiring, the BTU went so far as to launch its own appeal of the decision. In February 1976, during the first year of Phase II, Councillors O'Neil and Kerrigan were invited to address a rally of the American Federation of State, County, and Municipal Employees. At the rally the two councilors reaffirmed their opposition to court-ordered busing. Several months later, in May 1976, a group of white members of the Building and Trades Council disrupted a meeting between the Council's Third World Workers' Caucus and construction company owners, where the minority workers were negotiating an affirmative action agreement. The Third World Workers were denounced by Hicks, who is alleged to have said, "These third world people want nothing but chaos."[28] Another local union that opposed the order was the Boston Patrolmen's Union, whose president Chester Broderick was a featured speaker at a ROAR rally.

While some of the established organizations opposed the order to desegregate, a number of community organizations sprang up in response to the order. These included organizations such as ROAR and MCAFB. ROAR was especially effective in mobilizing resistance to court-ordered busing. They held rallies, marches, motorcades, and demonstrations throughout the city, both in the white communities and downtown.

On the eve of Phase I, ROAR organized a crowd of 8,000 people in opposition to the order. Prior to that, members of the organization had thoroughly canvassed South Boston. During Phase I ROAR had little trouble organizing well attended events On December 16, 1974

ROAR held a motorcade in various parts of the city: East Boston, South Boston, Hyde Park, Dorchester, and Roslindale. In March of 1975 they held a national antibusing rally in Washington, D.C., then in the spring they held their first National Conference in Boston. The organization was quite creative in coming up with fundraising events. In the fall of 1975 they held a benefit football game, and a Bike-a-thon from Charlestown to the North End. That fall they also sponsored a boycott that emptied South Boston and Charlestown High Schools of their white students.

Throughout the crisis of the mid-1970s, members of ROAR were accused of being involved in activities that were more disruptive than parades, motorcades, and bike-a-thons, and some of the statements attributed to them were quite inflammatory. When Phase II was ordered in May 1975, Pixie Palladino, a ROAR leader from East Boston and candidate for the School Committee, stated that, "The plan is a prescription for chaos and violence."[29]

ROAR members are also accused of having disrupted a meeting of the court-mandated biracial "Citywide Coordinating Council," as the Council was holding district hearings for the Roxbury-South Boston District. The Council is one of many organizations formed under court mandate. In addition to disrupting the February meeting, ROAR members are accused of having infiltrated the organization to nullify its effectiveness in assisting in the implementation of the order.[30] But one busing opponent stated to me that Garrity supported his involvement on the Council so that the antibusing viewpoint could be represented.

Prominent members of other organizations formed during this period have also had inflammatory remarks attributed to them. A member of the South Boston Information Center is said to have made the following remark about the president of the local NAACP:[31]

> Old Gorilla-face Atkins is at it again in trying to stir up the chowder. . . . Well if Garrity closes Southie and Atkins is not wiped out and NAACP headquarters with him, I'm going to be the most surprised and disappointed person in Southie.

I interviewed several persons who had been affiliated with the SBIC, and none of them verified that such a statement was made. A former president of the Center told me that making derogatory remarks was against the goals of the Center. This individual made the following statement about the use of insulting language and participation in violent acts:

And just for the record, never engaged in that, never condoned it, never thought it was a good idea. Because much of what we were doing was a public relations kind of thing too. We were trying to, in our very naive and unprofessional way—We instinctively knew that, Jesus, in order for us to do something about busing . . . we can't behave like a bunch of KKK members. . . . There are certain things you do and there are certain things you *don't* do. You don't stone buses; you don't use terms like "n——r." You behave! You just say, "Hey, we want our children to go to, to be allowed to go to neighborhood schools." There's the argument right there.

While on the subject of the Ku Klux Klan, this informant told me of how representatives of an out-of-town hate group tried to set up a storefront in South Boston. The informant prided himself on having been instrumental in convincing the hate group's representative that his services were neither needed nor appreciated in South Boston. Another informant told the same story when I met with him several months later. After twenty years both persons had the same recollections of how the hate group was run out of South Boston. This leads me to conclude that the story was indeed accurate.

When I asked another person who was an SBIC volunteer if there was a toleration of racial epithets within the center, the response was, "You wouldn't get me in if there was." This individual, along with her husband, was involved with the SBIC during the busing crisis. I interviewed the two of them together. At one point the husband made mention of how he and the aforementioned SBIC president protected a black reporter from being attacked by a crowd outside of South Boston High School. He provided me with the name of the reporter and the news channel he worked for, presumably so I could check the veracity of his story.

These anecdotes substantiate one of the findings of Jonathan Kelley. In his quantitative research on "The Politics of School Busing," Jonathan Kelley states that opposition to busing is not necessarily an indication of racism. Except for among the educational elite, this opposition is not routinely paired with conservative views on most other social and political issues. Kelley reported the results of a factor loading study that compared whites' attitudes toward busing with attitudes toward seven other issues regarding race, such as school integration, interracial friendships, laws proscribing mixed marriages, the integration of neighborhoods, and black presidential candidacies. What Kelley discovered was that the other items have high factor loadings, but busing does not. The other seven items correlated highly with one another, indicating that they are part of a single "attitude syndrome."[32] Attitudes toward busing, however, do not appear to be part of that syndrome. On the other seven items the correlations between any one and a scale composed of the others average .56, with the lowest being .42, yet the correlation between busing and racism is only .18.[33] Even attitudes toward school integration are not closely correlated with attitudes toward busing. This means that many opponents of busing support school integration but oppose busing as a means to achieve that goal.[34] In a study focused on Boston, D. Garth Taylor similarly found that opposition to busing and classic racist attitudes were not mutually inclusive.[35]

Kelley found that the correlation between opposition to busing and racism was only found among the "elites." He concludes that this is because the elites dominate the political structure and have constructed busing as a race issue. I believe that this conclusion is based on Kelley's overly narrow definition of "elites." My definition not only includes political leaders (many of whom benefit from race politics), but also from leaders who have no political aspirations whatsoever, and who therefore do not have a need to frame the busing issue as a racial issue merely to generate votes. When interviewing these elites who have no desire to enter into electoral politics, one is less likely to find classic racist attitudes. Many of these elites are found in neighborhood organizations that are not formally connected with political machinery.

ROAR could be considered by some to be an organization connected to the political careers of certain supporters, which might account for the racially inflammatory rhetoric attributed to some of its supporters. But even with this organization there was a softening of tone as Phase II approached. On September 9, 1975, ROAR issued a public statement urging calm as Phase II began. Apparently the leadership of ROAR wanted to distance itself from the violence that characterized the first phase of implementation. J. Anthony Lukas is one who believes that this represented an ideological split in ROAR between moderates, who might have made a deal with Mayor White, and thus wished to see no more violence, and others who were less concerned about being in good favor with the mayor. The division became more evident in 1976 during the Democratic presidential primary. Dapper O'Neil served as the manager of insurgent Democrat George Wallace's campaign, a bandwagon that School Committee freshman Pixie Palladino jumped on, while Hicks supported Washington Senator Henry Jackson, a far more moderate foe of forced busing. On February 25, 1976 the split was made official, with the Palladino faction forming "ROAR United," while Hicks' regulars formed ROAR, Inc.[36]  *Copyrighted Material*

During this period of time, there were organizations, black and white, who were supporting desegregation. The core of white support for the decision came from Pixie Palladino's community of East Boston. There a woman named Evelyn Morash formed an organization called East Boston for Quality Education, whose goal was to prepare the community for Phase II. Morash later served on the Citywide Coordinating Council. Meanwhile a community newspaper, the *East Boston Community News* editorialized in support of desegregation.[37]

The biracial support for improvement of schools in the black community can be traced back to the early 1960s. Around 1960 a group of black and white activists formed a group called Citizens for Boston Public Schools (CBPS). Among the activities the group was involved in were attendance at Boston School Committee meetings and researching educational issues.[38] In 1961 CBPS endorsed a slate of five candidates for the Boston School Committee including a black candidate named Mel King. Though King did not win, he later became a fixture in electoral politics in Boston. In 1963 the CBPS again endorsed a slate of candidates for the School Committee.

Meanwhile the traditional civil rights organizations were heavily involved in educational issues. On June 11 of 1963 members of the Boston Branch of the NAACP appeared before the School Committee and asked that the Committee recognize the existence of *de facto* segregation in the Boston Public Schools, as well as the poor condition of the schools in the black community. The Committee denied that there was any segregation, *de facto* or otherwise. On the following day an organization called the Citizens for Human Rights advocated a boycott of the public schools in protest of segregation and inferior facilities for black students.[39] In 1964 the Boston NAACP decided to support a "stay out" scheduled for February 26. On that day some 9,000 students missed classes, more than 20 percent of the students in the city.[40]

The advocacy of the school boycott represented a departure from the policies of the national NAACP. Nationally the organization preferred litigation to public protest. The members of the Boston chapter were showing a level of activism not normally associated with the nation's oldest civil rights organization. But the Boston NAACP did not abandon litigation; attorneys affiliated with the NAACP provided the legal assistance during the federal court case. The second oldest civil rights organization, the National Urban League, also had a reputation for avoiding public protest. As with the NAACP, the Boston chapter of the Urban League departed from the national organization. In 1967 Mel King became the director of the Boston chapter, renaming it the "New Urban League."

Among the issues the New Urban League was involved with was educational development. By the time desegregation was being implemented, another organization was at the forefront of the struggle to desegregate. Freedom House, a local settlement house, was often referred to as the black community's "Pentagon" during the busing crisis. One informant for this study was heavily involved with Freedom House during the 1970s. The informant explained the support the business and professional community gave to Freedom House:

> We had teams of people for every situation, event, emergency, educational process. There was, a team could be made up of a loaned executive. The large corporations and companies would ask people to get volunteers who were on loan from their desk jobs. They had marketing, whatever they were doing, corporate jobs, to come to Freedom House and to other satellites around the city in the minority community to lend their expertise and the resources of their company. . . . You had all of the core of black officers, volunteers, the firefighters, the police department. You had social workers, the black social workers organized. You had the black teachers. . . . The ministers were on board. You couldn't have had a much more organized (community).

## Reactions of Boston's White Leadership During Phase II

Phase I took its toll on Boston, with violence, school closings, threats, and increased expenditures to ensure public safety. Many leaders, including those who opposed the order, were anxious to avoid the same situation in Charlestown, which would be covered by Phase II. They did not wish to see a repeat of what occurred the previous year in South Boston and sections of the High Wards. Leaders in Charlestown had a chronological advantage over those in South Boston and the High Wards, and they capitalized on this advantage. Many thought that Charlestown was as much of a hotbed of racial hostility as Southie was, therefore the community elites worked to prevent this hostility from manifesting itself the way it did in South Boston.

The interviews I conducted with South Boston community elites, as well as documented evidence in news reports, indicates that antibusing leaders in South Boston were disturbed by the violence in their community, and worked to calm things down after the situation got out of hand. The South Boston experience alerted Charlestown leaders to the possibility of their community also exploding upon the implementation of Phase II. While they did not abandon their opposition to busing, they looked at other approaches so that there would not be a repeat of South Boston. According to testimony given to the U.S. Civil Rights Commission before the implementation of Phase II, antibusing leader Gloria Conway, publisher of Charlestown's community newspaper *The Patriot,* printed statements in her newspaper admonishing "Townies" to refrain from violence.[41] During the same hearing before the Civil Rights Commission, it was also brought out that the Charlestown Boys' Club was regularly meeting with the Headmaster of Charlestown High School to help bring about a peaceful implementation of Phase II.

In Charlestown the Catholic archdiocese played a key role in preventing the violence. When Phase I was ordered by Judge Garrity, the archdiocese's official position was in support of the order. As Charlestown awaited Phase II, the Roman Catholic clergy became much more involved than they had been the previous year. A diocesan official had the following to say about the increased involvement of the clergy just before Phase II:

> There were some things I think that the community learned from South Boston. I know the clergy did. I know we did. . . . The South Boston clergy literally took a walk on the issue. And, some were, I couldn't say to a man . . . but pretty much they said, "I don't wanna get involved."
>
> At that time we had a new cardinal who . . . was not welcome in South Boston as a priest. (The parish priests felt that) "If I get associated with the cardinal who is seen as very much in favor of the busing and all this sort of stuff, one of those liberals." The priests, I think many of them felt they'd be guilty by association.

This informant also spoke of the actions the clergy took to prepare the Townies for Phase II:

> I think the larger community learned some lessons from South Boston in terms of having some other people on the buses. There were some clergy on the buses. Several evenings, and several days in late August the buses made dry runs, parents came on the bus to see where their kids were gonna go. They had open houses in some of the grammar schools. One day it was the high school, another evening junior high, another couple days, it was some of the

grammar schools. . . . They organized to welcome black parents
when they came in. In other words, have people at the schools to say,
"How are you?" . . . It's hard to measure the effect of that. . . .

Part of the Charlestown experience was that those involved from
the clergy end had all served together at one time over in the South
End at the Cathedral. So they had some ministerial roots in the
black community. They just had a different pastoral ministerial
background than some of the others in South Boston had had. And
I think they also developed sort of an ecumenical approach. They
were also involved with a Baptist minister, an Episcopalian clergyman, and a Congregational clergyman. And there were very minute
minuscule populations in that Irish neighborhood, of non-Catholic
Protestants. But (the priests) worked with them, and that helped,
because they also then began to try to meet with priests in Roxbury
and clergymen in Roxbury, black clergy in Roxbury. . . .

I think in Charlestown they did learn from the South Boston experience.

This diocesan official strove to make it clear that the clergy were
not solely responsible for the calmer reaction, but also the political
leadership in Charlestown, particularly its newly elected state representative Dennis Kearney. In 1974 at the age of 25, Dennis Kearney was elected as a state representative in a district that covered
Charlestown and East Boston. Kearney was from an Irish family in
Eastie, but he was popular among the Townies also. The diocesan official made the following complimentary remarks about Kearney:

I think the community was lucky to have him when they did. Dennis had worked closely with Charlestown priests in terms of the
neighborhood, and in terms of public safety. He watched what was
going on in South Boston the year and two years before, and the
neighborhood really destroyed itself in terms of even their business,
you know, the elderly really afraid to go out in the middle of the day
because they didn't know when buses were going to come, what kids
were going to do, go crazy. And it really sort of self-destructed in a
number of ways. The priests, in terms of their approach to the busing of children coming in from Roxbury, looked upon it in terms of
public safety. That in Charlestown you can be dead set against the
desegregation order or the busing, but you don't hurt kids; you don't
hurt children. . . .

(Dennis) bought into that. I mean he basically was a bit more open
than maybe previous leadership had been in Charlestown in terms
of, he had sort of brought a world vision.

Kearney's efforts to maintain peace in Charlestown were not merely behind-the-scenes efforts. In a public antibusing gathering on August 19, 1976, Kearney told hundreds of Townies that, "Although we're opposed to forced busing, we're not racists. . . . We're human beings. We are concerned . . . and we are as strongly opposed to violence as we are to the concept of forced busing."[42]

I interviewed one of the political leaders who worked in Charlestown during this period, and he too agreed that Charlestown benefitted from seeing what had happened in South Boston. About Southie, this person said, "They were the first, and there were no lessons to be learned (before) that. And again, a lot of it, again, at least from a citywide basis, maybe a lot of elected officials were still saying 'never,' when that wasn't the appropriate response."

The failure of city officials to reverse the decision during Phase I undoubtedly convinced leaders in Charlestown that busing was an inevitability. South Boston did not have the benefit of failed appeals. A public official I interviewed said that leaders in Charlestown had a clearer understanding that the order had to be obeyed. In an interview the informant told me the following:

> I can't speak to the dynamic in South Boston, but . . . I think that there was no equivocation in Charlestown, with respect to accepting the fact that it was coming. So to stand up and give speeches and talk about how we're gonna stop this didn't seem to make very much sense. Indeed the true, the true, the true thing to do out of concern for the people in the community was to help them cope with it as much as possible, and prepare for it, knowing that you couldn't change it.

The above informant had this to say about what his role was in working with his constituents regarding the busing issue:

> And my attitude at the time was, there's nothing I can do to change this order. I wouldn't deceive my constituents into thinking that I could. . . . I felt that these people were getting screwed. And I felt that the more violence there was, and the more disorder, the more screwed they get.

A community leader who worked outside of the political arena made similar observations when speaking with me:

> I do know that we tried to handle it differently than South Boston. With all due respect to my good friends in South Boston. Our

position, and the position that I advocated and maintained and still maintain: we should do nothing to drive the young people out. And if in fact we believe that it is the right of the parents to choose the school, then we in no way should oppose any parent's choice of putting a child on a bus. . . . And we shouldn't do anything in any way to promote violence or obstruct people's right to, parents' right to exercise educating their kids. . . .

(But) in Charlestown's case, (Charlestown High) wasn't the first choice of a majority of kids going to high school, as opposed to South Boston. South Boston was in fact the first choice for the majority. So they felt far more—Without putting words: we try to stay away from each other's turf. They would feel much more threatened at the high school level than our community would.

When Phase II began in September 1975, there was far less violence and disorder than there had been the previous year, even at Charlestown High. A very active member of the black community, Ellen Jackson of Freedom House, was interviewed during the opening of the 1975–1976 school year. Mrs. Jackson stated that, "By and large schools' opening is an improvement from last year. . . . It's hard to tell why. Maybe it can be attributed to efforts on the part of community agencies this summer. . . . Many realize desegregation is an inevitability."[43]

## The Case in Buffalo

The school desegregation case in Buffalo was filed in federal court in 1972, the same year it was filed in Boston, but the decision came two years later in Buffalo, in 1976, while Boston was going through Phase II. The Buffalo case, *Arthur vs. Nyquist,* was decided on April 30, 1976 in the U.S. District Court of the Western District of New York.

The judge in the Buffalo case was John J. Curtin, a man who was similar in many ways to Judge Garrity. Curtin was born to an Irish-Catholic family in South Buffalo, and grew up in a middle-class section of South Buffalo called "Roanoke Park." He describes himself as a "fifth generation South Buffalonian."[44] Curtin received his early education in Catholic schools, then went on to Canisius College, a Jesuit institution in Buffalo. He then received his legal training at the University of Buffalo's law school and graduated in 1943. Curtin and

Garrity share the characteristics of ethnicity, similar age, and a Jesuit undergraduate education. But unlike Garrity, Curtin could not be considered as an "outsider" to Buffalo. Though the judge now lives in North Buffalo (which is within the city limits), he has close family ties to South Buffalo. His parents remained there until their death, and his brother Dan was an orthopedic surgeon at Mercy Hospital, a Catholic hospital in South Buffalo.[45] Because of his background, some were surprised when Judge Curtin ruled that Buffalo had intentionally segregated its schools and ordered the Buffalo Board of Education to develop a plan to transform the Buffalo Public Schools into a unitary system.

The "Buffalo Plan," as it came to be known, was implemented in three phases over a five-year period. In Phase I, which began in 1976, there were school closings in both the black and white communities, closings that resulted in more racial balance. There were also changes of the feeder patterns, which brought about more racial balance in high schools. Phase II, which began in 1977, was the closing of neighborhood schools in the black community and their transformation into specialized "magnet" schools that would attract students from throughout the city. Students from the white communities would be bused to the magnet schools, while many blacks from the former neighborhood schools were bused into white communities. Phase III, which began in 1980, mandated the removal of grades pre-kindergarten through two in three predominately white schools. The white students would be bused into receiving schools in black communities. These schools were now called "Early Childhood Centers," with special programs not previously offered in neighborhood schools. The students would remain there until completing grade two, then they and the black students at the schools would be sent to white communities to schools serving grades 3-8, known as "academies." In 1981 Judge Curtin ordered the School System to "expedite" Phase III beginning that fall. Phase IIIx (meaning "three expedited") began in the fall of 1981.

Phase IIIx required the busing of over three thousand white pre-K to grade 2 children into the black community. Between Phase III and IIIx, a total of 13 white schools in peripheral areas lost their grades pre-K to 2, while children of those grades were bused into the inner city. White elementary school students from South Buffalo, Riverside, the far East Side, and the Lovejoy District were sent to the inner city for the earliest grades. For grades 3-8, black students from the Ellicott, Masten, and Fillmore Districts were sent to schools in the outer city. It was hoped that this use of forced busing would complete the transformation to a unitary school system.

## Reactions of Buffalo's White Leadership

Persons familiar with the Buffalo school desegregation case will agree that opposition to desegregation and busing was as strong in Buffalo as it was in Boston. The antibusing movement traveled a similar path in both cities. Louise Day Hicks had a powerful counterpart in Buffalo in the person of Alfreda Slominski. Five of the thirty-five persons from Buffalo whom I interviewed made this comparison. While Mrs. Slominski never achieved the national fame of Mrs. Hicks (none of the Boston interviewees mentioned her name), Slominski's early political career was quite similar to that of Mrs. Hicks'.

Alfreda Slominski was appointed to the Buffalo Board of Education in 1962, the same year that Louise Day Hicks joined the Boston School Committee. She was appointed for a five-year term. When her five-year term expired in 1967, she ran citywide for an at-large seat on the Common Council, which she won. That was the same year in which Hicks left the School Committee to run citywide, but for the office of mayor. In 1969, midway between Hicks' two races for the mayoralty of Boston, Slominski ran for mayor of Buffalo. Like her Boston counterpart, she was defeated in her bid.[46]

From the time she was on the School Board, Slominski was a strong opponent of forced busing. In January of 1966 she publicly spoke out against busing white students into black neighborhoods. When she perceived Superintendent Joseph Manch as favoring a busing proposal, she urged a boycott of the schools and led a picket on Manch's office, demanding that he resign. Slominski stated that there were so many persons willing to side with her that it would be impossible to jail every one of them. After being elected to the Common Council on an antibusing platform, Slominski led the fight against constructing portables to facilitate integration.

During Slominski's 1969 race for mayor, the councilwoman ran on a neighborhood schools and law-and-order platform. She also advocated a change in the city charter so that members of the school board would be elected rather than appointed. This, Slominski undoubtedly felt, would place more busing opponents on the Board of Education.

In 1971, while Hicks was running citywide in Boston for the office of Mayor, Slominski was running citywide in Buffalo for an at-large seat on the Common Council, a race which she won. Just as 1974 was a propitious moment for Hicks to return to the Boston City Council, 1972 was equally propitious for an opponent of desegregation in Buffalo to enter the Council. The year 1972 marked the height of the battle between the forces pushing for desegregation and those advocating neighborhood schools. On January 24 of that year, New York State Education Commissioner Ewald Nyquist ordered the Buffalo Board of Education to come up with a desegregation proposal. When the Board refused to do so, Nyquist said that he would issue a mandate. He traveled to Buffalo on February 21, 1972, and was met by angry demonstrators who were opposed to forced busing. They physically prevented Nyquist from entering City Hall. Slominski was one of four city council members in the unruly crowd.

In 1972 there was also a great deal of racial turmoil in several of the local high schools in the peripheral areas of Buffalo. One informant, a former member of the Board of Education, described the tensions as "race riots . . . that (were) like war." The rioting led to some of the high schools being closed for several days. Allies of Slominski used these events as evidence that further desegregation of the schools would be doomed to failure.

Slominski, however, was not very active in the antibusing movement after 1972. In 1974 she successfully ran for the position of Erie County Comptroller. Once in that office she began to focus more on county matters. Having left her municipal office, she did not mobilize opposition to the *Arthur vs. Nyquist* decision in 1976. Her leadership on this issue had been short-lived.

As stated earlier, Mrs. Slominski's opposition to busing dated back to her days on the appointed Board of Education. While on the Board she was one of several members who advocated defying the state's order to desegregate the schools. The Board members defied Commissioner Allen in 1966, and they defied Commissioner Nyquist in 1972. Despite this defiance, there was no withholding of funds, which is why Nyquist was named as the defendant when the case was brought to federal court.

## Mobilization in Buffalo's Black Community

The case in Buffalo would not have materialized had it not been for the efforts of the local NAACP and other segments of the civil rights community in Buffalo. In 1962 the NAACP publicly presented its case before the Buffalo Board of Education. In a public statement the NAACP alleged that Buffalo's public schools were racially aggregated and that the black schools were in an inferior condition. When the Board of Education did not respond favorably, education advocates in the black community presented their case to state officials. In December of 1964 a biracial group named Citizens' Council on Human Rights (CCHR), under the representation of an attorney named Norman Goldfarb, petitioned State Education Commissioner James Allen to address the issue of segregation in the Buffalo Public Schools. This action led Allen to order the desegregation of the schools, an order ignored by the Board of Education.

In addition to the NAACP and the CCHR, a local civil rights organization became involved with the issue of the public schools. That organization was Build Unity, Integrity, Leadership, and Dignity, more commonly known by its acronym, "BUILD." In 1967 William Gaitor, the president of BUILD, denounced the slow pace of school desegregation in Buffalo.[47] BUILD was created in 1967 as a coalition of over 100 civic, religious, business, labor, social, youth, and other groups. It was formed with the assistance of Saul Alinsky, a Chicago-based national activist.[48] In the year of its formation, BUILD began a study of the Buffalo Public schools, and in 1968 it issued the results of its findings. The report, entitled "Black Paper Number One," condemned the schools, cited a lack of black teachers, and expressed the need for more community control.[49] Nevertheless, the Board of Education was no more receptive toward BUILD than they had been to the NAACP or the CCHR.

### Efforts of Buffalo's New Board of Education

In 1974 the City of Buffalo underwent a charter change mandating that the seven-member appointed Board of Education be replaced by a nine-member elected Board. This was a revision supported by antibusing leaders, who anticipated that the city's white majority would elect an antibusing school board. The election was held on May 4, but it was preceded by a campaign in which busing was the major issue. The majority of the candidates were opposed to busing, but the local press boasted that the candidates took the high road and avoided mudslinging. After the votes were counted, it appeared that the antibusers held the majority, but the new Board was composed of three blacks (one man and two women) and six whites (three men and three women). One of the black members, Florence Baugh, had run at-large and received a substantial number of white votes and the endorsement of some of the Lutheran churches in South Buffalo.

From the point of view of the black community, there were other positive developments resulting from the elections. The members of the new Board of Education were less adamant than the old Board in opposing desegregation. This may have had less to do with the membership than with the developments in Boston immediately following the installation of the Board members in Buffalo. Several interviewees told me that the events in Boston provided an example of what to try to avoid in Buffalo. They saw the many similarities between the two cities and their cases, and realized that there was a potential for the same type of outcome in Buffalo. Therefore they worked to prevent this from happening.

Informants who had not sat on the School Board, but who nonetheless were quite familiar with the case, agreed that chronology was on Buffalo's side. One white informant, a current elected official in Buffalo, said the following concerning his observations of that period of time:

> I mean *nobody* wanted to have happen in Buffalo what happened in Boston. So I think even if you harbored racial feelings, I think you bit your tongue to avoid riots in the streets.

Those who supported the plaintiffs acknowledged that their opponents worked to avoid a Boston-style reaction in Boston. One such person told me that, "Boston happened first. And we saw those horrible television depictions of what happened. And maybe that was the lesson that we didn't want to emulate." A community leader who worked intensely with the plaintiffs said the following about the potential for a Boston in Buffalo:

> I think Boston was probably a catalyst for a lot of other communities. Because communities looked to see what was going on in Boston and said, "We can't be another Boston. And therefore how do we handle this?" In Buffalo there was no resistance. Nobody said, "We're not"—Oh there were one or two people. But they were not the real leadership. In Buffalo they said, "We're gonna abide by the judge's order."

The cooperation with the court was very evident. An informant with very close ties to the legal team representing the defendants said that there was a collaborative effort among the Board of Education, the Court, and the plaintiffs even while the case was appealed. I found through my research that this cooperation began two months before the decision was rendered. On February 11, 1976 the Board of Education came up with Phase I of the desegregation plan. This plan mandated the closing of ten schools, five which were predominantly white, and five which were predominantly black. In three of the white schools that closed, the students were sent to schools with significantly higher black percentages. There was also some rezoning of feeder schools. There were three schools where students who were previously zoned to overwhelmingly white high schools (South Park and Riverside), were changed to be zoned to predominantly black high schools (Kensington and Bennett). It is difficult to imagine Boston's Board developing a pre-decision plan that would result in white students being reassigned to schools that were predominantly black.

What further distinguishes Buffalo from Boston was that prior to a 5–4 vote on the above plan was a unanimous vote to move toward integration. Florence Baugh, one of the three black members, had been elected by the other members as President of the Board. She and the Superintendent of Schools, the late Eugene Reville (who was from South Buffalo), made a decision that everyone had to be in agreement to cooperate if they were going to proceed with desegregation. So before any specific plan was drawn up, the members voted 9–0 to begin the process of desegregating the Buffalo Public Schools. Once the decision was rendered, none of the members publicly denounced it.

What was crucial to the smooth implementation of Phase I was the support it received from two of the highest-ranking persons in the school system: Board President Florence Baugh and Superintendent Eugene Reville. Reville assumed the position of Superintendent in 1975 upon the retirement of Joseph Manch, who had been Superintendent for 18 years. Dr. Manch was reluctant to take the initiative in dismantling Buffalo's dual school system. He was especially leery about the use of busing to remedy desegregation, yet he was not one to propose other effective means to desegregate the schools. In February 1972, when Buffalo was under state pressure to desegregate, Manch traveled to Albany to join the superintendents of the other four largest cities in New York State as the "big five" urged the State Department of Education to avoid the use of busing for school desegregation. Though the state ultimately did not withhold funds from Buffalo, the case was making its way through the federal court, where the city was less likely to avoid being forced to desegregate. It was at this point that Manch announced his retirement. One former member of the Board of Education said that she believed Manch retired in 1975 because, "I think he saw integration was coming."

Harrell R. Rodgers, Jr. and Charles S. Bullock III would see the departure of Manch as a development favoring the desegregation of the public schools. In a study of school desegregation from 1969–1971, they found a positive correlation between superintendent change and desegregation.[50] In Buffalo Manch was replaced by a superintendent who was more willing to address the demands of the black community. But more significant than the departure of Manch was the departure of the appointed school Board at almost the same time. It would seem to many that an elected school Board would be more receptive to the white community, which held the majority of the votes. An elected Board would be less likely to take the political risks of cooperating with the federal court. The Boston School Committee certainly did not take those risks. The appointed Buffalo Board indicated its willingness to listen to the civil rights community in the 1960s when it voted to fund the QIE program and to construct portables. These measures, however, were opposed by the City Council, which had to face voters every two years. Nevertheless it was the appointed Board who developed the student assignment plans that were being challenged in court, and who refused to cooperate with the State Department of Education in developing a plan to end *de jure* segregation and racial imbalance in the public schools.

To the surprise of many, the elected Board proved to be more receptive to the courts than the appointed Board was. This is not necessarily evidence of an increased moderation on the part of the elected members. The failure of the appointed Board to develop a desegregation plan was due to the fact that members of that very Board were accused of having illegally segregated the Buffalo Public Schools. For them to have backtracked and changed their own student assignment plan would have been an admission of guilt, something that one rarely sees in public life. Though the elected Board had members who were strongly opposed to busing, none of the members elected in 1974 had been involved in the student assignment plans that were being challenged in the federal court. Therefore they had no reason to feel defensive about the existing plan. This, plus the desire to avoid a situation where the court assumed broad powers, and a willingness to avoid conflict, led the members of the new School Board to cooperate with the court.

When Eugene Reville assumed control over the school system, the case was being heard in the federal court. It was common knowledge that the city was not doing well in the case and would be found guilty. Therefore the new superintendent and the newly elected Board of Education began to put together a plan that would be acceptable to the federal courts.

Phase I was considered as a temporary measure; the Board was required to develop a substantial plan that would have more permanence. The Superintendent made two strategic appointments of deputy superintendents, which greatly assisted him in developing and selling the plan. One of the appointments was of a black administrator named Claude Clapp. Mr. Clapp had a long and distinguished career as a teacher in the Buffalo Public Schools. He eventually went into administration and was in line for the superintendent's position when Dr. Manch retired. He was bypassed, however, in favor of Mr. Reville. The selection of the Irish-American South Buffalonian over Claude Clapp dismayed some in the African-American community of Buffalo, but appointing Clapp as a deputy superintendent gave Reville credibility in that community. To bolster that credibility, Reville appointed a well-known black public official, Kenneth Echols, as director of the Office of Integration. Another strategic appointment was of Joseph Murray, from an Irish-American family in the Riverside area on the North Side. Murray would prove to be an invaluable asset during Phase II.

From the outset it was understood that Phase I would be a very temporary stage of desegregation, lasting only during the first year. The Board was under federal pressure to develop a more substantial plan to desegregate the schools. The Board under President Baugh, along with the team of Reville, Murray, and Echols, decided to seek parental input from throughout the community. Beginning in November of 1976 they held meetings in every section of Buffalo. In the white communities they made it clear that the order could not be evaded.[51] Rather than give white parents false hope, they asked them what they wanted as improvements for the public schools. They were most interested in finding out what curricular offerings could be added.

In subsequent meetings the Board explained to white parents that they would be able to accommodate many of their requests, but in order to partake of these innovative curricular offerings, their children would have to be bused to "magnet schools" in the black community. Throughout the black community neighborhood schools were closed down and replaced by citywide magnet schools with curricula that would hopefully attract white students. For example, Woodlawn Junior High School became Buffalo Traditional School, with emphasis on traditional methods of pedagogy; Clinton Junior High became

Buffalo School of the Performing Arts, with specializations in dance, vocal music, instrumental music, etc., and School 17 became City Honors School, an examination school for gifted students. The work of the School Board and the Superintendent in securing white parents' support is what Mark A. Chesler, Bunyan I. Bryant and James E. Crowfoot call a "consistent positive approach." This involves the use of two plans: one being the desegregation plan itself and the other a plan to generate community and school support for the plan. Chesler, et. al. state that this would involve "reach(ing) out to a variety of community groups to present information, hear complaints, and solicit input."[52] A key to the success of such an approach is the involvement of parents in devising the plan to desegregate the city schools, which ensures their later acceptance of the plan. Jennifer Hochschild wrote that, "If citizens become involved early in the process, if their roles and responsibilities are clear, if their work is relevant and actually influences the process, they may improve the plan and increase white acceptance. But these conditions are seldom met, and . . . their outcomes usually come at the relative expense of minorities."[53] Buffalo was one of those few cases where these conditions were met. Murray, Reville, and Echols listened to the parents' suggestions and incorporated them into the plan for Phase II.

On the negative side, as Hochschild would predict, minorities did not reap all of the benefits of the plan. Phase II would require the mandatory transfer of black students whose neighborhood schools became magnets (unless they managed to gain admission into the magnet), but depended upon white students volunteering to be bused into the inner city. This differed from Phase I, wherein some elementary schools in peripheral areas were shut down and white students rezoned to schools with larger minority populations; or where there was a change of feeder patterns, rezoning some white students from predominantly white to predominantly black high schools. It was only on the part of white students that Phase II would be voluntary. The Board worked under the knowledge that if there were insufficient numbers of white students volunteering to be bused into the inner-city, a third phase would have to be implemented requiring the mandatory reassignment of white students. Anxious to avoid more mandatory reassignments, the Board worked to convince white parents to send their children on buses to the inner city.

One strategy that Reville and Baugh used was reaching out to parents who were against desegregation, many of whom lived in South Buffalo. The Superintendent and Board President met with these parents and were able to convince some of them to send their children to magnet schools. This made it easier to bring other parents on board. I interviewed one of the South Buffalo parents who was convinced to come on board, and this individual indicated to me that Reville and Murray's success was partly due to their relationship to South Buffalo. This parent had the following to say about the Superintendent and his deputy:

> You have to keep in mind Gene Reville was born in South Buffalo, okay. And see the Judge (Curtin) was born and raised in South Buffalo. . . . And of course Joe Murray married someone from South Buffalo. So, you know, so these people that were on there knew the feelings in South Buffalo.

A former member of the Board of Education gives the same level of praise to Mr. Reville for the smooth transition. When I asked this former member what might have been the major difference between Buffalo and Boston, I was given the following answer:

> Well, you know, I think there was one major difference; that was the Superintendent. Florence Baugh was President of the Board at that time. . . . And what they did, they went to the community first, which did not happen in Boston. And they went in some very hostile areas. But they were able to develop positive facts about what the children would be getting within the school setting, that sort of turned even the South Buffalo parents around. Because some of the South Buffalo parents who swore they would never send their children in the black neighborhood, sent them into the black neighborhoods and became leaders in the Parent Teachers' Organizations. But I think talking directly to the people, letting them vent their concerns was one of the best things. . . .
>
> [The] Superintendent was wonderful. And he had the support of the Mayor, who did not want his city disrupted. He may not have wanted desegregation, but neither did he want his city torn apart. But going directly to the people, getting their input, and developing magnet schools that the parents wanted for their children was quite a difference, I think.

It took a major sales effort to convince large numbers of white parents to buy into these magnet schools in the black community. This is where Murray proved himself an invaluable member of Reville's staff. A person who served as a consultant to the plaintiffs had this to say about Murray:

He's a genius at organization. And what he did was, he went out into the white communities and pre-empted all the bigots and all the racist remarks and co-opted people who were opponents. And convinced them that there was gold at the end of that rainbow, when those children got on those buses. And did a beautiful salesmanship job. He really made it happen. And we have to give him credit for that because we had no problems like Boston, nowhere near.

A current member of the Board believes that the outreach to influential persons in the Buffalo community was quite helpful. This person too gives Reville and Murray credit for this effort:

> And what was great is that Mr. Reville and Mr. Murray and Board members didn't just reach out to parents. But they reached out to ministers, church people, got them to buy into it. Business leaders. I mean they did a public relations job like you wouldn't believe. So that you not only had the Board and staff out there talking about the need to do this. But you had ministers on Sunday preaching from the pulpit that this was the right thing to do, that this was the human caring thing to do. This was the Christian thing to do. And I think when you build coalitions like that, where you reach out and you involve all sections of the community in the decisionmaking, I think that's how you're more successful.

What was witnessed in Buffalo was a commitment from the Superintendent and his top level staff. Ernest R. House sees the "central office staff" as being as valuable as the Superintendent in bringing about educational innovations. House said that their contact with the outside world makes them key to this process. This contact allows them to serve as "propagators or inhibitors of innovation."[54] In Buffalo Joe Murray's position as Deputy Superintendent allowed him more flexibility than the Superintendent to travel throughout the city. Immediately after Judge Curtin's decision, Murray became well known among parent groups and Parent Teacher Associations throughout the city of Buffalo. His intimate knowledge of Buffalo was a tremendous asset. One informant had the following to say about Murray's work throughout the city:

> Reville's a good spokesman, but Murray knew what was going on. He knew where the bodies were buried. He knew who he could call on to make things happen. This openness, the public meetings, going right to those communities and holding meeting after meeting after meeting, with their slide presentation. Oh it was beautiful!

They did up visual aids and all kinds good stuff. Not so much asking people what they want, but telling them, "This is what you need!" And, you know, he just put a positive twist to it. And it stuck.

Daniel U. Levine and Connie Campbell state that, in addition to commitment from top level administrators, magnet school programs must be launched with widespread publicity "in order to attract students all over the city and to build confidence among middle-class families in the quality of instruction in such a school."[55] Levine and Campbell's research was done before Buffalo's Phase II, so they are not able to use Joe Murray's work as an example of the successful publicity of magnet programs. The examples they cite are Cincinnati, Houston and Boston. They praise Boston for printing literature in seven languages describing the magnet school programs. But the consensus among persons I spoke with in Boston was that not enough was done to publicize the magnet programs.

I asked several of the Boston interviewees if there were Buffalo-style efforts on the part of the superintendent and/or School Committee to sell the magnet schools, which were a part of Phase II in that city also. They felt that there was very little official effort to sell the magnet schools in the white community. An informant who played an integral role in the development of Boston's secondary school magnet programs lamented the underutilization of the magnet schools: "From the time they have been here they have never been well utilized to any great extent. . . . No, they didn't sell the magnet schools." Another Boston informant, an African American, cited an occasion where a School Committee member tried to prevent the informant's daughter from attending a magnet school in predominantly white East Boston:

> My kids were bused in first and second grade. Bused to East Boston, which was not part of the deseg order. East Boston is not part of that whole order. When they voluntarily decided they wanted to be part of it, [they] created magnet schools out there. . . . I think it was math. At the beginning of school, the first day, [School Committee member] Pixie Palladino, Pixie was sitting there holding on a seat telling them, "I don't want these black kids here! . . . "
>
> And I marched my kids in that building and said, "Take your seat. She doesn't own this building."

In Buffalo there were no incidents of elected officials doing anything even remotely similar to that. The School Board there was far more cooperative.

## Cooperation of the Buffalo Media

A number of the Buffalo interviewees also give credit to the local media for being very helpful during Phase II. During the summer of 1977, just before Phase II was implemented, Reville and Murray launched a massive public relations effort to get white parents to send their children to magnet schools. They received a great deal of help from the media. Local radio stations broadcasted advertisements about the magnet schools and encouraged students to take part. A high-ranking official at the Board of Education office said that, "Everybody joined together, including the press. . . . They even got the *Buffalo News* and the press involved. That's a big plus, when you have the press putting out articles. That leads to some kind of positive results." As a result of the efforts placed into Phase II, the magnet schools had lengthy waiting lists of white students hoping for a spot in the inner-city schools. Many of those on the waiting list were suburbanites whose parents were willing to pay tuition and transport their children to the inner city to receive their education in *public* schools.

Another informant, one who was involved in the integration effort, said one thing positive about Buffalo as compared to Boston was that, "The newspapers didn't exploit the issue." In Boston the consensus seemed to be that the media was bent on exploiting the issue. This consensus was shared by desegregation opponents, such as the SBIC member who complained about the press stationing itself at South Boston High, and proponents such as the Roxbury community activist who made the following statements:

> I think the news media was the worst culprit of all, even above the politicians. Because it was the news media that capitalized on the events that were taking place, publicized them all over the world. Added to them, and never once put anything that was of a good nature during this whole period of time. I say that because we went to, we went to the *Globe* to locate some of their thousands of pictures in order to do a slide show. And we were looking for some slides that would be good. Not one of them depicted anything nice that went on then at all. They just concentrated on those five areas where the problem was, not the others. And there were at that particular time, I believe, over 200 schools in the school system. And they concentrated on those five.

An official in the U.S. District Court that issued the Buffalo order, when speaking of the media in Buffalo's case, summed it up by saying, "There was good cooperation from the media. We had good cooperation from the, not only TV, but radio stations and newspaper as well."

I verified these statements by researching articles from the *Courier Express* from 1972 through 1981. The *Courier* was one of the two daily newspapers in Buffalo, the other being the *Buffalo Evening News,* commonly referred to as the *News.* I looked at the *Courier* because during much of the period it was the only one of the two that published Sunday editions, with special features on topics such as school desegregation. The *Courier* folded in 1983, but this was long after the third phase of desegregation had gone into effect.

Through my research of *Courier* articles, I was able to verify the cooperation of the media. When the Board of Education came up with its plans for Phase I, the plan was publicized as one that required no forced busing. The May 19, 1976 headline in the *Courier* reads, "School Board to forward no-busing plan to court."[56] Four months later, when school re-opened after a teacher's strike, the same newspaper printed an article stating, "No incidents were reported as a result of the busing. As they did on September 8, opening day of school,[57] parents, priests, ministers, and nuns rode the buses to try to maintain order in case of any disturbance."[58]

In May when Phase I was unveiled, the *Courier* chose to ignore the fact that there were *mandatory reassignments* affecting both black and white students, with many of these reassignments taking place on a bus. In September, however, after Phase I began without a hitch, the *Courier* admitted that there was "busing," and estimated that some 3,000 students were transported by yellow school buses as a result of the court order. This figure does not take into account the number of secondary school students who had to be provided with passes to take public buses to their new schools. The fact that the newspaper waited until Phase I was peacefully implemented before correctly describing the plan is an indication of a desire to maintain peace throughout the city.

### A Decade of Opposition from Elected Officials in Buffalo

Many Buffalonians were surprised at how peaceful the reaction was to the desegregation plan. Not only had the events in Boston caused many to worry about a repeat in Buffalo, but there was also the vivid memory of the racial turmoil that took place in the schools in 1972. That year saw race riots at several of the peripheral schools where blacks were still very much in the minority. It was also the year when the antibusing movement was at its peak in Buffalo. This was reflected in the Common Council. During the winter of 1972 the Council sponsored six antibusing bills and confirmed busing foe Carol Williams as a member of the Board of Education. It was also that winter when Commissioner Nyquist was physically prevented from entering City Hall, blocked by some members of an antibusing crowd that included four members of the Common Council. One action at that rally, however, demonstrated the willingness of some of the councilmen to avoid the expression of racial hatred.

At the February 1972 antibusing rally, one of the participants held up a sign saying, "Wallace for President." Councilman Daniel Higgins (D-South Buffalo), an ardent foe of busing, requested that the protester remove the sign. He stated that the sign was racially inflammatory and indicated that such was not the aim of the rally. This was in contrast to an antibusing rally in Boston several years later, where one of the members of the City Council was flanked on both sides by confederate flags,[59] and where Wallace's local campaign for the U.S. presidency was headed by a member of the Boston City Council.

There were other events where antibusing members of the Common Council worked to prevent or calm racial disturbances. During that time, when there were racial disturbances at Kensington High School on the Far East Side, two elected officials went to the school to help calm things down. One of them was Arthur O. Eve, a black member of the New York State Assembly, and the other was Councilman Charles Volkert (R-University District), an ally of Slominski, and a very strong opponent of busing. Eve, Volkert, and Ted Kirkland, a popular black policeman, walked to the front of the school, where blacks and whites were facing each other off. They brought the students together, went inside and, conversed about the school's problems. This prevented the situation from becoming violent.

A similar situation happened after the court order, when there was some racial violence between black and white students at South Park High. This tension was resolved when at-large Councilman Gerry Whalen of South Buffalo (who ran as Gerry "No Busing" Whalen) went to the school, joined by two black members of the Council, George Arthur (D-Ellicott District) and Council President Delmar Mitchell. The three spoke with the students and calmed things down. One informant credits this type of behavior for keeping Buffalo peaceful during the transition. This informant, who later served on the Council himself, gives credit to the Council of the 1970s for preventing a Boston-style situation:

> Some members of the City Council really led the opposition. But once the order came, they weren't about to foster violence. Those people, I remember Jerry Whalen, definitely pulled his wings in. . . .
>
> They got a group of the antibusing parents together to calm the kids down and calm the parents down. They said, "Look, it's over! We're gonna bus; we're gonna cooperate. And it has to be non-violent." And it worked.
>
> I think there were some friendships. So in other words, Gerry respected George Arthur, who was the plaintiff in the case. They were great friends. So while they disagreed on the issue, they were good enough friends to trust each other and to try to let busing work once it had been ordered, and to try to do it in a non-violent fashion. . . . I think that was the big reason, is that people who were philosophically opposed decided that there wasn't going to be any violence in Buffalo. . . . Because frankly, had Jerry taken a walk on the thing, or said the wrong things in the wrong places, or even Slominski for that matter. . . . Had those people fanned those flames, boy, we could have been in for some serious problems.

Whalen's neighbor and colleague on the Council, South District Councilman Higgins, again made clear his opposition to desegregation in 1976 after Curtin's decision. Curtin was dismayed by statements that Higgins made at a meeting at School 67 in South Buffalo. The judge stated that Higgins and Joe Hillary, South Buffalo's representative on the Board of Education, were behaving in an "inflammatory manner."[60] Despite this, in the fall of 1977 Higgins enlisted the help of businessman Joe Pirakas, head of the Federation of South Buffalo Community Organizations (consisting of more than 30 groups in the community), to assist him in meeting with South Buffalonians to try to convince them that Judge Curtin and Superintendent Reville were not traitors to their community.[61]

In the 1977 election there were nine Common Council seats up for election, but the issue of desegregation was not a major focus of the candidates, not even in the ethnic enclaves where resistance was fiercest. The major issue in that election was the Erie County Democratic Committee. Insurgent Democrats (both black and white) in all nine council races were challenging the "Machine," which at that time was headed by an Irish-American attorney named Joseph Crangle. Therefore the major issue was not school desegregation, but each candidate's independence from or ties to Crangle.

There was perhaps more potential for violence in 1981 when Judge Curtin ruled that Phase II had not gone far enough and ordered the busing of large numbers of white children below third grade to schools in the inner city. On April 1 of that year Councilman James Keane (D-South Buffalo) sponsored a resolution against forced busing. Keane labeled the Phase IIIx plan as "The threatened forced busing of our babies."[62] The resolution passed by a 9–4 vote, with four black councilmen voting against the resolution. The fifth black member, Council President Delmar Mitchell, voted with the white members.

Other than their vote on the resolution, members of the Council were not very vocal in their opposition. There was a public hearing on Phase IIIx on April 8, but the *Courier* makes no mention of any public officials being present, as they undoubtedly would have been nine years earlier. When the plan was unveiled in May, Councilman Dan Quider (D-North) accurately predicted that, "Parents will voice their strong opposition to this very loud, clear, and quickly, but I don't see any organized protests . . . and I don't anticipate any."[63]

Two of the informants I interviewed stated that one reason why the IIIx forced busing was peacefully implemented was because the residents were somehow made to believe that this was not forced busing, but merely an extension of the popular magnet school program. What was helpful in convincing them of this was the fact that the receiving schools in the inner-city would be "Early Childhood Centers," with pre-kindergartens and other special facilities for the students, facilities that did not exist in neighborhood schools in peripheral areas. An employee of the Board of Education credits the shrewdness of Murray and Reville for making the residents believe that IIIx was not forced busing. When I asked this person if the parents objected to the forced busing of IIIx, I was given the following explanation:

> They still don't feel they're being, at that time they didn't feel they were being forced. They thought they had another opportunity to get their child into pre-k, because it was such a popular grade. And was an all, don't forget that before then we didn't have pre-k, we didn't have all-day pre-k. In Phase II we only had half-day pre-ks. The only full-day pre-k was Montessori and BUILD Academy. I mean that was 30 students, that was all you could take, 35 students

at the most. So out of citywide, that's not many students. . . . But you know what? Buffalo is shrewd. I mean, you gotta understand what they did. And I go back to these two gentlemen (Reville and Murray), and I go back to the elected Board. I mean, like Florence Baugh. Florence was like a sister out in South Buffalo. Now as staunch as what she, you know, of course Florence Baugh has charisma. . . .

Another informant, a former city councilperson, had the following to say about the public's perception of the Early Childhood Centers in the inner city:

People were convinced that those were great schools. The Early Childhood Centers were great schools. And it didn't become an issue. Ah they didn't like the fact that their kid had to be on a bus for 45 minutes, but they also had an alternative. If they really felt strongly about it, there was a strong parochial school system that they could send their kids to for a hundred bucks a year at that time.

Another former city councilperson gives praise to the Superintendent:

I think it's because of the way it was structured, and the quality that was being offered, the programming being offered to attract white families to neighborhoods that they may not have been accustomed to being in or visiting made a difference, I think. A parent being convinced that their child was going to get a superior education in these Early Childhood Centers versus the neighborhood schools.

I think again there was a lot of public awareness and meetings that Gene Reville, God rest his soul, I think was a major force. And allowed the desegregation that happened here, more smoothly than it did in Boston.

I told a member of the Buffalo Board of Education what many of the Boston interviewees, black and white, told me, and that is that white Bostonians would never have accepted a Phase III with the forced busing of kindergartners. In Boston, kindergartners are exempted from Garrity's order. I told this Buffalo Board member that to include kindergartners would cause a tremendous uproar in Boston. The member gave the following response about Buffalo's Phase III:

These are pre-ks, so they're even younger than kindergarten. Three, three years, nine months is the youngest child on that bus. And there is anxiety. There's no question. . . . "These are children that are barely able to function on their own. They're barely able to be independent of their parents. You're asking us to send them into harm's way." And that was the reaction in the early '80s. . . . It was not something that was easily accepted at first.

When I asked the informant how they were able to pull it off, credit was given to the resources of the ECCs and the salesmanship of the Superintendent. The informant gave a description of the benefits of the Centers:

> The early grades in the pre-k through the second grade age group are set up so that every classroom has both a teacher and a teacher aide, *every single classroom*. And so that the benefit for the child is that, and for the young children, the very young, is that the maximum class size is 20. For every classroom there are two adults in the classroom. And educationally it's the best model that we have in our district, other . . . than the Montessori, in that having the interaction of two adults in the classroom with 20 children or 25 young children gives the ability of the classroom teacher to do a far better preparation with teaching, and the children succeed far better. And I think parents saw that as an asset.

About the Superintendent's role in convincing the parents, this Board member said:

> Well again, the salesmanship of the Superintendent. . . . Gene Reville is somebody that actually I think singlehandedly brought together a team of his administrators, and went out and cajoled, lobbied, and convinced the community that they should take the chance, that there wasn't a risk in terms of race relations. But if there was a safety concern that those folks had out there, he was going to make sure that they could see hands-on that there was not going to be an issue, that it could be cured by something that the school district would do. . . . So it wasn't something that he was somebody that sat back and took a passive approach in convincing people. He was very active in trying to convince people. . . .
>
> Reville's role couldn't be understated, I don't think. And the Board, Florence Baugh was the Board President, as I recall. Very articulate, confident woman.

The ability of the top level school board personnel to convince the public to accept the desegregation plan is evidence of the power of the leaders to steer the biases of the public. Robert Dahl would state that the elites are able to create a "false consensus" among the masses, by influencing their attitudes, ideas, and opinions.[64] In Boston the leaders were able to create the consensus among the public that (1) their children's lives would be endangered if they were to be forced to attend school in the black community, and (2) the decision could and would be reversed. In Buffalo the leaders worked to prevent perception number one among the public. Using their power as elites, they gained the consensus, perhaps false, that Phase IIIx should be supported because it was merely the extension of the popular magnet school program.

The interview data shows that much of the opposition in Boston might not have occurred had the local leadership acted as did Buffalo's in 1981 and neglected to inform the masses of the implications of the desegregation decision. In Boston many of the masses were unaware of the case and the impending forced busing until they were mobilized by the rallies and parades held by the antibusing forces. One individual from South Boston, who did not hold any community leadership role prior to the court case, said that before Garrity's decision the members of the community were not aware of the case. The informant said that, "None of us knew a federal district judge from the district court judge up South Boston Court. We didn't know anything about the law." When I asked how the people became aware of the case, credit was given to the efforts of "a lot of people who had been involved in the antibusing movement, or what they anticipated would be forced busing. The Louise Day Hickses, and Rita Graul, and Virginia Sheehy." Another individual from South Boston answered the following to the question of how people in the community became aware:

> The community—I don't remember at what point—but community activism is what happened. When they hear of many, many marches. . . . There were rallies and community meetings, people taking to the streets. . . .

A former elected official from South Boston had the following to say about how the community became informed of the implications of the decision and mobilized to oppose it:

> There was such an organizational effort over here. . . . There were meetings on a weekly basis, sometimes two or three meetings a week in the different communities. People traveled from community to community. South Boston contingent would go to Charlestown, Charlestown would go to Southie. . . . And it was your representa-

tives that were bringing the message back, the people that you had. . . .

Two opponents of busing whom I interviewed were not as laudatory of the efforts to mobilize opposition to the decision, but they also credit these efforts for making the public aware of the court order. One informant had the following to say about the Boston School Committee at that time:

> I think what you had, you had a lot of citywide rhetoric coming out of the Boston School Committee at the time. But, so one can say that the citywide elected officials, especially the School Committee, obviously made it an issue.

Another opponent of the order criticized some of the antibusing organizations and elected officials who affiliated with them:

> Some of them fanned the flames of prejudice. Through their own ignorance and immaturity, they appealed to the emotional aspect of it. They antagonized different groups, trying to solidify themselves with their constituency, instead of reaching out trying to reason and come up with common solutions. Adamant groups were formed like R.O.A.R. Restore Our Alienated Rights, in South Boston, was a very active antibusing group. They'd parade, and they were violently against busing. And of course when it happened, people were all up in arms, all emotionally involved in it. And it was difficult to reason with them.

In Buffalo there was no such mobilization against Curtin's decisions, including his 1981 decision to begin massive forced busing of students in the earliest grades of elementary school. The failure of Buffalo's antibusing leaders to organize marches and demonstrations to rally support, and the decision of the School Board to allow the public to see Phase IIIx as a mere extension of Phase II's popular magnet schools is what led to community acceptance of forced busing. This demonstrates that the masses do not rally against such innovations without being mobilized by persons considered as leaders. This was particularly true in 1981, by which time the issue of busing had lost its salience among the voters. Having lost its salience, most persons did not have strong opinions on the issue. Their opinions are provided to them by those who are more closely connected with the public schools, namely the Board of Education. In the days when Buffalo had a School Board who strongly opposed

school desegregation, the board members did not present information to the masses favorable to desegregation, nor did they convince
the public of the consequences of disobedience. In 1981, when there
was a Board whose members favored compliance with the court, they
presented information favorable toward integration, and convinced
the parents that their children would benefit from attending the
Early Childhood Centers. The superior level of information the elites
hold on particular issues makes it contingent upon them to mobilize
the public's support or opposition to an innovative reform. In this
case the leaders mobilized support, whereas the leaders in Buffalo in
1972 and Boston in 1974 mobilized opposition.

### The Busing Issue and Mayoral Politics in Buffalo

The Buffalo desegregation case was temporally extended over
the administrations of three different mayors: Frank Sedita, Stanley
Makowski, and James Griffin. The last of these mayors had the most
consistent record of opposing school desegregation, but Sedita eventually made clear his opposition to busing. Early on in his tenure as
mayor, Sedita developed a reputation as a liberal, and he hired more
blacks in City Hall than any other previous mayor, if not more than
all previous mayors combined. When he ran for re-election in 1969,
he received the lion's share of the black vote, running far ahead of
Slominski and a black Democrat who was running as an independent. But like Mayor White in Boston, Sedita could not hope to remain mayor if he supported busing.

Sedita demonstrated his opposition to busing in 1972 when he,
a Democrat, appointed a Republican, Carol Williams, to the Board of
Education. In a letter Sedita wrote that he was appointing Williams
because of her opposition to busing, a practice the Mayor referred to
as "playing checkers with our students."[65]

Sedita retired in early 1973, and was replaced by Councilman
Stanley Makowski. When Makowski was on the Council, he was the
only white member to join the three black members voting against
the law barring portables. As mayor, Makowski had a record that
won him praise by the persons I interviewed who were advocates of
desegregation. One member of the Common Council described
Makowski as a "highly religious man" who "saw the world in terms
of right and wrong, good and bad. . . ." A former member of the Council said the following about Makowski:

[He] had a lot of faults and inadequacies, but certainly one of them wasn't his racial attitudes. . . . He was a very charitable, very sincere person. Perhaps not a leader, but clearly could've appealed to people's better instincts, and did that, I believe, in this case.

In September 1995, months after I concluded my Buffalo interviews, the Board of Education opened an Early Childhood Center in the heart of the inner city, and named it after Stanley Makowski. Makowski's successor was nowhere near as supportive of the plaintiffs in the school desegregation case. James D. Griffin, a very conservative Democrat from South Buffalo, became Buffalo's mayor on January 1, 1978. Prior to becoming mayor, Griffin was a state senator, where he assumed a leadership role in the fight against busing. In 1972 Griffin was one of a bipartisan group of legislators who went to Albany trying to convince Nyquist to avoid the use of busing as a remedy of desegregation. Griffin also worked with Slominski in the fight for an elected Board of Education.

Griffin's campaign for mayor was during the fall of 1977, just as Phase II was being implemented. Nevertheless, he did not make desegregation an issue, focusing instead on crime and his opposition to the Machine. County Comptroller Alfreda Slominski crossed party lines and campaigned for Griffin, but even with this antibusing veteran at his side, Griffin's camp avoided the school desegregation issue. They did not criticize the magnet school publicity campaign that ran simultaneously with the mayoral race. Throughout Griffin's first term as Mayor, he maintained that Curtin's decision was the law, and it had to be obeyed, whether or not one agreed with it.

Phase IIIx, requiring massive forced busing of white students, came into effect while Griffin was campaigning for a second term as mayor. Griffin threatened to appeal the decision to expand busing, but he made no threats of disobeying the court, nor did he provide his constituents with any hope of having the decision overturned. In preparation for IIIx, Griffin attended a meeting at School 65 in Riverside and told the overwhelmingly white audience, "It's that judge over there that is making the decisions. If he says 'bus,' there's not a thing you or I can do about it, unfortunately."[66]

Throughout his tenure as mayor, Griffin was vociferous in his opposition to Judge Curtin's decision, and he tried to prevent the city from allocating money to fund certain aspects of the decision, but he never threatened to disobey the decision. Some of Griffin's strongest detractors were interviewed by me, and they all agreed that Griffin stressed following the judge's order as the law, and they said that as

a candidate for mayor and as mayor, Griffin did not make school desegregation a major political issue, as was done in Boston.

All mayors have at their disposal the powers of local law enforcement agencies to quell disturbances, but the Boston case demonstrates that even these powers, plus a desire of the mayor for calm,
are not enough to *prevent* the occurrence of violent antibusing
demonstrations. What is necessary is for the mayor and other influential officials to persuade opponents to obey the decision and to refrain from violence. Mayor Griffin historically had been more
strongly opposed to busing than Mayor White was, but unlike White,
when massive forced busing was imposed on white students, Griffin
immediately acknowledged that he could not change the decision of
the court, and he publicly admonished his constituents to accept the
decision as law and to refrain from illegal protests. Some felt that this
may have been part of the reason for Buffalo's peaceful transition.

## The Role of Biracial Nongovernmental Organizations in the Buffalo Case

One cannot underestimate the contribution of neighborhood organizations in making desegregation successful in Buffalo. Several
of the informants I spoke with give credit to the grassroots community organization BUILD (Build Unity, Integrity, Leadership, and
Dignity). BUILD was created in 1967 under the guidance of Saul
Alinsky, a white activist from Chicago. Three of the interviewees in
Buffalo also spoke of the involvement of local white activists in the
school desegregation struggle. The Citizens' Council on Human
Rights (CCHR) whose membership was predominantly white,
worked closely with the NAACP, and the CCHR Chairman, the late
Norm Goldfarb, was listed as a plaintiff in the *Arthur vs. Nyquist*
case. None of the interviewees in Boston spoke of the involvement of
white-led organizations in the struggle to desegregate that city's
public schools, but in Buffalo the CCHR and the NAACP worked together as plaintiffs in the case. The CCHR served as a link between
the local civil rights community and other predominantly white organizations, such as the Buffalo Teachers Federation. An informant
who was an official in the CCHR had this to say about the work with
the Teacher's Federation:

> We went around talking to the teachers' organizations asking people
> to come together to begin to work on a solution to this before the

Court ruled. And then once the Court ruled, then many of those groups had no control over what happened. We met with the teachers, the Buffalo Teachers at that time at their delegate assemblies, and with their executive committees, explaining, going over step-by-step what happened. And that maybe if we would now start to fashion a plan, when the court ruled, the court might take that into consideration that there had been some good faith efforts. But we were rejected at every point. . . . But I think we were making some inroads. . . .

When the order was finally issued by Judge Curtin, the Buffalo Public School System was found guilty of staff segregation as well as student segregation. The finding of staff segregation directly impacted the Teacher's Union. There was a similar finding in the Boston case, and Judge Garrity ordered an affirmative action plan. The Boston Teachers Union (an affiliate of the American Federation of Teachers) objected to the plan and filed an appeal in federal court. In Buffalo the CCHR went back to the Buffalo Teachers Federation (an NEA affiliate) and tried to gain the union's cooperation. The CCHR official had the following to say about this effort:

> We had resistance with the teachers with the affirmative action, but the Judge said—It then stopped white teachers from becoming permanent. So we talked with the Teachers Association, said, "Unless you carry out the judge's order; unless we get the support of the teachers, you, your membership can't get permanent appointments." . . .

> The affirmative action spread, and they branched out more to get more black teachers to take those exams so that the white teachers could [become permanent]. They didn't come around because they felt sympathetic toward black teachers. It's that they couldn't get white teachers permanent unless they could get black teachers.

One former member of the Board of Education noted that five years later the Buffalo Teachers Federation was instrumental in helping to convince persons to accept Phase III. This informant had the following to say about the BTF's role:

> Mr. Reville set up teams of administrators and some teachers, along with the Teachers Federation . . . to go to these schools and talk directly with the parents before they really set up the program. In other words, he did the groundwork beforehand. So the parents knew; they had a chance to ask questions.

This is a very significant difference between the two cities. In Boston the teachers union led an appeal of the desegregation order, whereas in Buffalo the union helped sell a forced busing plan.

In Buffalo there were also white religious groups who were supportive of the efforts to desegregate the schools. This is a fact that was mentioned by two of the informants, and by Mark Goldman in *City on the Lake*. One of the informants, a former official in the Sedita Administration spoke of a ministerial association that was at the forefront in the local civil rights movement:

> These were white ministers who took a very active lead in issues of this sort. In fact as I recall, this (desegregation) was one of their key urban issues. There was Richard Prosser, who, a Presbyterian minister who ended up heading Friendship House in Lackawanna. He's dead now, died of cancer. A Saul Alinsky man, you know, and Dick was rough, he was tough.

> Dick and Norm Goldfarb (of the CCHR) together were something that Boston didn't have. Boston didn't have a Dick Prosser; they didn't have a Norm Goldfarb out in the battle. What you had out front in the battle there was a Louise Day Hicks. She stirred up the emotions, I think, in ways that Alfreda Slominski could not. Alfreda Slominski was Louise Day Hicks' counterpart in Buffalo. But there was nothing comparable to the organization of white ministers in Buffalo.

> There were even a couple of Roman Catholic priests who weren't a part of that group, but who were out front.

The informant who worked with the CCHR also credits the religious leadership in Buffalo. This person stated that compared to Boston, in Buffalo, "You had a different configuration of people, religious leadership, some of the political leadership was not as rabid in its approach."

When the order was issued by Judge Curtin, the local religious leadership did indeed cooperate. Archbishop Edward Head gave a similar order that Cardinal Medeiros gave in Boston: parents could not use parish schools as a vehicle to escape desegregation. In August 1976 the prelate sent a letter to be read in all Catholic parishes in Buffalo, saying that, "Catholic schools will not become havens for those seeking to avoid public school integration." Public school students would be accepted only if, "the receiving officer is morally certain that the request for admission is consistent with the above stated diocesan policy."[67] Head was more popular in Buffalo than Cardinal Medeiros was in Boston, hence his directives were not as likely to be opposed. *Copyrighted Material*

On the opening days of school in 1976, there was an interfaith group of ministers who demonstrated their support for peace by riding the buses with the students. Adult volunteers included nuns and priests from the Catholic archdiocese and a liberal coalition of Protestant ministers, the Buffalo Area Metropolitan Ministries.[68] In Jennifer Hochschild's 1984 work on the Boston School desegregation saga, she states that case studies "unanimously assert" the need for local elites to be involved in order to prevent racial violence. She specifically mentions the religious leadership. Hochschild looks at Wilmington, Delaware, which implemented a metropolitan-wide school desegregation program in the mid-1970s. There a religious coalition, the Delaware Equal Education Process Committee (DEEP), served as the "chief counterweight" to the local antibusing organization.[69] Persons from the Wilmington area give DEEP credit for bringing about the peaceful transition to integrated education in Newcastle County, Delaware. Likewise the religious leadership in Buffalo played a key role in facilitating a peaceful transition in that city.

There was also assistance from some unlikely groups. As stated earlier, Joe Pirakas, founder of the Organization of South Buffalo Community Organizations, went through that section of Buffalo trying to convince the residents that South Buffalo natives Curtin and Reville were not traitors to their community.[70] In the Lovejoy District of the far East Side, a neighborhood where antibusing sentiment rivaled that of South Buffalo, a local community agency also lent its support. Lovejoy, a heavily Polish-American district, had its own Alinsky type of organization, the Advisory Board for Lovejoy Elderly and Youth, known by its acronym ABLEY.

I interviewed a former activist from ABLEY, a person who shared the antibusing sentiments of many other Lovejoy residents. This individual informed me that Lovejoy's neighborhood school, School 43, was one of the first peripheral schools to participate in the Quality Integrated Education program, which was before Curtin's order. This activist explained ABLEY's role in keeping things calm when the QIE program first began at School 43:

> Initially there was quite a bit of resistance, but as time went by there was less and less. But I can remember having a whole bunch of parents and kids lined up on Lovejoy Street and waiting for the buses to go by, and I would be standing on the corner as [an official] of ABLEY trying to keep things. . . .
>
> But there were some, there were some racial problems. I used to walk around with a camera. Never had any film in it. But the minute

I'd start walking down the street with my camera, all of our kids would run like hell. And they ask me, they said, "Why you got the camera?" "If there's any kind of problem," I said, "and if anybody gets hurt, I'm gonna have proof that you guys were here instigating some problems." And I would just walk down the street with my camera, and I would raise it up, and they'd run like hell to get outta my way.

When Curtin's order came down, this individual, though still strongly opposed to the order, helped children from the Lovejoy district get safely to school in the inner city. In none of my interviews with Bostonians, nor in any of the readings, did I see evidence that leading opponents of Garrity's order transported children to school in Roxbury, North Dorchester, or Mattapan.

One should not assume that there was not a great deal of organizing in Buffalo against school desegregation. A difference between Buffalo and Boston in this regard is that as the Boston case was making its way through the federal and state courts, a cadre of organizations came to the forefront to mobilize opposition to the decision, whereas in Buffalo much of the antibusing mobilization took place well before Judge Curtin's decision was rendered. One of the first well-attended anti-desegregation demonstrations in Buffalo took place in June 1968 when 500 demonstrators picketed a model portable classroom, a life-sized facsimile of what would be used at peripheral schools to facilitate desegregation. Another well attended protest was the 1972 demonstration spoken of earlier where antibusing parents, supported by several elected officials, prevented Commissioner Allen from entering City Hall. One South Buffalonian I interviewed spoke of the antibusing activity during the early 1970s:

> It was frustrating because it took precedence over everything else. It was, really people were incensed. I don't think, you know it's always strange, it always took me strange. All these parent, parent-teacher groups became very active. All the various schools, public schools primarily in South Buffalo. . . .
>
> [Everything else] really took a back seat. Everything was busing, busing, busing. People were absolutely paranoid, and I supposed rightly so. . . .
>
> They went from PTAs to like an organized type of thing, where all the various schools were involved in what they call the—I forgot what the official name of it was—but it was a "no busing" issue, was primarily the issue. So as a result of that there became a very large vocal group.

The informant was undoubtedly speaking of the South Buffalo Advisory Against Forced Busing. This was one of the groups that formed in opposition to the threat of forced busing. A similar group formed in the Lovejoy District, with the rallying cry of the "Neighborhood Schools." These groups joined forces with the already established Western New York Parent Teacher Association (PTA) in opposing forced busing. The PTA was Buffalo's counterpart to Boston's Home and School Association and played the same role as the HSA in leading the fight against busing.

Despite this organizing in the early 1970s, these groups were very much muted in 1976 when Judge Curtin ruled against the city. They did not mobilize the antibusing forces in the way that the Boston organizations did. This is a point that I noted when speaking with the informants. In examining the statements I was provided with three different reasons for lack of organizing of the antibusing forces in Buffalo when the decision was rendered. One reason is that by 1976 there was no strong leadership on this issue coming from elected officials. Another reason was that some of the community leaders had been co-opted and hired by the School Board, and a third reason is that the white community had resigned themselves to the inevitability of desegregation, with the Boston case serving as evidence of the fact that the decision could not be overturned.

## A Muted Common Council

By 1976 Buffalo's most noted antibusing leader, Alfreda Slominski, was no longer on the Common Council. In a special election in 1974 she was elected as Erie County Comptroller, a position she held until her retirement in 1993. Mrs. Slominski was now removed from issues directly affecting the city and its schools. In her elevation to county politics, the antibusing movement lost a leader whom even her detractors praise for being highly intelligent and very knowledgeable on educational issues.

Another stalwart in the fight against busing was Carmelo Parlato, a Republican who served on the School Board from 1962 to 1972, and who was considered as an ally of Slominski. In 1972, however, Parlato was elected as a City Court judge. He then followed the judicial custom of staying out of controversial issues like school desegregation. By the time of Curtin's Order, the Common Council and the School Board had lost their most vociferous opponents of busing.

Some interviewees, however, do not believe that Mrs. Slominski could have generated the following that Mrs. Hicks had in Boston, even had she still been on the Common Council. They cite this as a reason why there was no ROAR-type group in Buffalo in 1976. Different reasons were given for Slominski's inability to mobilize the support that Hicks could mobilize. One informant said that Slominski's Republicanism and her poor relations with the Erie County G.O.P. were reasons why she never had a large following. The following are excerpts from this interview:

Alfreda Slominski didn't organize anything. Louise Day Hicks did organize. See too then in Buffalo, when you look at the small "p" politics, Alfreda Slominski was a Republican, the city was Democrat. She was not only Republican, but she was fringe, extreme conservative. The city was moderate in its politics, small "p" politics. And with the city being predominantly Democratic, she was like a noise in the wilderness from a political point of view. An embarrassment in some instances to her own party. . . .

Where in Boston the Democrats were raisin' all this hell, here in Buffalo it was one Republican woman, who was an embarrassment, and who the Democrats could sort of snicker about and figure that she would go away, she would disappear. She's an aberration on the political scene.

The informant is absolutely correct in saying that Mrs. Slominski did not enjoy good relations with the Erie County G.O.P. During the 1960s, and to some degree the 1970s, the Erie County Republican Party was a moderate organization that reflected the state of Republicanism in New York State at that time. The titular head of the state's G.O.P. was Nelson Rockefeller, whose liberalism earned him a rude reception at the 1964 Republican National Convention. The other very prominent Republicans in the state were also considered as liberal. The senior senator was civil rights champion Jacob Javits, the junior senator for a time was Charles Goodell, another liberal, and the mayor of New York City was John Lindsay, who was so liberal that he eventually changed parties. In Erie County the local Republican Party was an upper class moderate organization that shied away from issues like busing. In fact, one of the Republicans from the city, Joan Bozer, who now sits in the Erie County Legislature (the only Republican from Buffalo in the Legislature), was described by one informant as having been a "staunch member" of a group called Parents for Quality Integrated Education. The Erie County G.O.P. of the late 60s was not a party where Slominski could have gained a great deal of support. When she did run for mayor in 1969, the party leadership did not support her in the Republican primary, but she nevertheless won the primary.

One informant seems to feel that in order for a leader to marshal the forces that Hicks was able to marshal in Boston, that person needs to be from the area of the city with the strongest opposition to busing. In Boston the core of resistance was Hicks' neighborhood of South Boston. In Buffalo, the agreement among the interviewees (without any dissent among those who were asked) was that the core of resistance was South Buffalo, which was not Slominski's neighborhood. About Buffalo's antibusing forces, an informant said the following:

> They never really had a leader. There was no real focus. Well they did in Alfreda Slominski and Parlato, but they weren't *their* people. There was no real Irish American that really came forward as an avowed racist who could ride that horse. Griffin was around; he was in the State Senate at that time. But even he never really rode that horse. . . .

There was, however, one very strong voice against busing from South Buffalo, and that was of at-large Councilman Jerry "No Busing" Whalen. But despite the fact that Whalen used this as an issue in some of his campaigns for election, his leadership against busing was largely confined to the chambers of the Buffalo Common Council. One former member of the Common Council said that Whalen "may have been one voice of 15 at the time. So it really was inconsequential."

Another former member of the Common Council, one who has been strongly opposed to forced busing said that, "There was no organized leadership that was able to pull off an anti-movement." This former council member went on to say the following:

> I'm trying to recall the political situation, was there ever a pro-busing or antibusing slate? I don't think I've ever seen that where you really had people that were on opposite sides of the thing. I don't think that the political system in Buffalo used the integration as a cause one way or another.

The spouse of this former Common Council member said, "I think there was a lot of grumbling, but nobody ever organized."

## Phase IIIx Meets No Organized Resistance

When Phase IIIx mandated the massive involuntary transfers of white students, one might have expected a reinvigoration of the antibusing movement in Buffalo, but such did not happen. As previously stated, many of the parents were made to see this as an extension of the heralded magnet school system. One could not expect this belief to be shared by the leaders of the antibusing forces. Leaders usually have greater knowledge of political developments, and it would be unlikely for them to see the pairing of neighborhoods with inner-city Early Childhood Centers as anything other than forced busing. In fact, those opponents whom I spoke with expressed their discontent with Phase IIIx, despite the facilities of the Early Childhood Centers. They were dismayed that their neighborhood schools were no longer available to very small children. One South Buffalo parent who had been active in the antibusing movement during the early 1970s said the following about the Early Childhood Centers:

> Now with Phase III, no they don't have a choice, as far as that goes, unfortunate. But the choice they will say to people is, "Well, you can always apply to a magnet school." And it's not fair.

When I asked this parent why it was unfair, the response was, "Because that's not true. There are only so many seats available" in magnet schools.

My question to some of the interviewees was, if the antibusing leadership saw Phase IIIx as a massive increase in forced busing of white students, why was there not a strong opposition mounted? One former city councilperson said the following in response to that question:

> I think that busing was accepted. But I think that the reason for that was, soon as the magnet school system started, the whites themselves were moving their kids in buses themselves to what they considered to be a better education system. You understand? I don't think that the groups were together. The mothers weren't that involved, you know, as much of a turmoil as they were in the early busing, when busing first came out.

The turmoil certainly was avoided. When Phase IIIx went into operation on September 9, 1981, there was not one reported incident of violence. Police Commissioner James Cunningham was quite pleased with the way the opening day of school had proceeded in the city.[71]

Another reason given for the lack of mobilization among the opponents is that many of these opponents were provided with jobs with the Board of Education. Interviewees on both sides of the issue noted that many of the leaders of the antibusing movement had been provided jobs when Curtin's order came into effect. This was a lure difficult to resist in Buffalo in the 1970s and 1980s, with the closing and/or scaling down of many of the area's factories, such as Westinghouse, Bethlehem Steel, and Trico. Buffalo went into a seemingly permanent recession from the mid-1970s on. Many of the antibusing leaders were connected with the declining local industries, either through direct employment or, more often, through the employment of their spouses. Even those families who had not yet suffered from unemployment could not be certain that layoffs would not hit the factory of the families' breadwinners. Having steady *paid* employment was more of an incentive to many of the leaders than was *volunteering* to lead antibusing rallies.

One member of the Common Council spoke to me about a conversation with Superintendent Reville concerning the hiring of busing fooa!

> I said, "Gene, the reason why we didn't have any problem is that we hired a lot of the parents that were raisin' hell." He hired some of them. And so they went riding the bus with the children and watching out for others and that stuff. That's why we were able to open up and go through without any, without any disturbances.

A former member of the Council praised Reville's ingenuity in using employment to co-opt the leadership of the antibusing movement:

> Reville was a fox. Reville went out, he said, "If we're gonna have busing, we're gonna have to have bus aides. We're gonna have to have classroom aides to help monitor this." And he went out and made all these antibusing people, he went out and hired them. He hired them. He said, "Ma'am, if you're so much against this, you come in and monitor it. It's gonna happen. The order's there. You can monitor it; we'll pay ya to monitor it. You can ride the buses. We're gonna give you fi' dollars an hour to ride the buses, to be a monitor in a classroom." These people became the chief advocates afterwards. Not only were they employed, they saw how well it was working. It wasn't the nightmare. Didn't turn out to be the nightmare that they had envisioned. Really, I remember, he was a fox. Smart move.

One informant was not so laudatory about the use of jobs to buy out the opposition. This person, an opponent of busing, began working in City Hall in 1978 when the Griffin Administration assumed office. When asked how much of a political issue busing was in the late 1970s, this informant gave the following response:

> I don't think it was that much of a political issue. You know, really, in fact most of the groups that started—we had people that were dead against busing and everything else, and my first year working in City Hall, I'd go into City Hall, and jeez, these people, they'd gotten a job with the Board of Education. I said, "Jeez, weren't you the one that was always yelling about this desegregation order, integration order. And now you're working for the Board of Education?" They'd smile, "Oh you know, well you gotta do things." . . .
>
> And the councilmen, the councilmen did great with the patronage. That's all they had to do was agree with the Board of Education, and I know that. . . . You can see by just going over to the schools. You get people from my community, "I never knew so-and-so's wife was working at this school." Because the councilman, they call Reville up at the time, and now they've got Al Thompson. Sure they're gonna hire their friends. But to me it was an awful costly plan that they had.

The use of jobs to stifle the opposition to school desegregation is an example of appealing to the individualistic sentiments of people to gain their support for measures they would not ordinarily favor. By using school desegregation as a means to provide jobs to white ethnics, the Buffalo Board of Education and Superintendent Reville were appealing to the individualistic sentiments of people from communities like South Buffalo, while simultaneously securing their support for the enforcement of a court decision that they might otherwise view as an inappropriate governmental intrusion, despite its constitutionality. One cannot help but agree with the former Common Council member who said, "Reville was a fox!" His South Buffalo background made him quite aware of the individualistic desires of persons in his home community. He used these desires to the advantage of the School Board and the federal district court.

This doling out of patronage to buy off opponents of desegregation is a method that was not widely used in Boston, despite the city's reputation for old style politics. While it is true that Louise Day Hicks and many of her supporters were given jobs in the White Administration, I could find no reports that there was a large-scale hiring of leaders of antibusing organizations to work in the schools. I asked an official in the White Administration why this was not done. The following is the answer I received.

But you understand, the Mayor's Office didn't control the School Department. You understand? They could have done it if they had (controlled it). But they didn't. . . .

It appears from the above responses regarding patronage that the different governing structures of the two cities' school systems helped contribute to the different outcomes. The Boston School Committee is far more insulated from the Mayor's office and the City Council. This is reflected in the location of the School Committee Headquarters: it has its own building, away from Boston City Hall. In Buffalo the School Board offices are located in City Hall, the same building that houses the Mayor's Office and the City Council. The independence of the Boston School Committee prevented Mayor White from using patronage to buy off the leaders of the antibusing movement.

It is doubtful, however, that it was the Buffalo *Mayor's* greater degree of control over that city's schools that made the difference. Mayor Griffin was no more supportive of Curtin's decision than Mayor White was of Garrity's, and I uncovered no evidence that Griffin used patronage to gain the compliance of vociferous opponents. In relation to desegregation, patronage was used in Buffalo and not in Boston, because the Buffalo Board of Education had made a decided effort to cooperate with the judge, whereas the Boston School Committee resisted making such efforts. Had the Boston Committee been more cooperative in putting forth a desegregation plan, they too may have used patronage to hire leaders of ROAR, MCAFB, and the Information Centers.

## Chronology on the Side of Buffalo

A major difference in the two cities' desegregation cases was that Buffalo's court order came two years after Boston's. Throughout the interviews I was consistently reminded of a major reason why there was more cooperation in Buffalo, which was the same reason why Charlestown's leaders were somewhat more cooperative than Southie's: chronology was on the side of those who desegregated subsequent to 1974. One informant from Boston told me that he believes "that a decision was made in the United States between '74 and '76. . . . The idea that white racist mobs would be unleashed on black students across the country terrified the rulers of the United States, the government. Leave aside their opposition to busing, they had to find a way to modify that reaction." When one looks at the difference in the behaviors of the leaders of the two cities, the above statement sounds very plausible.

Both Boston and Buffalo's cases were filed in 1972, but Buffalo was fortunate enough to have its case decided two years later than Boston's. Had the chronology been reversed, perhaps the violence that occurred in Boston may have afflicted Buffalo, and Boston's antibusing leaders may have felt forced to cooperate, or the more moderate antibusing leaders may have taken the forefront of the struggle, since their approach would have been seen as more appropriate in dealing with an unyielding federal court. A consistent sentiment expressed by Buffalo interviewees was that they saw what was going on in Boston, and they wished to avoid it in Buffalo, just as the leaders in Charlestown tried to avoid a repetition of South Boston.

Boston did not have the advantage of having a very similar city to compare itself to in regard to the desegregation case. Without another metropolis for comparison, antibusing leaders in the Hub were not able to perceive that there may have been a need to convince the antibusing masses to keep their opposition peaceful. One informant, a high-ranking member of the White Administration, claimed that in the midst of the violent reactions to Boston's Phase 1, Councillor Hicks looked at him and asked in desperation, "What are we going to do?" The leaders in Boston were unable to foresee the violent reactions to Garrity's decision. Had they had an example to look to, some of them may have done as many of Buffalo's antibusing leaders did, and gone through their communities pleading for calm *prior to* the implementation of Phase I.

The masses involved in Boston's antibusing movement did not seem to realize that no amount of protest would change Garrity's decision. The School Committee was found guilty of having segregated the schools, and a remedy was in order. Protests could neither erase the finding of guilt, nor could they erase the legal mandate for a remedy of the dual school system. As one antibusing elected official in Buffalo said, "I think after the court order . . . the people realized we had to do it. . . . A federal court order is almost impossible to overturn." The experience of Boston demonstrated that. Bostonians did not have a nearby model as proof that a court order could not be overturned, even after the facts in the case showed that the School Committee had profoundly misbehaved in its student assignment process. By the time that Curtin gave his decision in Buffalo, antibusing leaders and their followers had no illusions that a reversal was imminent.

The Buffalo Board of Education also realized that desegregation was an inevitability. Therefore, despite the antibusing campaigns in the 1974 elections, they voted 9–0 to develop a desegregation plan. Not only did they avoid contempt citations (such as were handed against three of the five members of the Boston School Committee), but they were able to develop a plan that would minimize the disruptions of desegregation. Therefore they avoided the Boston situation, where the court felt forced to develop a plan because of the School Committee's refusal to do so. Though the Buffalo Board of Education did appeal the case, they simultaneously cooperated with the federal court and avoided having a plan developed without their input.

One informant who was a leading voice of opposition to school desegregation in Buffalo, but who was silent by the time of Curtin's decision, told me, "I took little pleasure in seeing what I felt were the accounts of opposition in Boston, and would never have wanted the same sort of opposition in Buffalo." In speaking with the Lovejoy AB-LEY member who transported children to schools in the inner-city, and who had previously walked through the streets with a camera, I asked what would have happened if the antibusing leaders had not worked to prevent violence. The response was, "I'm very (confident) that we would have had bricks thrown, and it would have been Boston. Sure, sure." Many of Buffalo's strongest opponents of busing were even more opposed to having their community disrupted by violent protests against Curtin's decision.

Members of the Buffalo Board of Education also used the Boston example to their advantage. The worries about Boston were not merely on the subconscious minds of the members of the Board, but the members pointed to Boston as an example to avoid. A former member of the Buffalo Board of Education told me that, "We were so happy that, in reading about Boston, it gave you some ideas how to counteract that kind of thing here." Another former Board member told me the following about how the Buffalo Board benefited from the example of Boston:

> We were familiar with Boston. We went to Boston to observe. We knew most people in the country from the large cities, because we were a member of the Council of Great City School Boards, and that's your 50 large cities in the country and their boards of education. . . . So I knew all those persons, all the superintendents and Board members from around the country, and particularly Boston. And talked much with the folks in Boston, the Board members. The white Board members. . . .

The whole issue of integration in Boston became a political issue, and the politicians rose to fame or to their demise on that whole issue. We didn't allow that to happen in Buffalo. And that was a decision. It was there in my mind, but we can't allow that to happen. Can never allow it to be taken over by the politicians. As often as we would say, as often as Gene Reville and Florence Baugh would often say, "the ball is in our court, and we must keep it there." Now that was a saying we would share with one another. "We have it in our hands, and we cannot allow someone to take it out of our hands and do with it as they would."

A supporter of the Buffalo plaintiffs, a person who also held elective office in Buffalo, gave the following account of how Reville and Murray met with antibusing parents in 1976 and used Boston as an example to avoid:

What they were doing was going into little small neighborhood meetings, talking with parents, and particularly in a lot of the white districts where there were parents, you know, "I'm gonna lay down in front of the bus. I'm not gonna let this happen." And there were some of those who even had people from Boston coming in and fanning the flames of hate. And we had members on the Council who, as elected officials, who were also trying to keep the schools segregated, and who were rabble-rousing. And so Reville, and there was a Joe Murray who went out and began to have these meetings to say, "Hey, look, to hell with Boston. We don't want—we use Boston to our advantage." We were able to say, "Hey, look! Don't let that what's happening in Boston happen here. Let us sit down and see how we can work this out and come together."

The use of Boston as a negative example for Buffalo officials to avoid is the converse of the process of "diffusion of innovations" from one state to another. Everett M. Rogers states that innovations are "communicat(ed) from one individual to another in a social system over time."[72] When applied to the states, it is assumed that officials in a state take cues from other states when developing programs. Quite often innovations are diffused from a state to a neighboring state. This is diffusion in a positive sense, which is what most of the diffusion literature focuses on. The Racial Imbalance Law of Massachusetts was a diffusion of a similar measure passed in neighboring New York State. In 1963 New York State Education Commissioner James Allen issued a ruling that school districts in the state were required to remedy racial imbalance. A school with an enrollment of over 50 percent minority was defined as racially imbalanced. In Massachusetts the Commissioner of Education Owen Kiernan did not have the power to enact a ruling, but he presented legislation to the General Court which was very much like Allen's ruling in neighboring New York.[73] That legislation became the Racial Imbalance Act. The RIA is an example of diffusion of an innovation from one state to a bordering state, and in this case Massachusetts used New York as a positive example. When Boston and Buffalo implemented these innovations, the diffusion was in the reverse order: from Massachusetts to New York, with a metropolis in New York *avoiding* the mistakes made in a Massachusetts city. Nevertheless it still followed the same process of diffusion.

Fred W. Grupp and Alan R. Richards state that today diffusion is accelerated because of the existence of professional organizations of public officials. They write that "most of these specialized groups meet regularly and publish journals or newsletters. They facilitate the exchange of policy and program development information among the administrators in the fifty states."[74] The former School Board member from Buffalo spoke of the Council of Great City School Boards as the organization through which members of the Buffalo Board of Education met with members of the Boston School Committee and learned of the mistakes to avoid. According to Grupp and Richards this is the same process by which innovations are diffused from one state to another.

Richard Rose refers to this reverse-process diffusion as *"Lesson- Drawing."* In lesson-drawing, public officials faced with the prospect of implementing changes often look at other instances when public officials were faced with a similar prospect. Contrary to the diffusion literature, Rose states that lesson-drawing can also be used in the negative sense, as is the case of Buffalo with Boston. Rose states that, "A Lesson can conclude with a positive endorsement or be negative, warning of difficulties in imitating what is done elsewhere."[75]

The examples officials use in lesson-drawing can be from an earlier time in history, or from the current time, but in a different geographical location.[76] When officials draw lessons across spatial distance, they look at other governments that are on the same jurisdictional level. Cities look to other cities, counties to other counties, states to other states. In searching for examples, officials are concerned with *geographical propinquity,* using nearby localities.[77] There is sufficient geographical propinquity between Boston and Buffalo for the latter to use the former as an example. In so doing, however, Rose states that the measures emulated (or avoided in this example) should be within the same policy area, as it is with this situation involving educational policies.

The use of Boston as an example for Buffalo was an example of lesson-drawing across spatial boundaries, but there was enough of a temporal difference (two years) for Buffalo's officials to capitalize on Boston's earlier mistakes. Buffalo's officials could look to Boston as a contemporary example of a similar school district undergoing desegregation, but there was enough of a chronological difference to demonstrate the dangers of following certain procedures.

## Chronology as a Causal Factor

Among the Buffalo interviewees, the most widely cited factor leading to the moderation of that city's antibusing forces was chronology. With Boston serving as a negative example, leaders in Buffalo worked to try to prevent such a reaction in their city. The interview data indicates that neither the antibusing leaders in Boston, nor those in Buffalo wanted to see violence committed by persons who agreed with their position. However, Boston's leaders, particularly those in the areas affected by Phase I, did not have the example of a nearby city to demonstrate the need to take the summer before implementation to stress to the masses the importance of the demonstrations remaining peaceful. While the majority of the demonstrators were indeed peaceful in Boston, there was a very visible minority who caused enough chaos and disruption to create a law-enforcement crisis.

Leaders in Charlestown took note of this chaos and disruption and spent the summer working to prevent problems before Phase II began. They were somewhat successful in that there were far fewer problems in Charlestown in the fall of 1975 than there had been in South Boston in the fall of 1974. Buffalo had the advantage of an additional year, and five hundred miles of separation between its antibusing masses and those few but visible leaders in Boston who placed personal aggrandizement ahead of peace. The leaders in Buffalo used this additional time to prevent a violent reaction and to develop a desegregation plan that would be somewhat more palatable to opponents of busing. Time was on the side of Buffalo.

In view of the information presented by the informants from Buffalo, one must conclude that chronology played a factor in motivating the leaders in Buffalo to act differently than their Boston counterparts. Leaders in Buffalo had the experience of Boston to benefit from, whereas Boston's leaders did not have the benefit of a larger, well-publicized, nearby, and very similar city.

# CHAPTER FIVE

❑

## Community Reactions to the Implementation of Busing

In Boston Phase I was met with the expected violence in South Boston, but the reaction in the middle-class High Wards was almost as volatile. The violence spilled over into the streets and strained the resources of municipal and state law enforcement agencies. Though Charlestown was somewhat calmer, there were nevertheless violent incidents in that community as well. This violence put a tremendous strain on the law enforcement personnel in Boston. But in addition to the violence was the non-violent reaction of white flight from the public schools. White flight had been occurring for a number of years prior to desegregation, but the Order temporarily accelerated it. Violence and white flight plagued the Boston Public School System during the years when desegregation was implemented.

When desegregation was first implemented in Buffalo, there was no violence. Nor was there any with the implementation of the third phase, when massive busing of whites was first put into effect. Data from the Buffalo Board of Education also shows that the desegregation orders did not lead to white flight from the Buffalo Public Schools. Furthermore, there has been overall academic improvement since desegregation was implemented in that city. This chapter gives an in-depth examination of how the two cities' white communities reacted to the implementation of desegregation.

### Trouble in the High Wards

The first major racial skirmish after Phase I began was at Hyde Park High School, in the southwestern edge of the city. Hyde Park is a section of Boston in the "High Wards," so named because it includes high-numbered electoral wards of the city. The High Wards area

includes Hyde Park, Roslindale, and West Roxbury. These were virtually all-white areas that were heavily middle class, while West Roxbury is a suburban area within the city limits. Though there are
many working class districts in the High Wards, the area is considered to be a middle-class Irish section of the city.

This area's higher economic status is perhaps what kept it from
receiving the unfavorable press that South Boston and Charlestown
received during the implementation of school desegregation. Many
associate the core of resistance with South Boston, but there was an
almost equal amount of resistance in the High Wards. One of the
anti-busing Information Centers was in Hyde Park, and Dapper
O'Neil, the antibusing city councilor, was a resident of Roslindale.
One of my informants from South Boston had very close relatives living in Roslindale and retained close ties to that community. When
asked what the feelings in the High Wards were about busing, the informant responded as follows:

> Identical to South Boston. I could transplant myself over there, and
> I'd be amongst the same. They might not have had the organiza-
> tions, but they were strongly, as strongly opposed to busing as South
> Boston was. . . .
>
> Hyde Park High School, you had your first stabbing there. . . . And
> I always remember saying that that was the first blood drawn. . . .
> And two white boys were stabbed by blacks. . . . That was before
> Michael Faith or any other incident. However, they didn't blow it up
> out of proportion. It wasn't as if it happened in Sou— If it had hap-
> pened in South Boston, if it was a black or a white, it wouldn't mat-
> ter who was stabbed, the media would have come in. . . .

The informant was correct in that there was more media coverage of negative incidents in South Boston than in other areas of the
city, except possibly for Charlestown. However, the first major racial
skirmish during Phase I did indeed occur at Hyde Park High School.
On September 19, 1974 a race riot broke out in the cafeteria of the
school, and police had a difficult time quashing the disturbance. In
the end five students were injured, and the school was closed the next
day. When school re-opened the atmosphere was quite tense, and
there were sporadic racial incidents. There were continued antibusing demonstrations in the neighborhood, demonstrations involving
both adults and students. On October 7, 200 white adults and children chased black students from a Roslindale restaurant to Roslindale High School.[1] This resulted in the arrest of 18 individuals, 5 of

whom were adults. On the following day 19 students were suspended from the school for their involvement in racial skirmishes.[2]

The troubles at Hyde Park reached a climax on October 15 when a white student named Joseph Crowley was stabbed during racial violence. This is the incident that the above informant was referring to. The stabbing touched off a race riot. According to testimony given to the Civil Rights Commission, there was also a stabbing at Roslindale High School during this time.[3] In response to these incidents, metal detectors were installed at Hyde Park.[4] Afterwards there was a relative calm throughout the remainder of the calendar year.

After the students returned from Christmas break, there were renewed racial tensions at Hyde Park High. On January 9 thirteen blacks and 2 whites were arrested in racial fighting, and on the following day white students walked out of Roslindale High School in protest.[5] Full-scale tensions resumed in May, with several days of race rioting at Hyde Park High School.

The tension at Hyde Park High School spilled over into the streets of the community. In October 1974 two white men were arrested on civil rights violations for carrying molotov cocktails outside of Hyde Park High School. The racial troubles outside of the schools became more frequent in the spring and summer of 1975. During May and June the homes of the few black families who lived in Hyde Park were subjected to continuous attacks by white youths. On June 19 a Jamaican family bought a home in Hyde Park and moved in. Within days their new neighbors threw rocks at them, smashed their windows, and uprooted their fence.[6] The following month the home of Reginald Budd, a black Hyde Park resident, was set afire by a kerosene torch.[7]

### Trouble at South Boston High School

While the troubles of Phase I began in the High Wards, South Boston was the area where the level of violence was most intense. Moreover, Southie was the focus of most of the media coverage of the antibusing movement, which led to the perception that antibusing violence was confined to South Boston during Phase I.

From the start of the 1974–1975 school year there were racial problems at South Boston High School. On the first day of school the buses transporting black students were stoned by residents standing on the sides of the streets, and the black students were taunted as they deboarded the buses. The first major racial skirmish occurred on October 2, 1974 when police officers from the elite Tactical Patrol Force (TPF) had to break up a fight at the school, a fight that caused eight students and three aides to receive injuries. The black students at the school were taken home early to protect them from further attacks.[8] By the end of that week attendance at the school was very low, as white students participated in a boycott. There were more racial skirmishes in late October, but these were dwarfed by what was to happen in December.

On December 5, there was a lavatory fight involving 30 black and white females, which resulted in the suspensions of a number of black students. Ironically on the next day 376 white students walked out of school in protest of what they saw as unfair treatment in favor of black students. On their way out about 25 or 30 white students trapped a black girl and spit on her while yelling, "N——rs eat sh—!"[9] On the next school day, December 9, three white girls were beaten by 7 or 8 black girls, which led to a day of sporadic racial skirmishes.

The skirmishes reached a climax on December 11, when a white student, Michael Faith, was stabbed in a racially motivated fight. When white students received word of the incident, they left the school and joined adults who were surrounding the building. The whites trapped 125 black students inside and refused to allow them to board the buses. Councilwoman Hicks, with Senator Bulger at her side, pleaded with the crowd to allow the black students to leave the building, but they ignored her. Rather they kept the black students trapped inside and chanted racist profanities in unison. The black students were able to leave only after a decoy bus was used to divert the whites. Then the policemen hurriedly sneaked the blacks onto buses and transported them back to Roxbury. In the operation injuries were received by 14 policemen and a larger number of South Boston residents. There were also four arrests.

Superintendent Leary closed South Boston High School for Christmas vacation one week early. When school reopened the following month, there was a relative calm throughout the winter. But when the weather became warm, the tensions rose again. On May 7–8 there were race riots in the school, and on May 9 500 residents of South Boston, adults and high school students, attacked buses transporting black students. As in Hyde Park, these tensions spilled into the neighborhood and led to a problematic summer on the streets of South Boston.

The racial violence that took place in the summer was a mere continuation of what had been happening on the streets of South

Boston throughout the school year. The first reports of after-school violence came from the Columbia Point Housing Project, a predominantly black development in Dorchester, very close to the South Boston line. On September 19 residents from Columbia Point complained that white men in cars were driving past the development, yelling racial insults, and firing at the buildings with firearms. Upon hearing these reports, the Police Department deployed troops from the TPF into the area. The residents of Columbia Point quickly became dismayed with the TPF after reports that the elite forces broke into a church and established it as headquarters.[10]

Complaints against the TPF were not confined to the black community. Residents of South Boston resented the Force's massive 24–hour presence on the streets of their community. On Friday night October 4, a brick was thrown through the window of a TPF cruiser. The policemen in the car chased several suspects into a bar called the Rabbit Inn. When an arrest was attempted, the patrons at the bar pulled the suspect away from the pursuing police officers and prevented the arrest. According to patrons, on the following evening TPF members entered the Rabbit Inn and began beating patrons and vandalizing the inside of the bar. The Boston Police Department offered few comments about the incident other than to say that TPF members entered the bar on October 5 in response to a report that an officer was in trouble.[11]

Two days after the Rabbit Inn incident there occurred an event that was captured in newspapers throughout the United States. A black man, André Yves Jean-Louis, was driving through South Boston to pick up his wife from work. He was stopped by a group of white men, dragged from his car and beaten to the ground. He was finally rescued when a police officer fired a warning shot into the air and the assailants fled.[12] There were repeated similar incidents in that month (October 1974). A black truck driver was assaulted when driving through Southie, and a black man was attacked while standing at a public transit station in South Boston.[13]

The high level of violence resumed when the weather became warm in the following summer. After school let out in June 1975, gangs of whites began hanging out on an overpass and throwing rocks at the vehicles of blacks on their way to South Boston's Carson Beach on the Atlantic Ocean.[14] On July 27 a group of six black Bible salesmen from South Carolina were attacked on the beach by a mob of whites. After beating the salesmen, many from the gang attacked a black Greyhound bus driver as he was leaving the company garage in South Boston.[15]

Members of the black community were outraged by the Carson Beach incident. They organized a "wade-in" at the beach, scheduled for August 10. When the marchers arrived at Carson Beach that day, they were met by a crowd of angry whites, and a makeshift sign on an awning saying, "N——rs Keep Out!!!" The whites were quick to begin throwing missiles at the black demonstrators, in plain view of the police. The response of the policemen was to charge the black demonstrators and force them back towards the water.[16] One of the persons I interviewed had participated in this demonstration. Though more than 19 years had passed, this respondent became very emotional when reminiscing about the behavior of the policemen on Carson Beach on August 10, 1975:

> When we went over for the peace march to Carson Beach, and the police drove their horses into the water where the kids were swimming. I mean, every law—

I interrupted the respondent by asking if it was indeed the police who charged into the crowd of non-violent black demonstrators. The respondent continued:

> THE POLICE! The mounted police. They went after the black kids in a few pockets. Because my daughter was with some of her white friends when we had the Carson Beach. Louise Hay—Day—I get so aggravated when I think about this. I don't think about it often, Steve. You're lucky. I don't think about it, and I don't do this anymore because it's a very stressful and discouraging situation that we had to face. We cried many a day. . . .

In the week following the wade-in at Carson Beach there was a wave of racial violence in black and white areas of Boston, especially in Roxbury and South Boston.

Blacks were not the only victims of the violence in South Boston. An activist from the community, Tracy Amalfitano, publicly supported school desegregation and subsequently became the victim of the wrath of some of her neighbors. The windows of her house were smashed, her car was vandalized, and the beauty salon owned by her sister was destroyed.[17] There were FBI reports of plans of more massive property damage: the destruction of bridges and tunnels connecting South Boston, East Boston, and Charlestown to the rest of the city.[18] This would certainly have prevented the implementation of

Phase II, which extended busing into Charlestown and East Boston, the areas accessible to the rest of Boston only by traversing water.

## Trouble in the Town

Phase II of the Boston desegregation plan included Charlestown, that economically depressed section of Boston that lies north of the Mystic River. Charlestown was thought by some to be as resistant to desegregation as South Boston, and many expected a similar level of violence. But as noted in the last chapter, the community leaders worked tremendously hard to prevent Charlestown from exploding in 1975 the way the High Wards and Southie exploded in 1974. While the level of violence was far lower in Charlestown, there were nonetheless several violent incidents both at Charlestown High School and on the streets of the Town. Most of the violence occurred in the evenings as a result of tensions between youths and TPF forces stationed in Charlestown.

The opening day of school in September 1975 at Charlestown High passed without a major incident, and the situation inside the school was comparatively calm for more than a month. The only injury occurring during the daytime on the first day of school was at nearby Bunker Hill Community College, where a black student was attacked, sustaining an injury to his arm.[19] There were walkouts of white students on September 30 and October 3, but the first major racial skirmish occurred on October 10.[20] Ten days later a race riot at the school led to the suspensions of four whites and five blacks. Only minor injuries were reported. On the following day the black students arriving in Charlestown refused to leave the buses out of fear for their safety in the school.[21] On the morning of October 24 a group of 125 demonstrating white students sat on the steps of the main stairway outside of the school and prevented the black students from leaving their buses and entering. When the white students refused to leave, the black students were finally sent home for the day.

There was a relative peace inside the school for three months, but on January 22 tensions resumed when white students again barricaded the main staircases and prevented the black students from leaving the school. At 12:45 p.m. the police were able to sneak the black students out through a fire exit and into an alley beside the school, where buses were waiting for them. Aware that they had been outsmarted, the white students threw stones at the buses as they left the alley.[22] One person, however, was not able to escape attack: a black teacher was assaulted by a group of white students.[23] The other major act of violence to occur that winter was after the basketball team of Charlestown High played the team of the predominantly black Jeremiah Burke High School. After the game was over, white students stoned the bus transporting members of the Jerry's team.[24]

There was considerably less violence inside Charlestown High than there had been the previous year at Hyde Park and South Boston High Schools, with no school closings nor stabbings. Nevertheless on the streets there was a high level of violence. On the opening day of school, several youths hung a black man in effigy from the roof of the Town's Bunker Hill Housing Projects, with a sign saying "N——r Beware." Later they set the effigy afire in a raucous public demonstration against busing. Seven months later it appeared that they were going to act out this scenario with a live victim. On April 4 a black attorney named Theodore Landsmark walked toward Boston City Hall in the midst of an antibusing demonstration. A group of students from Charlestown High attacked Landsmark and speared his face with the pole of an American flag that they were carrying, then proceeded to beat Landsmark. This incident was observed by press photographers and placed in newspapers throughout the country. On the following night a group of white males beat and robbed a black man who was walking through Charlestown.

Much of the wrath of antibusing Townies was also directed at the Boston Police Department. During the demonstration in which the black man was hung and burned in effigy, members of the TPF came on the scene to clear the area and make way for the buses. This set off a confrontation that led to a fight between TPF members and antibusing demonstrators.[25] Throughout the fall and winter there were regular skirmishes between the TPF and youngsters who pelted them with missiles. This reached a climax on February 16 when about 100 youngsters assembled outside of the Bunker Hill Housing Project, erected barricades, and began pelting police cars with rocks, shattering their windshields. That night six officers were sent to the hospital for injuries sustained in the rioting. A white reporter for the *Boston Globe* was also beaten. Riots continued nightly for most of the week. In addition to squad cars, the demonstrators also vandalized the Charlestown branch of the Boston Public Library, the high school, and a butcher shop, where they entered inside and looted some of the meat.[26]

The halls of Charlestown High School were much calmer than the streets surrounding the school. In comparison to the trouble spots in Phase I, blacks in Charlestown High were somewhat safe.

The clergy, political leaders, and community leaders were able to prevent a recurrence of what happened in the High Wards and South Boston during the first phase of school desegregation.

## Violence in East Boston and Other Areas Not Directly Affected by the Decision

In addition to the High Wards, South Boston, and Charlestown, East Boston was regarded as an area very resistant to school desegregation. "Eastie" is a largely Italian community that lies on a peninsula apart from the rest of the city. It is connected to Boston by the Sumner and Callahan Tunnels, and by water shuttles that transport passengers to Logan Airport, which is in Eastie. Because of its isolation from the rest of the city, Eastie had very few black residents when Garrity's order was rendered. The local high school, East Boston High, was 100 percent white. There were several vocal residents who did not wish to see any change in the racial composition of Eastie.

During the first phase of desegregation, Eastie and Charlestown were temporarily exempted from busing. A few of the most volatile opponents of desegregation allowed a rumor to be spread that if Eastie were to fall under the order, the Sumner and Callahan Tunnels would be blown up, thus preventing passengers from traveling to or from Logan Airport. Some Bostonians believe that Judge Garrity took these threats to heart when he crafted the plan for Phase II. In this plan Eastie was exempted from mandatory busing, but some of the area's schools, including East Boston High, would be transformed into magnet schools to attract black students.

Some residents of Eastie were not even willing to accept this compromise. On January 20, 21, and 22, 1976 white students in Eastie walked out of the school in protest against plans to make Eastie a magnet technical school beginning in September 1976. Students and adults took to the street and blocked traffic at the tunnel exits, fought with several police officers, and overturned automobiles.[27] When the magnet school program was put in place in the fall, Eastie's own Pixie Palladino, then a member of the Boston School Committee, tried to prevent black students from taking their seats in one of the magnet schools in East Boston. This incident was briefly described in the last chapter.

As in other white areas of Boston, non-white residents of Eastie were neither safe in the streets nor in their homes. In May 1975 the homes of five Puerto Rican families in Eastie's Maverick Housing

Project were set on fire. The director of that community's "Little City Hall" blamed the violence on school busing.[28] The following month the home of a black family was firebombed. This was followed a week later by an hour-long race riot on one of Eastie's streets.[29]

Sporadic race-related violence was also occurring in areas of the city that were not known for racial hostility. On August 11, 1975 there was an outbreak of racial violence in Haymarket Square, a tourist area adjacent to downtown Boston. This violence occurred at a television forum where blacks and whites were discussing the Carson Beach incident of the previous day.[30] In September 1975 the John F. Kennedy birthplace in Brookline, Massachusetts was set afire, resulting in $75,000 worth of damage. On the sidewalk in front of the former Kennedy home someone had scrawled "Bus Teddy."[31] Three months later, the South End headquarters of the Boston branch of the NAACP was bombed, and in February a black student from Tufts University was attacked by a gang of whites at North Station, a very busy transit terminus that is adjacent to the famous Boston Garden sports arena.[32]

## Black-on-White Violence

Though many of the initial reported incidents of racial violence were acts committed by whites opposed to school desegregation, from the first month of Phase I there were also incidents of race-motivated black-on-white violence. One of the informants from South Boston told me that, "There were also other incidents going on in other neighborhoods, maybe in retaliation. . . ." The retaliative motive certainly was the case in black-on-white violence at predominantly black Dorchester High in September 1974. After the first race riot occurred at Hyde Park High, black students at Dorchester High retaliated by attacking white students. White students at the school were allowed to leave early that day to avoid further attacks. Later that day black students stoned buses of white students leaving Dorchester.[33] On October 8, the day after the beating of Jean-Louis, white students were attacked at English High. This resulted in 19 injuries, three arrests, and a spillover into the streets, where neighborhood stores and other buildings had their windows smashed.[34] Later that week black members of Dorchester High's football team rescued a white girl from being assaulted by a group of black youths.[35]

The beating of Jean-Louis also led to violence on the streets of Roxbury. Shortly after the violence at English, cars parked outside of the Roxbury building of predominantly white Boston Technical High School had their windows smashed by neighborhood youths. When members of the TPF tried to move a crowd of blacks away from the bus routes at the end of the day, a battle ensued between blacks and the police. Missiles were thrown at the police, and a television cameraman was injured. One arrest was made. Nearby at the Mission Hill Extension housing project, groups gathered and attacked white motorists. The violence at Mission Hill Extension lasted into the night and resulted in the injuries of 14 blacks and 24 whites. At Roxbury's Dudley Street subway station there were also stonings of white motorists, along with vandalism and looting of stores in the area.[36] In the aftermath of the August 1975 Carson Beach incident, there were more retaliatory acts by blacks against whites. White motorists driving past the Mission Hill and Columbia Point housing projects were stoned by angry blacks, while several automobiles were set ablaze.[37]

The most serious incident of black-on-white violence to occur was the April 1976 beating of Richard Poleet. Poleet, a white auto mechanic, was stopped by a group of teenaged youths as he drove past the Orchard Park Housing Project in Roxbury. Poleet was dragged from his car and beaten with cinder blocks. He lapsed into a coma and died the following month.

## Why Did They Riot?

The violence that took place in Boston during school desegregation can be classified as protest against government institutions. On the part of the white community it was a protest against the state and federal courts who ordered the desegregation of the public schools, and on the part of the black community it was a protest against the criminal justice system whom they felt tolerated and possibly condoned violence from white protesters. In his analysis of antibusing protests in Boston, D. Garth Taylor gives explanations as to why the protesters involved themselves in illegal activities such as boycotts. While much of Taylor's analysis looks at participation in school boycotts, the conclusions he has arrived at are equally applicable to more severe forms of protest such as violence. It would have been difficult, if not impossible, for Taylor to have examined variables leading to participation in violent acts, because participants were less likely to admit involvement in these acts than they were to admit involvement in school boycotts. Nevertheless, much of what Taylor concludes regarding boycotts can be generalized to violent acts also.

The key concepts that Taylor looks at were first elucidated by William Gamson, Bruce Fireman, and Steven Rytina. They speak of a *legitimacy frame of reference* and an *injustice frame of reference.* With the legitimacy frame of reference, the actions, statutes, and decisions of governmental institutions are accepted, even by those who disagree, because opponents believe that the decisions were arrived at fairly and that they will not lead to social harm. Persons who are dissatisfied with the enactment of a policy take solace in the fact that in the future this same decision-making process will result in the adoption of policies that they favor.[38] With the injustice frame of reference, the opponents of a policy view it as unjust, as having been arrived at unfairly, and as being socially harmful.[39] Persons operating from the injustice frame of reference are more likely to engage in illegal acts to protest against a policy.

Taylor sees Boston as a classic example of a setting with a historical background that will lead to persons adopting the injustice frame of reference. Boston's history of state government denying autonomy to the city, and the ethnic implications behind this denial, made that setting ripe for opposition to the Racial Imbalance Act and the SJC's order to desegregate. School desegregation was regarded as a modern day version of the infamous "Boston Bills" that imposed state policy upon an opposing populace in the city of Boston.[40] This is evident by the name of the most prominent antibusing organization: Restore Our *Alienated* Rights. The name itself embraces the notion that Bostonians have been alienated from their rights, subjected to an injustice at the hand of the state government and federal court.

Taylor emphasizes, however, that history alone will not lead the masses to adopt an injustice frame of reference. In order for this frame to be adopted on a large scale, there is a need for political leaders to become involved. Using a term of Norman Frohlich, Joe Oppenheimer, and Oran Young, Taylor speaks of the importance of *political entrepreneurs* in leading the public to adopt an injustice frame of reference.[41] The political entrepreneurs are instrumental in mobilizing protest against policies regarded as unjust. Taylor states that in order for opposition to take the form of protest, two conditions must be met. The first condition is that members of an opposing group must be made aware that the adoption of a policy is an abuse of authority by the decisionmakers in power. This is called "attention calling." The second condition is that the members of the group must become aware of the fact that there are many others who share their opposition to the unjust action. Attention calling fosters group cohesiveness and helps gain commitments to protest against the hated policy.[42] The political those individuals who call attention to an injustice, coordinate the opposition, and mobilize action against the policy.

Frohlich, et. al. state that mobilization requires that a person develop an organization and collect resources, all for the provision of a collective good. These actions for the purpose of mobilization are viewed as a service.[43] One who performs this service in exchange for public office is a political entrepreneur. Taylor stated that political entrepreneurs mobilized protest against busing by alerting persons to the injustice of this measure being imposed upon Bostonians by the state and federal government, and served to remind people of how this measure related to historical oppression by the state government. Opponents of desegregation did not view busing as a mere loss in a fairly played game. They saw it as an unjust action being used against them. Twenty years later this sentiment was still shared by opponents of desegregation. The following are some of the statements made by various white Boston interviewees who were opponents of desegregation:

> This was going to affect all the children. This was government coming in, and it was going to affect everything, different neighborhoods, not just this neighborhood. This would be uprooting families.

> What they were trying to do is break the black community up. . . . What they were trying to take the black community and spread them around. That's what they were doing. Because they feared— You go down to Washington and you get public records and things like. They feared the blacks all in one community. They wanted to dilute their political power and to break them all up.

> [The antibusing protest] wasn't opposing black kids, wasn't opposing black people. It was opposed to . . . the intrusion of the government. The kids coming—going out of their community hurt them the most. Plus the curriculum. What was the government going to do with it?

> You know, this is where they live, this is their church, this is their supermarket. This is . . . related to the neighborhood. Concept of a community, or at least were a community at that time with families. We looked at it and still do look at it, that deseg as implemented by that court order was an attack on the family. Nobody has a right to tell a parent where to send a kid to school.

> I don't think Judge Garrity had to craft an order the way he did. And I just think that he ordered the maximum possible impact because, 'These are just a bunch of white racists, and I'm gonna teach them a lesson.' That's what I believe. I believe that was an element. . . .

And that's what was attacked: your right, your right to that sense of neighborhood identity was being taken away. And it was taken away by people who had no clue as to what they were doing. Who had no understanding. The Judge Garritys in the world and the liberal press didn't have a clue as to what people in these communities were up against.

And until this day I think it's absolutely outrageous that students, school children, are not allowed to attend neighborhood schools. They're being denied that right because of their race. . . . Now we had a case of neighborhood school children being denied the right to attend schools. But yet the court in this case said, no, racial balance is more important, or integration is more important than the right to attend schools, not attend schools based on race. I mean you still have to think of it, Steve, the fact that Steven Taylor's kids cannot go to the school closest to home, because Steven Taylor's kids are black. I think that we can all agree, yeah that was offensive. For the Steven Taylors of this world, for the Linda Browns of Topeka, Kansas. And if it's offensive, how can people say that my kids, because they're white, can't go to neighborhood schools.

I think there was a great deal of misunderstanding on how you could live in America and have the government tell you what you have to do. . . . The Irish fled the Famine and the plight of persecution of the Irish in Ireland. I think people just could not understand. Everything that we've principled our life on and fought for, which is freedom for all people. Now being questioned. We can't do what we thought we had come to the country to do, which is make our own decisions.

D. Garth Taylor states that another part of the injustice frame of reference is the belief that a policy will be socially harmful. The following comments demonstrate that many opponents in Boston saw busing as a socially harmful experiment, often used purposely to punish communities:

They never achieved equal education; they achieved equal stupidity. And that's what the busing accomplished, equal stupidity. . . .

We feel that it's been a failure. An absolute and total failure. . . . It's been a disaster. It hasn't done anything to enhance racial relations. And unfortunately it has done little on an educational basis to help education. . . . I believe, I truly believe that a lot of the sadness that has been reflected on our community, with the acceptance of drugs. I'm not saying it wouldn't have happened without busing. It clearly accelerated it. And it magnified it. You know the sense of loss, frustration, the easy out, the structure of values. All those things, the hypocrisy, all those things, you know.

We lost a sense of community, and we still haven't regained it. I think we're seeing that loss of community with how our young people act out today. I think that's why you see kids that join gangs.

The above statements were made two decades after Phase I, so they reflect hindsight about the perceived injustice of busing, and the social harm some opponents believe it has caused. Prior to busing, much of the prediction of social harm would be the violence that busing would lead to. Taylor reported on a study that shows that antibusing opponents who saw Hicks and Kerrigan as being more defiant in regard to busing were more likely to predict social harm and view busing as unjust than were those who saw Hicks and Kerrigan as being conciliatory. As is reported in the previous chapter, both of these antibusing leaders exhibited strong defiance at times and conciliation at other times. Those opponents who saw the leaders in the former role more often predicted violence, and were more likely to feel that the rights of children and parents were being violated.[44] This shows that when leaders are more defiant, their constituents are more likely to adopt the injustice frame of reference, a frame that can lead to illegal protest.

Taylor states that "injustice motivates disobedience."[45] Those who believe that a measure is unjust are unlikely to believe that legal protests will do any good. Hence they become involved in illegal protests. They feel that such protests are their only hope for achieving positive results.[46] This explains why much of the protest was violent. Rioting is generally a measure resorted to by persons who feel powerless, and who believe that legitimate means of protest will not be effective. Conversely, persons who feel that the system has produced them a number of victories are more likely to accept defeat. In this legitimacy frame of reference, they feel certain that they will win in future struggles, and they are comforted by past victories. In Boston, however, both the whites and blacks who engaged in rioting did not feel they had a record of victories to ensure them that the system worked for them. One prominent member of Powder Keg, a Charlestown antibusing group, wrote the following statement about engaging in violent activities:[47]

. . . Maybe the people dumping trash and causing commotion feel that this is the only way we can be heard. We lost in the courts, and

we lost at the polls. What is left? Put our kids on a bus??? Obey a
law that to us is completely wrong?

With the white community, particularly with those who were not
affluent, there was the memory of scores of political defeats at the
hands of the Yankee establishment or the state government. Memory of these defeats was stirred up by leaders who reminded their
constituents that their rights were again being "alienated." In the
case with busing, the elected representatives of the opponents were
usually consistent in their opposition. But they were overruled by the
appointed justices of the SJC and by the appointed judges on the federal bench. Though there was a fairly high vote turnout in the Irish
neighborhoods of Boston (particularly in the High Wards), this did
not help the communities avoid busing. This was a defeat that could
not be reversed at the polls or by other legitimate means. This is
what led to the violence in the white communities.

In the black community, bad experiences with the criminal justice system, the lack of any elected officials on the municipal level,
and poor representation on the police force and in the judiciary led
many to believe that they could not expect law enforcement officials
to take measures to end the attacks against persons like Ted Landsmark, André Yves Jean-Louis, or the students at Hyde Park, Southie,
or Roslindale High Schools. This frustration is what led to rioting in
the black community. Again it was an injustice frame of reference,
but whose anger was not directed toward the school desegregation
policy. A peaceful implementation of desegregation in Boston was impossible with both the black and white communities feeling that they
were victims of injustice, and that the system as it existed was inhospitable toward their concerns.

The phenomenon of rioting occurs after a group has come to believe that they will not receive justice through legitimate means.
Most of the large-scale inner-city riots the past 17 years occurred in
response to police brutality, which often led to the death of the victims. The riots usually did not take place immediately after an incident of brutality was made known to the public, but after the accused
assailants were acquitted in courts of law. Likewise with school desegregation, the violent antibusing protests did not occur until after
the defendant school committee was defeated in the courts, and the
desegregation plans were implemented. The implementation
brought home the harsh reality that the governmental system had
ruled against those opposing busing. The feeling of desperation, coupled with the belief that the ruling was unjust, brought about vio-

lent reactions among busing opponents who feared the worst with the implementation.

The irony is that, though the leaders' actions are what lead the public to adopt an injustice frame of reference, the leaders rarely openly support the masses involving themselves in rioting or other violent activities. This disdain for some of the violent actions of the masses is precisely the sentiment expressed by the previously quoted leader of the SBIC:

> And just for the record, [I] never engaged in that, never condoned it, never thought it was a good idea. Because much of what we were doing was a public relations kind of thing too. We were trying to, in our very naive and unprofessional way—We instinctively knew that, Jesus, in order for us to do something about busing . . . we can't behave like a bunch of KKK members. . . .

While the leaders are essential in convincing the masses to adopt the belief that they are the victims of an injustice, once this belief is adopted, no actions of the leaders are required for the masses to involve themselves in violent actions. Often the leaders lose control of some of the most volatile members of the public, as was the case in Boston. During my interviews with antibusing leaders, the informants indicated that they were displeased with the violent incidents that occurred in protest of the court decision.

## Measurable Costs Involved with the Implementation of the Order in Boston

Opponents of busing can point to some basic statistical data as evidence that school desegregation had some undesirable effects. None can disagree that busing created a law enforcement crisis that put a strain on the city's budget. Nor can any disagree that it accelerated the pace of white flight from the Boston Public Schools, which eventually decreased the amount of interacial contact between black and white students. The loss of white students from the school system was a major problem because it was accompanied by white families leaving the city. This had the potential of reducing the tax base at a time when more tax dollars were needed to cope with the law enforcement demands that were accelerated by school desegregation. Though the implementation may have been successful in initiating

the dismantling of the dual school system, the increased law enforcement demands and the acceleration of white flight give the impression that desegregation has failed. Many of the white political
leaders interviewed, as well as their constituents, seem to be more
concerned about the tangible costs associated with desegregation
than they are with the dismantling of the dual school system. For
this reason, desegregation has been regarded as a failure among
many white residents of Boston.

The law enforcement costs were considerably high from the very
beginning of Phase I. According to the U.S. Civil Rights Commission,
the deployment of extra TPF forces at Hyde Park High, South Boston
High, and other trouble spots resulted in more than $750,000 in over-
time costs from September through December of 1974 alone.[48] When
looking at the entire police force, the overtime costs from September
1974 to January 1975 totaled $4,623,828.16.[49]

On October 9, 1974, after the Jean-Louis beating, Governor Sargent ordered the deployment of 350 state policemen to South Boston.
They remained there for much of the entire school year, with their
numbers fluctuating between 63 and 300.[50] Governor Sargent also
ordered an increase in the number of Metropolitan District Commission (MDC) police officers deployed in South Boston. The police
force of the state-run MDC was sent to augment the forces of the
Boston Police Department, and the additional troops were placed under the control of the Boston Police Department. Initially 25 MDC
police officers were assigned to desegregation duty, but from October
to January there were 100 working under such assignments.[51] Sargent also activated 500 troops of the Massachusetts National Guard,
but he chose not to dispatch them to Boston.

One public official who consistently complained about the costs
associated with busing was Mayor Kevin White. In a letter to Judge
Garrity, Mayor White wrote that the additional law enforcement costs
during the first 18 days of school topped $2,000,000. White further
wrote that the Boston police force had "strained all its personnel and
exhausted every resource available to it," and that the force was "no
longer able to preserve public safety and also ensure the implementation of the federal court order in South Boston."[52] Toward the end of
Phase II, White stated that busing was costing the city $20,000,000
annually, with much of the money used for law enforcement.[53]

There was also the possibility that the problem of increased
costs would be exacerbated by the acceleration of the rate of middle-
class whites moving out of the city of Boston. Like most urban centers, Boston had been losing population since the conclusion of World

War II, primarily white residents moving to the suburbs. But this white flight was accelerated in the mid-1970s when the schools were desegregated. A close look at census data, however, shows that if the desegregation of the schools had an effect on white flight, it was only temporary. Table 5.1 shows the changes in population during the post-war years.

**Table 5.1**
**City of Boston Population from 1950-1970[54]**

| Year of Census | White Population | Non-white Population | Percent Change in White Population |
|---|---|---|---|
| 1950 | 758,700 | 42,744 | — |
| 1960 | 647,938 | 68,399 | −14.59 |
| 1970 | 524,709 | 116,362 | −19.02 |
| 1980 | 393,937 | 169,057 | −24.92 |
| 1990 | 360,875 | 213,408 | −8.39 |

The above table shows that, after a peak in 1950, the white population of Boston had been declining. This decline began possibly two decades before the desegregation case was initiated. From 1950 to 1960 there was nearly a 15 percent decline in the white population, and from 1960 to 1970 the decline was 19 percent. Between 1970 and 1980, the decade when desegregation was argued in the courts and implemented, the decline rose to nearly 25 percent, but in the following decade the decline in white residents was down to eight percent, lower than it had been during the decade of the 1960s. This decline in the 1980s was superceded by an increase in the number of non-white residents, which led to the first overall *increase* in population since the decade of the 1940s. If there was an increase in white flight brought about by the implementation of desegregation, it was only temporary, and followed by a *decline* in white flight. Perhaps the decline during the 1980s was a statistical correction of the 1980s, meaning the desegregation order accelerated white flight and merely led to the departure of whites who may have waited until the 1980s to depart. Their departure prior to the 1980s may explain why the level of white flight was so low during that decade. If one were to look at scores rather than decades, there is virtually no change in white flight. From 1950 to 1970 the rate of white flight was 30.0 percent, and

from 1970 to 1990 (the score when desegregation was implemented)
the rate was 31.2 percent, virtually unchanged.

More pronounced than white flight from the city during desegregation was the decline in white enrollment in the Boston Public
School System. White enrollment had been slowly declining as the
white population of the city decreased, but the annual rate of decline
of white enrollment had been 2.95 percent during the ten years prior
to the implementation of the court order, with the largest decline being 5.8 percent in 1973, the year preceding the court order. In 1974
however, there was a decline of 16.11 percent, in 1975 there was a decline of 7.9 percent, in 1976 there was a decline of 16.53 percent, and
in 1977 the decline in white students was 8.02 percent. During the
same period of time, the minority enrollment *increased* by an average of 5.47 percent annually, with an increase of 2.23 percent in 1974
the year Phase I was implemented. In 1975 there was an increase of
6.57 percent, followed by a decline of 2.88 percent in 1976, and an increase of 3.52 percent in 1977. The following graph shows the enrollment of white and non-white students in Boston from the 20
years 1967 to 1986.[55]

One cannot, however, blame declining white enrollment exclusively on white flight from the city and/or its public schools. Much of
it was the result of declining birth rates since the 1950s. Though the
birth rates of minorities also declined during the same period of time,
that decline was offset by increasing in-migration of minorities.

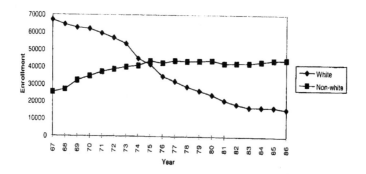

**Figure 5.1**
**Boston Public School System Enrollment 1967 to 1986**

Table 5.2 shows the fertility rates per 1,000 for the decades from 1960 to 1990:

**Table 5.2**
**Children Per 1,000 Women Aged 35–44 years**
**City of Boston[56]**

| Year of Census | Fertility Rate for Women aged 35–44 | Change from Previous Decade |
|---|---|---|
| 1960 | 2,685 | — |
| 1970 | 3,379 | +25.85 |
| 1980 | 2,364 | −30.03 |
| 1990 | 1,620 | −31.47 |

The above table focuses on women aged 35–44, because that is the age group that consistent data is available from the U.S. Census Bureau from 1960 on. In 1980 that age group is the primary group where persons would have children who were affected by the desegregation order, and who would be enrolled in the school system during the 1970s. As Table 5.2 shows, there had been a significant decline from a decade earlier, when women of that group would have children who were enrolled during the 1960s. Therefore the declining fertility rates played a role in the loss of white students from the school system. And unlike with minority children, there was no in-migration to compensate for the loss.

One reason why many whites were easily able to leave the Boston Public Schools was that an extensive parochial school system was operating in the city. Prior to the order, however, the public schools were also popular in the enclaves most resistant to busing. I examined U.S. Census data from 1970 to determine the percentage of white students in public schools that year, and then I looked at data from the 1980 Census to see the change after busing was implemented. I focused on the neighborhoods with the most resistance, which were the High Wards, South Boston, Charlestown, and East Boston. For each of the neighborhoods I looked at the number of children from grades K-12 who were enrolled in public schools and non-public schools, the number of white students in the communities, and the number of non-white students. Since the census does not identify public or non-public school students according to race, I attempted to determine the highest possible percentage of white students in non-public schools (or the lowest possible percentage in public schools). This was quite simple for the 1970 census data because in each of the four communities the non-white population percentage was minuscule. In no census tract was the non-white population in excess of ten percent; in most it was less than one percent.

The 1980 census data provides information on the number of elementary and high school students according to race, and the number of private school students and public school students, but not according to race. Therefore I used a formula to estimate the number of white students enrolled in private schools. In order to arrive at the estimate, for each community I subtracted the number of students enrolled in non-public schools from the total number of white students enrolled in elementary and secondary schools, and assumed that the difference is the number of white students in public schools. This is based upon the hypothetical assumption that all students enrolled in non-public schools are white. This, of course, is an incorrect assumption, but it assisted me in determining the absolute *minimum* number of whites in public schools. To this number I added the total number of students attending non-public schools, which is the *maximum* possible number of white students attending non-public schools, an overinflated estimate. By dividing the estimated number of white students in non-public schools by the estimate of the total number of white students, I was able to come up with a figure representing the absolute maximum possible percentage of white students in each community who attended non-public schools in 1980. The following table lists the four communities and the percentage of white students in non-public schools:[57]

### Table 5.3
### Percentage of White Students Enrolled
### in Boston Public Schools

| Community | Public School Enrollment in 1970 | Public School Enrollment in 1980 |
|---|---|---|
| South Boston | 69.78 | 57.10 |
| Charlestown | 66.30 | 46.75 |
| High Wards | 70.57 | 54.26 |
| East Boston | 75.01 | 70.76 |

What the above data shows is that even with the inflated estimates of non-public school attendance, a majority of the white students in the four neighborhoods combined still attended public schools in 1980. There was, however, a significant increase in the percentage attending non-public schools. My deflated estimate of white students attending public schools shows that in 1980 57 percent of South Boston's whites attended public schools, 47 percent of Charlestown's white students, 54 percent of the white students in the High Wards, and 71 percent of the white students in East Boston. This high utilization of public schools explains why many white parents in Boston were angry with school desegregation. Had most of their children been in parochial schools, their children would not have been affected. Instead the majority were sending their children to public schools, even after busing was implemented.

## Buffalo's Experience with Desegregation

The first phase of Buffalo's desegregation program was scheduled to begin on September 8, 1976 with the opening of school. This was a preliminary program requiring the transportation of 3,000 students on school buses, in addition to some secondary school students whose reassignments required their transportation on public transportation. When the buses rolled on September 8, the students riding them were accompanied by clergypersons, nuns, and parents who were trying to ensure a peaceful first day. There were no incidents on that day, but the following day the teachers went out on strike, delaying the second day of school for nearly three weeks, making September 27 another "first day of school." Again on that day the children being bused were accompanied by concerned adults, and again there were no racial incidents. The September 28, 1976 issue of the *Courier Express* carried a front-page article stating that, "No incidents were reported as a result of the busing."[58] This was quite a difference from Boston two years earlier.

In 1977 Buffalo entered into Phase II of its desegregation plan. In this phase selected inner-city schools were transformed from neighborhood schools into specialty magnet schools open to students from all over the city. Because all of the magnet schools were in predominantly black communities, there was a shortage of seats in neighborhood schools that served black students. This necessitated the use of predominantly white schools to accommodate displaced black students. Phase II was a mandatory desegregation program for the displaced black students, but it was voluntary on the part of white students. Because of the voluntary nature of the program, it did not evoke much opposition from the white community.

During the first five years of desegregation, Buffalo had not been tested as severely as some other cities undergoing desegregation. The limited scope of Phase I, and the voluntary nature of Phase II resulted in few white students being forced to transfer to predominantly black schools. In 1981, however, the federal court ordered the implementation of Phase IIIx, a massive busing program requiring the mandatory transfer of thousands of pre-kindergarten through second grade white students to "Early Childhood Centers" in the inner city. The implementation of this phase mandated the busing of 6,411 elementary students, half of whom were white students from pre-kindergarten through grade 2 being sent to the inner city, and the other half being minority students from grades three through eight sent to schools in peripheral areas. This resulted in the mandatory reassignments (through forced busing) of 30 percent of the white elementary school student population and 15 percent of the total white student population.[59]

When Phase IIIx began on September 9, 1981, there were 14,000 students in Buffalo being bused, close to thirty percent of the total number of students. But despite the large numbers of students affected by busing, the first day of Phase IIIx went without problems. The September 10 edition of the *Courier Express* featured the headline "Everyone Cooperates as Busing Commences," and a byline saying, "A day without incident."[60] Buffalo's police Commissioner James Cunningham was quoted as saying, "It's gone terrific."[61] He went on to say, "We had no incidents relating to busing, thank God."[62] An integration specialist from the New York State Department of Education observed the first day of schools, and later made the following statement:

> We saw not one picket, not one so-called protective parent hanging around. . . . I was impressed. I just finished visiting Louisville, St. Louis, Chicago, and Milwaukee—and this is not the way it usually goes.[63]

The integration specialist could have added Boston to that list of cities where "this is not the way it usually goes." There was a world of difference in the reactions of white parents of the two cities when their children were being sent to schools in black communities. Nearly all desegregation experts would have to concede that Buffalo's implementation was a success. Some, however, may argue that it is unfair to compare the two cities, due to the voluntary nature of much of Buffalo's plan. Christine Rossell compares Buffalo with Dayton, Ohio, and downplays the mandatory side of Buffalo's plan. Rossell asserts that "in Buffalo mandatory reassignments followed five years of successful voluntary desegregation, and the mandatory reassignments were identified with a highly popular preschool program that has always had a surplus of applicants."[64] This, however, is an inaccurate description of Phases I and II in Buffalo. With Phase I in Buffalo there were some mandatory reassignments brought about with the closure of white elementary schools and the reassignment of some of the students to predominantly black schools, and the redrawing of high school zone boundaries, resulting in some white students being reassigned to predominantly black high schools. Another inaccuracy of Rossell is that the pre-school program was "highly popular," and had "always had a surplus of applicants." The Early Childhood Centers, with their pre-kindergartens began on a pilot basis in 1980, when Phase III was implemented, and was not placed in full swing until 1981 with IIIx. It is true, however, that many white parents perceived the Early Childhood Centers as being part of the popular magnet school program, as was stated by some of the interviewees.

Rossell went on to say that Buffalo's mandatory reassignments were not too unpopular because they affected "only 15 percent of the white student population."[65] It must be noted, however, that in Phase I in Boston, mandatory reassignments affected approximately 16 percent of the projected white student population,[66] but it was nevertheless very controversial. As stated earlier, Rossell wrote that Phase IIIx resulted in the reassignment of 30 percent of the total elementary school population.[67] From the perspective of parents of elementary school students, Boston's plan was milder. Kindergartners were exempted from Boston's plan, and it did not result in the reassignment of 30 percent of the white elementary school students, as it did in Buffalo. Had Boston's plan placed such a burden on elementary school students, parents would have been even more opposed to the plan than they already were. Though they may not have thrown bricks and bottles at elementary school children, they would have undoubtedly been up in arms if 30 percent of the white kindergartners, first- and second-graders would have been required to catch a bus from neighborhoods like Hyde Park and Southie into Roxbury.

I asked several respondents in Boston if the white community would have accepted the busing of kindergartners. The following are some of the answers given to that question:

"No, absolutely not!"

"That would be tough. I think that would be tough."

"That's a little much."

"Oh my God! No way!"

Only one informant from Boston believed that such a plan would have been acceptable to the whites in his city.

A more peaceful but potent protest against desegregation is flight from the public school system. As the last section explains, in Boston the desegregation order was met with unprecedented levels of white flight. One of the interviewees from that city told me that before busing was implemented in Boston, he warned that busing in Boston would create another Detroit, with an overwhelmingly non-white school system. In Buffalo, however, desegregation seems to have had no effect on white flight, in any of the phases. As was the case in Boston white flight from the public school system was a product of post-war suburbanization and of declining birth rates. Table 5.4 shows the population of Buffalo according to race from 1950 to 1990.

**Table 5.4**
**City of Buffalo Population from 1950–1970[68]**

| Year of Census | White Population | Non-white Population | Percent Change in White Population |
|---|---|---|---|
| 1950 | 542,432 | 37,700 | — |
| 1960 | 459,293 | 73,466 | −15.33 |
| 1970 | 364,367 | 98,401 | −20.67 |
| 1980 | 252,365 | 105,505 | −30.74 |
| 1990 | 212,449 | 110,968 | −15.82 |

The above table shows that the decline in Buffalo's white population, which was first noticed during the decade of the 1950s, increased during the 1960s to above 20 percent, and to a high of over 31 percent during the 1970s, the decade when desegregation was first implemented. However, during the decade of the 1980s, which was the decade when large scale busing of white students was imposed, the rate of decline was just under 16 percent. But this decline cannot be attributed to busing, since there was no simultaneous acceleration of the decline in the number of white public school students during the years when the various phases of Buffalo's plan was implemented. Table 5.5 shows the rates of white enrollment decline in the Boston and Buffalo Public School Systems.[69]

**Table 5.5**
**White Enrollment Change in the Boston**
**and Buffalo Public Schools**

| Change in Boston's White Enrollment | | Change in Buffalo's White Enrollment | |
|---|---|---|---|
| YEAR | %CHANGE | YEAR | %CHANGE |
| 1968 | −3.77 | 1968 | −2.1 |
| 1969 | −2.86 | 1969 | −3.2 |
| 1970 | −1.03 | 1970 | −3.6 |
| 1971 | −4.23 | 1971 | −5.1 |
| 1972 | −4.20 | 1972 | −9.4 |
| 1973 | −5.80 | 1973 | −7.8 |
| Implementation of Phase I | | 1974 | −5.3 |
| 1974 | −16.11 | 1975 | −8.7 |
| Implementation of Phase II | | Implementation of Phase I | |
| 1975 | −7.90 | 1976 | −2.6 |
| 1976 | −16.53 | Implementation of Phase II | |
| 1977 | −8.02 | 1977 | −4.6 |
| 1978 | −9.67 | 1978 | −4.9 |
| 1979 | −8.18 | 1979 | −8.0 |
| 1980 | −8.75 | Implementation of Phase III | |
| 1981 | −13.58 | 1980 | −1.8 |
| 1982 | −10.58 | Implementation of Phase IIIx | |
| 1983 | −8.99 | 1981 | −2.0 |
| 1984 | +0.15 | 1982 | −2.5 |
| 1985 | −0.25 | 1983 | +0.6 |
| 1986 | −6.28 | 1984 | −4.3 |
| | | 1985 | −2.4 |
| | | 1986 | −0.8 |

In the eight years preceding the decision to desegregate the Buffalo schools, there was an average annual white enrollment decline of 4.47 percent, with a 7.8 average in the last four years prior to 1976, and an 8.7 percent decline in 1975. In 1976, however, the rate of decline plummeted to 2.6 percent. That rate began a slow rise up to 1979, where it reached 8.0 percent, but then in 1980, with the implementation of Phase III and the first Early Childhood Centers in

the inner city, the rate dropped to 1.8 percent, and was 2.0 percent
the following year, when Phase IIIx was implemented. This rate of
decline was lower than in the surrounding suburbs. It was also less
than the white student decline of 4.5 percent in the Diocese of Buffalo Public Schools from September 1980 to September 1981. Much
of this was because 400 children left the diocese schools to enroll in
public magnet schools. Within a year the enrollment in Buffalo's
Catholic schools was down 30 percent. In the first six years of Phase
IIIx, the average rate of white decline was a mere 1.9 percent, which
was considerably lower than the trend for other school districts with
similar racial compositions.[70] By the end of the 1980s the number of
white children in the elementary school grades (the grades affected
by Phase IIIx) was reported to have actually been *increasing*.[71] The
fact that there was a decline in the number of white students attending schools in the surrounding suburbs indicates that the decline was related to regional factors, not to desegregation. The 1970s
and 1980s was a period of time when western New York lost many of
its manufacurating industries. It was also a time when there was a
declining birthrate, which further contributed to the drop in the
number of white students attending public schools. As with Boston,
the declining birthrate of non-white families was offset by in-
migration of non-white families into the city. With white families,
there was no in-migration to offset the decline. Table 5.6 shows the
change in fertility rates among women aged 35–44 in Buffalo.

**Table 5.6**
**Children Per 1,000 Women Aged 35–44 Years**
**City of Buffalo[72]**

| Year of Census | Fertility Rate for Women aged 35–44 | Percent Change fromPrevious Decade |
|---|---|---|
| 1960 | 2,434 | — |
| 1970 | 3,188 | 30.98 |
| 1980 | 2,696 | − 15.43 |
| 1990 | 1,909 | − 29.19 |

The steady decline in the fertility rate following the "baby boom"
has contributed to a decline in white students enrolled in both public and parochial schools. But in Buffalo the parochial schools were
more severely plagued by declining enrollment than the public

schools were. Christine Rossell credits the city of Buffalo's magnet schools for the success in luring students from private and
parochial schools to public schools. She notes that in 1977 128 children left private and parochial schools to enroll in Buffalo Public
Schools. The number reached 309 in 1980 and peaked at 391 in 1981
the year Phase IIIx began. The number stabilized at just over 300,
with 326 students leaving private and parochial schools in
1986–1987. In the first eleven years of desegregation some 2,848 students left private and parochial schools to attend Buffalo Public
Schools. Eighty percent of these students were white.[73]

Table 5.7 looks at Buffalo's four communities that showed the
most resistance to desegregation (South Buffalo, Little Italy, Black
Rock/Riverside, and Polonia) and compares public school attendance
in 1970, before desegregation, with public school attendance in 1990,
after the three phases were implemented. As with Boston, this information was gathered from Census Bureau data. For the 1970 data, I
looked at only those census tracts which were in excess of 90 percent
white, which eliminates one South Side tract and 5 of the tracts in
Polonia. This was done to ensure that the information is confined to
white students. For the 1990 data, I used the same formula used to
estimate non-public school attendance in the Boston communities.[74]

## Table 5.7
### Percentage of White Students Enrolled
### in Buffalo Public Schools

| Community | Public School Enrollment in 1970 | Public School Enrollment in 1990 |
|---|---|---|
| South Buffalo | 51.71 | 67.34 |
| Polonia | 52.65 | 62.70 |
| Black Rock/Riverside | 71.27 | 79.68 |
| Little Italy | 71.27 | 88.31 |

The above data does not necessarily represent a massive white
flight from non-public to public schools. Rather it demonstrates that
the *proportion* of whites in public schools in the selected neighborhoods has increased significantly, while the proportion in non-public
schools has declined. The numbers in both public and non-public
schools has declined since 1970, but the rate of decline has been
much higher for non-public schools.

I agree with Rossell that the magnet schools have played a large role in luring whites away from private and parochial schools in Buffalo. But a more significant factor may be the economy of the city of Buffalo. There are fewer parents who can afford to send their children to non-public schools, or who can afford to join the white flight to the suburbs. Boston, on the other hand, went through an economic revitalization during the 1980s, and gained in population between the 1970 and 1980 census. Real estate values skyrocketed, particularly in the city. This forced some low and moderate income whites and blacks to move to the suburbs, while the low unemployment rate helped many to afford to send their children to non-public schools.

Figure 5.2 compares the Boston and Buffalo Public Schools in terms of total white enrollment.[75]

## Academic Improvements in Buffalo

An earlier section of this chapter includes a quote by a Boston opponent of busing who said, "They never achieved equal education; they achieved equal stupidity." In an article on Buffalo's desegregation plan, Rossell presents data that demonstrates that in Buffalo, at least, desegregation did not lead to "equal stupidity." Rossell compares academic performance of Buffalo students in 1976 (before the order) with 1986, ten years after the order. This data comes from standardized tests given to students in grades three and six. Table 5.8 presents the findings:[76]

**Table 5.8**
**Achievement Test Data of Elementary School Students in the Buffalo Public School System**

|  | Percent scoring above State Norm | |
| --- | :---: | :---: |
|  | *1976* | *1986* |
| Third Grade Reading | 68 | 76 |
| Third Grade Math | 78 | 96 |
| Sixth Grade Reading | 55 | 76 |
| Sixth Grade Math | 54 | 91 |

The above findings reflect an average increase of 16 points for reading and 26 points for math over a ten year period.
*Copyrighted Material*

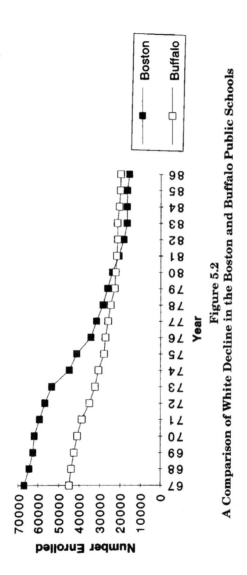

**Figure 5.2**
**A Comparison of White Decline in the Boston and Buffalo Public Schools**

The improvements were not solely confined to magnet schools. Rossell looked at the three types of elementary schools in Buffalo: magnet schools, grades 3-8 "Academies," and neighborhood schools. There was little difference in the percentage scoring above the state norm in the three types of schools.[77] Rossell also sees evidence that the increase was not limited to students of higher socioeconomic levels. Typically when comparing students from lower and upper socioeconomic levels, test scores from students in the former levels decline as the students progress through the grades. Rossell says that in 1986 such a decline was not observed.[78]

Buffalo's Public Schools have also received more than their share of awards for academic accomplishments. Data from 1988 shows the academic success of the public schools after more than a decade of desegregation. That year there were 165 New York State Regents scholarships awarded to students from the Buffalo Public Schools, a figure up 100 percent from 1977. In 1988 there were also 14 Regents Empire Awards given to students from the Buffalo Public Schools. In Buffalo there was a higher percentage of third and sixth grade students who passed pupil evaluation tests in reading and math than there was in any other city in the state. And in 1988 eight of Buffalo's city schools received presidential citations. This was a higher number than any other city in the nation.[79]

# CHAPTER SIX

◻

# Informants' Explanations of the Community Reactions

The timing of the two cities' court decisions was the most obvious difference that contributed to the leaders' diverse reactions, but there were other factors involved. This is made very clear through an examination of the data provided in the interviews with the leaders. But in addition to the timing, the informants confirm that their cities had political idiosyncracies that impacted the behavior of the leaders when desegregation was ordered by the federal courts.

Many of Boston's Irish Americans viewed busing as the latest of unwanted reforms being forced upon them by a political culture that had been hostile toward them. Hence the implementation of busing opened up very old wounds that had not yet completely healed. This is the reason why white political leaders of Boston, most of whom were Irish Americans, were not disposed toward being conciliatory with the courts when desegregation was mandated. The cultural conflicts in Buffalo were less severe than in Boston, hence the leaders in the white ethnic communities were less confrontative when faced with moralistic reforms such as school desegregation. Historical factors motivated Boston's leaders to behave in the manner they did when faced with the desegregation order. This is made evident by the statements made during the interviews I conducted in that city.

While conducting my interviews in Buffalo, I was constantly reminded of the fact that Buffalo had black elected officials on the municipal level. At the time the desegregation order was rendered in Buffalo, one-third of the members of the School Board and one-third of those on the Common Council were black. In Boston there were no blacks on either the School Committee or the City Council. The presence of black elected officials in Buffalo had a moderating impact upon the behavior of white elites who may have been opposed to the court order.

## Boston: The Legacy of Cultural Conflicts

Political historian Doris Kearns Goodwin wrote that "In Boston, ethnic conflict became fossilized as the politics of resentment. . . . Through several generations the stifled Irish evolved a peculiar Boston culture which would, during the busing crisis of the 1970s, be revealed to be remarkably cohesive. . . ."[1] Other analysts have also postulated that the busing crisis in Boston was an outgrowth of old resentments between the city's Irish-American community and the economically dominant and erstwhile politically dominant Yankees. D. Garth Taylor states that Louise Day Hicks tapped these resentments in her mayoral campaigns of 1967 and 1971. A central plank of her platform was "removing the politics from city administration."[2] Taylor believes that Hicks was referring to the continued involvement of the General Court in the administration of the city government.

Because of a difference in political cultures, legislators from Irish-American communities historically had given little support for many reform-minded ideals, and likewise there was little support in that community for the RIA. Progressive measures such as abolition, prohibition, child labor laws, and women's rights were seen by Irish Catholics (and by their church) as unnecessary government intrusions into the personal lives of people.[3] In the 1960s and 1970s this same feeling was held about civil rights measures, particularly those directly affecting Boston, as the RIA did.

In contrast to the views of the Irish community, the moralistic political culture of the Protestant Yankee legislators led some of them to deem it appropriate for the government to enact legislation to correct what they perceived as social ills. This extended to civil rights reforms of the 1950s and 1960s. Yankee domination of the Massachusetts G.O.P. resulted in a state party that was liberal on many social issues, more liberal than the national party. The Massachusetts Republican Party was supportive of civil rights, and, as one of the informants notes, a Republican governor signed the RIA into law, a law which specifically applied to predominantly Irish Boston.

Desegregation opponents in the Irish community of Boston saw themselves as again being discriminated against by a hostile power structure that was trying to victimize the Irish community by imposing unwanted reforms. There is an acknowledgement that the ranks of the traditional elites have been joined by some well-to-do Catholics who have left the city, hence many informants in Boston no longer identify their nemeses as being "Yankees." Rather they refer to them as "liberals," which is politically synonymous with the word "reformers." They identify these reformers by their residence, and point to the fact that they live in suburban communities that are not affected by their reforms. These are communities that were once Yankee strongholds and which still retain much of that character. Over the years they have become more ethnically diverse, with more Catholics and Jews residing there, but they have not become economically diverse. Hence the battle lines remain the same: individualistic working class Irish Catholic urban dwellers versus moralistic upper middle-class and upper class suburbanites.

One informant, a former official in the White Administration, said the following when asked if the historic Irish versus Yankee tensions might have led to some of the problems related to school desegregation:

> There was a long strain between the Yankees and the Irish. But Yankees and Reformers, regardless of the accuracy of the ethnic designation. Yankees and Reformers were synonymous, and "Liberals." So you've got that combination of this is the same old thing of their pressing down their reforms on us. Reform, of course, was a terrible word among the Irish, because it always meant skewing the system so it would exclude the Irish. And rewriting city charters, so you know. . . . Taking away the Licensing Board, the police commissioner. So in that sense, yes, there was certainly that very strong perception.
>
> I suppose the same thing was said about your judge [Curtin], but that Garrity right from the outset was a traitor. . . . The Irish upper class became part of the enemy.

Another informant spoke of the enemy and agreed that they were Yankees, but said, "We don't identify them as Yankees. We identify them as liberals." This person included the *Boston Globe* in this characterization and noted that the Taylors, the family that publishes the Globe, are Yankees.

The use of the word "liberal" by some of the informants has a different meaning than it usually has in U.S. politics. In many respects some of the most prominent antibusing politicians could be considered as political liberals. Their strong support for social programs and organized labor classifies them as such. Some of the elected officials who spoke against "the liberals" had voting records that were far from conservative. Moreover, some have consistently endorsed liberal Democrats over conservative Republicans in congressional, gubernatorial, and presidential races. Louise Day Hicks maintained her ties with the Democratic Party, refused to run as George Wallace's running mate in 1968, nor would she support the Republican slate that year. During the one term she was in Congress, she drew a 62 percent rating from the liberal group Americans for Democratic Action, yet received only a 28 percent rating from the conservative Americans for Constitutional Action.[4] In her 1972 race for re-election to the U.S. Congress she received the endorsement of George McGovern.[5] Some of the informants who spoke against the "liberals" have since campaigned for nationally known liberals such as Michael Dukakis, Kevin White, and even Edward Kennedy. One informant, a leader of an antibusing group, railed against "white liberals," yet at the same time he expressed some beliefs that one could consider quite "liberal":

> I became defensive of Teddy Kennedy and did some functions for him (in 1994), which I thought I'd never do. . . . He came back and mingled with the common folks."

As for the Republicans, this informant referred to Newt Gingrich as "That idiot," and had the following to say about the Republican platform:

> Many of (the Irish community) are still strong construction unionists, they're also starting to see that the Republicans are just lying through their teeth to them. I think Congressman Livingston (R-LA) said it all. When some of the more legitimate Republican pro-lifers were trying to put amendments on the Welfare Reform to take care of the young children and the babies, and things like W.I.C., and they said, "Well, yes, we're pro-life, but it's important to balance the budget and save the taxpayers' money." In other words, the Republicans' traditional god: money. And they're now starting to see this.

This informant, who also mentioned the suburban addresses of the "white liberals" who supported busing, was apparently not using the word "liberal" in the same sense in which it is more commonly used in the U.S.

The suburban addresses of white supporters of busing was an issue brought out by many of their antibusing detractors. An informant who once served as a volunteer with the South Boston Information Center noted that both Judge Garrity and Martin Walsh, a U.S. Justice Department official working on the Boston case, lived in elite suburban communities:

But then again, the people who were promoting it, that lived in Dover and Wellesley, they didn't want to participate. But Garrity, there's another guy up there, his name is Walsh. He's an ex-priest. And his wife is an ex-nun. But anyway, this guy works in public relations in civil rights. And his wife I think has a job also. And they live in Wellesley. And Garrity lives in Wellesley. So these people are making plans for you and I, and they exclude themselves.

The last informant appears to ignore Garrity and Walsh's ethnicity and group them with the suburbanite outsiders. This is a viewpoint held by others, that residence in elite suburban communities makes a person out-of-touch with the concerns of the Irish community, and therefore an outsider. Many informants who expressed a great deal of anger at Garrity do not mention the fact that he is Irish on both sides of his family. Rather they look at him as a typical Wellesley resident who is bent on punishing the Irish community. This is the sentiment expressed in a statement made by an Irish-American former elected official whose district included both Irish and Italian residents. When I asked the individual if the perception was that the order was a latter-day example of Yankees oppressing the Irish, the response was, "Oh yeah! Judge Garrity from Wellesley." It was not Judge Garrity from Worcester, or Judge Garrity, the grandson of Irish immigrants from County Sligo, or Judge Garrity, the member of the Clover Club, or even the husband of the former Barbara Mullins. All of these reminders of Garrity's ethnicity were forgotten and buried beneath the fact that he resided in suburban Wellesley. In responding affirmatively that this was an example of Yankee discrimination against the Irish, the informant made the following remarks:

> The bottom line is, I believe that the desegregation order in this city was punishment. It was punishment. It was punishment to the white—I won't say Irish, because I don't have an Irish thing. But to white ethnic people for the actions of their elected leadership. . . .

Here the informant is putting Garrity in the role of the moralist Yankee, using the government to correct a social ill, and to punish an entire ethnic group for perpetuating that social ill.

While the above informants identified their opponents as suburbanites who are targeting urban dwellers, there were some who specifically identified the supporters of school desegregation as being "Yankees" who were oppressing the Irish community. This was a view expressed by several Irish-American informants. The following is an excerpt from a conversation I held with the former head of an anti-busing organization:

> Once again the Yankee overlords were looking upon both the descendants of their servants and the descendants of slaves, who they brought over. And one thing that I always wanted to point out. That when they were being so self-righteous about slavery in the South, they were causing their own form of slavery in the sweatshops of Lawrence, Fall River, and New Bedford. Although it wasn't totally the Yankees. Because some of the ethnics that made it, at first did not perceive what was involved. . . .
>
> It was this aristocracy; it was the suburbanites that were telling you what to do with your children. But they weren't putting their children on the buses. But even of the new elite, Ted Kennedy's kids, Wendell Garrity's kids, Kevin White's kids, they never did. Michael Dukakis' kids, they never were going to get on a bus. And I think it ironic to this present day, the town of Weston has still not dealt with having affirmative action guidelines within the town.

A former member of the Boston School Committee had the following to say about Yankee suburbanites making decisions for Boston:

> You hear a fellow that lives up in Worcester way, Judge Garrity, is dictating school policy. And then the *Boston Globe* of course were, the Protestant Yankee group that controlled the *Globe,* who all lived in the suburbs. And there's great resentment against the *Globe.* . . . People that didn't live and work in the city were telling us where our children had to go to school. Tremendous amount of resentment by that. The powers that be that were mandating it were these very same people. They were not residents of the city. They didn't have their children going to the public schools. And that was it.

A former elected official from South Boston said the following when asked whom the people in his community identified as the persons who singled out white ethnic neighborhoods to be picked on:

> The Establishment. The so-called, you know, the rich people from over there. The Yankees, the Protestants. All kinds of phrases, but really what it was is the power structure.

Many of the informants did not specifically state that this was a class issue, with working class communities being placed under restrictions imposed by persons from wealthier communities. They chose instead to identify their tormentors as "suburbanites," "liberals," or, in some cases "Yankee Protestants." There were several, however, who framed the struggle as rich versus poor. The individual who described the order as a punishment of white ethnic communities, also saw it as a class issue, where the poverty in affected white ethnic communities made them vulnerable to victimization:

It was a class outcome that penalized poor whites, without any regard for their plight and that sense of neighborhood identity. . . . These are poor people, Steven. . . .

And I believe that, that the Judge Garritys in the world and the liberal press didn't have a clue as to what people in these impacted communities were up against. And it's no excuse for a lot of the bad behavior, clearly. But it is, it is part of what created the level of opposition that did exist.

A former member of the Boston School Committee said the following when asked to give a possible reason why the suburbs were excluded from the court order:

And the people who represented the inner city voted against the Racial Imbalance Law. All those who lived outside and had no black kids in their system were, they were strong liberals who wanted the Racial Imbalance Law.

It was unfair. Because they've been the same people (interrupted by a call). It was like a snob zoning bill, where you had to have an acre to build a house. Well they'd all vote for that. Of course that kept the poor and the blacks out.

Another elected official from South Boston spoke of a classist bias of representatives of the media:

Those that editorialize go home to their suburban house. It's very easy for the elite, or those that had more means to tell us how to live our life. When they didn't necessarily live in a housing project, or were blue-collar workers, as were the people in all of these neighborhoods.

Later in the interview the above individual said the following:

People that are much better off, that are much better educated, that knew nothing about what it's like to work three jobs, have ten kids.

Raise them in a three decker, and say, "You ignorant folks, you don't know. There's something wrong with you; you're bad. And we're gonna fix that." There's a total lack of understanding.

The above informant and other South Bostonians I spoke with felt that their community was specifically singled out for scrutiny and social change. Some expressed a belief that Phase I of Garrity's order was limited to South Boston and Roxbury, with the other white neighborhoods unaffected for the first year, when in actuality, Phase I included all white areas of the city save for Charlestown and East Boston. But the residents of Southie have ample justification for their charge that their community is negatively regarded.

In his book *South Boston, My Hometown,* historian Thomas O'Connor notes that geography and ethnicity separated Southie from the rest of Boston. This contributed to the insularity of the community, whose residents were intimate with neighbors and resented outsiders characterizing their neighborhood as "slums," "shacks," and "tenements." They also resented a press description of South Bostonians as "shanty Irish," and the community as "a spawning ground of politician and prize fighters, policemen, and plug uglies." O'Connor said that this castigation by outsiders made the community residents feel closer to each other.[6]

These characterizations continued into the days of the busing controversy. J. Anthony Lukas spoke of the 1967 race for mayor and said that the Globe's endorsement of Kevin White over Southie's Louise Day Hicks was a classist bias against a woman "who represented the frumpy world of the Irish middle class."[7] *Newsweek* magazine used its coverage of Hicks' candidacy as a means to castigate the residents of South Boston. Of Hicks' supporters, *Newsweek* said,

"They looked like characters out of Moon Mullins, and she was their homegrown Mamie-made-good. Sloshing beer at the long tables in the unadorned room of the South Boston Social and Athletic Club sat a comic-strip gallery of tipplers and brawlers and their tinseled overdressed dolls. . . . After Mrs. Hicks had finished reading off her familiar recitation of civic wrongs the other night . . . the men queued up to Louise their best, unscrewing cigar butts from their chins to buss her noisily on the cheek, or pumping her arm as if it were a jack handle under a trailer truck."[8]

Such attacks by the press intensified South Bostonians' anger at the media and "the Establishment." Furthermore, it has convinced many that their community is specifically singled out for attack by the Establishment. These feelings were articulated by one informant, an elected official from South Boston. On the walls of this person's office was displayed a sign saying "Irish Need Not Apply," a relic of days of old. I asked if people in South Boston still have lingering resentments about the discrimination their community has historically faced, and if busing was a reminder that their community is still under attack. The following is the response:

> We don't wake up in the morning and say, "Jesus, the world is against us." We sort of go with the flow. But yes, we do feel that there are some instances when South Boston has been singled out. We're too white. We're too parochial in our thinking. We're Irish Catholic bigots. Jeez, we're against abortion. We don't lead integrated lives. We are as politically incorrect as a neighborhood can be. But I think that really bothers the people at the *Globe*.

> Now bear in mind that the people at the *Globe*, by and large, the people who make the decisions don't live in the City of Boston. They live in affluent suburbs, which, other than maybe a black doctor, a black law professor or attorney, pretty much in a white setting. And, so they really feel that South Boston or any other predominately white neighborhood should be integrated....

> A major player in all this has been the *Boston Globe*. They early on, even before the federal court order. Maybe a year earlier, even before that. Wrote an editorial, "We'd like to root out separate society, one black, one white, root and branch," and all that rhetoric. And they said that, "We place stock in South Boston." And they figure, if we can rule the roost in South Boston, if we can make it work in South Boston. If we can put in their place any (unintelligible word), teach them a lesson kind of thing, the world is ours.

A former volunteer with the South Boston Information Center (SBIC) expressed a feeling that real estate interests might be behind the singling out of Southie for social experimentation. The following is what this individual said to me after I asked if there was the perception that South Boston was being picked on:

> Well, let me say about this community here. This community here, the location is an ideal location for developers.... I'm not a John Bircher or anything like that, O.K., but like Boston Wharf, big companies that own a lot of property on the Waterfront. So they don't look, in other words, they're always making money. So they're always looking down the road for their grandchildren and their great-grandchildren. To make money.

There was a black schoolteacher, I can't think of her name. You
know all this is coming back to me. She taught at South Boston
High School. And she opposed busing. She opposed busing. She was
there before busing, and she was respected by the children. . . . But
one day she overlooked the high school, looking down over the, and
she said, "South Boston is a developer's dream. It's on a hill head-
ing down. So you could imagine taking a block at a time and you
know, years to come, could you realize here on Boston Harbor this
property here? It's all hill, and every view we could build homes.
Everything could look out to the harbor."

When you look out of the high school, and you look down, and you
could build homes all the way down like Frisco, to the bottom, over
the water and Boston Harbor. She said it was a developer's dream.
Now whether or not that was, who knows?

The above informant's spouse, who was also a volunteer with the
SBIC, agreed and added the following:

I think that we're very, very vulnerable. . . . The real estate factor
part of it. But I also think that they do their studies as far as the income, the age, how many people in this community can fight back,
if they're old, predominately older or senior citizens, because they
live a long time in South Boston. Yes we do have three develop—
housing developments here. Have the people got the wherewithal to
fight back? Fight the element that's going to start pointing the fin-
ger and doing the dictatorship towards us. And I think they do all
their homework ahead of time, and I think they do know.

And they knew enough to manufacture racism, didn't they? That's
all they have to do is pit one against the other. Then they could walk
right in. Don't open the door, just walk right in, just steamroll right
in. Once they created that racism and got us arguing amongst each
other, we took our minds off of everything else, and we were fighting each other.

What this couple is, in effect, saying is that there is a possibility
that the developers were using busing as a means to foment anger
and cause longstanding residents to flee communities that could become prime real estate property. And indeed over the past twenty
years there has been a great deal of development and gentrification
of existing homes in South Boston, Charlestown, and East Boston.
Real estate values have risen so high that longstanding residents
have been forced to leave. They are being replaced by the so-called
yuppies, who rarely have as strong ties to the communities as the

persons whom they have displaced. The above couple feels that the implementation of busing helped expedite the process of gentrification and displacement of those residents who have generations of ties to the affected communities.

Another informant, the former elected official from South Boston who earlier identified his community's opponents as "Yankees and Protestants," looked at the historical victimization of South Boston, and saw busing as one of the latest of a long series of indignities heaped upon Southie. When I mentioned to the informant the history of the Irish community in Boston facing discrimination, this individual said, "Yeah, especially this community." The following is what this person told me about the history of Southie's victimization:

> This place over here in the years past was a cow pasture. And the rich people from Beacon Hill used to take their animals over here, and they would do their grazing over here. So obviously then that was the place you also threw your garbage, so it was the first garbage dump. I mean this is the history of this country. We had the first insane asylum. We had the first penal colony over here. We had the first tuberculosis hospital over here. That's the history of this community. "If you're gonna sh— on it, put it over there."
>
> And every time we've had something, we've had to fight for everything. We got the biggest huge oil dump. I mean there's a beautiful oceanfront community, and what do they do with it? They bring in, all the gas and fuel tanks are stuck right there. We have a beautiful canal that was in there. What do they do? They turn and put Edison plant right there.
>
> Busing was another. I mean, sh—, throw it over here. They got the power plant that spews off the coal and the dust and the dirt. All of us over here have respiratory problems as a result of that. And all these other things that have passed over— yeah [busing's] the same thing. God knows there is the cemeteries we had over here. Paupers' graves, you know, we had them over here.

The above informant felt that the local press was involved in the singling out of South Boston, and that this was because of the ethnic character of the community. In the following statements the informant makes it clear that this anti-Irish discrimination was prevalent into the 1970s:

> We had a very ultraliberal press who, over all the years that I've known it, that I've served, never had any respect for in particular

this community or the Charlestown community. For two communities that were predominantly Irish. Allegedly predominantly Irish. Because when you look at the ethnic makeup of the city of Boston, we're predominantly Canadian in most respects. But nobody ever turns around because the name may have been a Mulverhill from Ottawa, and there was still a Mulverhill from South Boston or Charlestown. So they kinda zeroed in on those two communities, and they said, they being the press who tremendously influenced the federal court decisions, "You can't back down. If we're going to win this fight, you've got to break two communities." And that was the wrong thing to say and the wrong approach to it. But that's what they chose to do.

Among the above informants there was the perception that, just as in the early part of the century, the ethnic communities were being victimized, with busing being used as the vehicle (no pun intended) to punish them. Some, such as the couple who worked with the SBIC, saw this as a conspiracy. The following are more excerpts of the interview with the couple:

> It's almost a conspiracy. . . . I always say this: what they were trying to do is break the black community up. I always say this. Because the black community together is so powerful. What they were trying to do, that's the white community, they were trying to take the black community and spread them around. That's what they were doing. Because they feared—you go down to Washington and you get public records and things like. They feared the blacks all in one community. They wanted to dilute their political power and to break 'em all up.

In an essay entitled "The Paranoid Style in American Politics," Richard Hofstadter speaks of such feelings that one's group is a victim of a conspiracy of public officials. Hofstadter says that in this style of politics, "the feeling of persecution is central, and it is indeed systematized in grandiose theories of conspiracy."[9] Another aspect of the paranoid style, according to Hofstadter, is the view that the "enemy possess(es) some especially effective source of power: he controls the press; he directs the public mind through 'managed news.'"[10] This was certainly seen with the Boston opponents of desegregation. A constant theme was that the *Boston Globe* was in opposition to the people of South Boston and other communities where antibusing sentiment was strong. No opponent interviewed stated that the *Globe* was supportive of desegregation because the editors believed in the righteousness of the cause of desegregation. Rather it was believed that the *Globe* was trying to punish the resistant communities.

What is interesting is that the black community also was dissatisfied with the *Globe* and its coverage of the busing crisis. As noted in Chapter Four, several of the black interviewees were very critical of the *Globe*. One was angry that the *Globe* mischaracterized her as a welfare mother, when she had never been a welfare mother, and others felt that the media gave far more coverage of the viewpoints of the opponents of desegregation than of the proponents. This is supported by Christine Rossell's study finding that the *Globe* primarily focused on negative events surrounding implementation.

Rossell's findings notwithstanding, there was a strong perception in South Boston and other communities that the *Globe* strongly favored desegregation and was trying to punish those communities who opposed it. This is consistent with what Hofstadter refers to as the "paranoid style." Hofstadter, however, is looking at right-wing conspiracy theories that have long been discredited by sane and rational individuals: theories such as the "Illuminati," or those espoused by anti-Catholic or anti-Masonry movements of the nineteenth century. He also speaks of the fear of plots by worldwide communism.

Other analysts have dismissed conspiratorial interpretations as the elements of irrational fringe politics. Thomas Dye and Harmon Ziegler also looked at political movements that view events as part of a conspiracy, and who identify those who are part of the conspiracy. Dye and Ziegler call this "scapegoating," and state that it is a measure utilized by lower-class and less-educated individuals who want simple explanations of complex social phenomena.[11] The Boston respondents certainly identified several culprits in this conspiracy: the media, the liberals, the suburbanites, and the Yankees. These are the scapegoats, the objects of the busing opponents' anger. However, the informants of my study are community leaders, and were not necessarily lower-class and less-educated individuals. Though they represented working-class constituents, being leaders they were often more educated and usually had higher incomes than typical working-class people. Nevertheless they did identify scapegoats. This was not done as an effort to simplify things, but was done based on a knowledge of historical facts.

Hofstadter, Dye, and Zeigler downplay the fact that conspiratorial interpretations are often the result of legitimate concerns. Dye and Zeigler based their findings upon research of *followers* of fanatical fringe groups that espouse conspiratorial interpretations of events. This has led them to dismiss such interpretations as "paranoid," or the result of other personality deficiencies. However, what my informants' conversations reveal is that elites are also prone to view events as a part of that belief in the existence of a conspiracy, even if unfounded, is not the exclusive domain of irrational fringe groups. That is why leaders in both the Irish and the black communities in Boston feel that they are victimized by institutions of the Establishment, such as the media. Both communities share a history of poverty and discrimination by the Establishment. These historical realities have contributed to the perception of a conspiracy. The possible inaccuracy of a perception does not negate the historical background that led to the perception. One non-Catholic respondent stated the following about the history of discrimination in Boston:

> "Irish need not apply" was not just a story, you know. Point of fact, they were subject to all kinds of discrimination for years and years, so there's been that factor as well, and that resentment of the power structure.

Nevertheless, a major social disadvantage of members of a group having the perception that they are persecuted is that there is little desire to cooperate with those who are believed to be the persecutors. Had the community leaders in Boston viewed the *Morgan vs. Hennigan* decision as a mere court order that must be obeyed, they may have been disposed to cooperating with the court to develop a school desegregation plan, as was done in Buffalo. In Boston, however, due to historic circumstances, the decision was seen as the latest of a long series of plots to punish the community, and to prevent residents and their democratically elected officials from controlling their own neighborhoods. Cooperating with the court would have been viewed as taking part in an insidious plot designed by unsympathetic outsiders. The interview data demonstrates that many prominent Bostonians who opposed desegregation did not see cooperation with the court as a viable option. This is particularly true of elected officials who feared retribution at the polls were they to cooperate with the courts.

## Ethnic Tensions Downplayed in Buffalo

In my interviews of white elites in Buffalo, I tried to determine if the opposition to busing in that city was in any way connected to historical patterns of discrimination, as was the case in Boston. Though Irish, Poles and Italians faced discrimination in western

New York, the intensity paled in comparison to what was faced by the Irish Catholics in Boston. Another major difference is that in Buffalo there was far more ethnic diversity among elected officials. Because of the severity and persistence of the electoral "reforms" in Boston, persons from ethnic backgrounds other than that of the dominant ethnic group stood less of a chance of gaining electoral office on the municipal level. Therefore, while Boston's roster of elected officials was nearly exclusively Irish during the post-war era, in Buffalo the roster included Poles, Italians, and blacks. And during the 1970s the antibusing movement in Buffalo included members from all three white ethnic groups. But even in Buffalo's Irish community, which was thought to be the most resistant ethnic community, the level of anger against desegregation was far less than in Boston.

The high level of discrimination that the Boston Irish faced contributed to the resentment that made busing tumultuous in that city. I questioned Buffalo opponents to see if indeed this resentment was lacking in Buffalo, which led to a much milder opposition to busing. In my interviews with white elites in Buffalo, I asked questions similar to those I asked white elites in Boston concerning the relationship between a history of inter-ethnic tensions and anger about the desegregation order.

Because of the greater ethnic diversity among elected officials in Buffalo, I had more non-Irish white respondents there than in Boston. These respondents tended to rate the Irish community as being most resistant to desegregation. I asked them why they thought this was the case, and I also asked them about the resentments felt in their particular communities. Three of the informants were individuals who had grown up in the old First Ward, and who later held elected positions, representing the First Ward and neighboring South Buffalo. I asked them if there were feelings of resentment because their community may have been selected for the social experiment of school desegregation. The following is the answer given by a strongly antibusing informant when I asked if there was a perception that the community was being picked on:

> Well, you know, when you have the integration order from the judge, it's like they, you couldn't pick out anybody that they picked on. It was across the board.

A second antibusing informant who grew up in the Ward told me the following when I asked if the people in the Irish community felt that they were being targeted:

Well, I don't know, really. Just trying to, you know—I don't think they'd say "picking on them." It's just that [Judge Curtin] was making bad decisions as far as a lot of people were concerned. It's not a kind of thing with picking.

I mentioned that the residents of South Boston felt that they were being attacked from all sides, and asked if such was the case in South Buffalo (including the old First Ward). The informant said that this was the case "in some areas, in some individuals, but it wasn't widespread."

The third informant from the old First Ward said that the people did feel that they were being put upon with the implementation of busing, but this individual did not mention higher status individuals as the victimizers, as was done in Boston. Upon being asked if the people in the Irish community felt as if they were picked on, the individual responded as such:

> Yeah, I would think so. Mostly because South Buffalo was predominately Irish, although there was a pretty good sprinkling of Italian and Polish as well, but predominately Irish. And a lot of them, my father came to this country when he was 12 years old. . . . And he grew up in New York primarily and came to relatives. But he used to always say, when he landed in New York, and he was only a kid. And learned a trade, learned a bricklaying; he was a mason. Bricklaying trade, and couldn't get a job 'cause all over New York they'd have signs, "Irish need not apply." So we had all that in the back of our mind. And South Buffalo was a very self-sustaining, I guess. They worked, most of them were in the trades, the construction trades, or laborers here, policemen and firemen later on.

> So a lot of them had that kind of a definite background that they really had to pull themselves up by the bootstraps. And they had a natural resentment to anything being forced on them that they didn't think was in their best interest, that they weren't getting a fair share of.

I asked the above informant if in South Buffalo there was any lingering resentment because of such past discrimination. The following was the answer:

> Yeah, I would say so. Yeah, yeah. Because it was kind of built in. They, the income level was probably, wasn't middle income. Probably is now, but then it wasn't. It was probably in the lower income level. So they're really scratching. There were, a lot of them would escape it

by making the sacrifice of sending their kids to parochial schools. And they'd go to, you'd have Timon, you have Mercy. They had Ryan, Bishop Ryan, and they also had all the parochial schools. A lot of them were doing that. And they would, up to that point tuition wasn't a big issue, but as time went on it really became a big issue because it became more expensive. And they really couldn't afford it.

I asked who the people felt was trying to victimize their community. The informant said the following:

Well they felt that, I think the sense that I got was that they resented it because they were paying for it twice. They had to pay for it in their taxes for the school system, and then they were paying it again in their tuitions.

This informant did not identify any specific culprit or social group that the culprits might have come from. The anger was more about having to pay taxes for public schools their children did not attend.

Another informant also spoke of the resentment yet did not identify any human targets of this resentment. This individual, an Irish American from North Buffalo, had served in an upper-level administrative position in the Board of Education. This person said that the feeling was, "I've never done anything to anyone. Why should you pick on me and our children?"

Three other informants with ties to South Buffalo denied that the people in their community feel as victimized by outsiders as the people in South Boston feel. One informant, a North Buffalonian with very close family ties to South Buffalo, spoke of how the people of South Buffalo were distrustful of outsiders, but made the following remarks when asked if the people felt that busing stirred up resentment at being picked on by outsiders:

I don't know. I don't. And I always, 'cause I went to school in South Buffalo, Bishop Timon. And you knew you weren't from South Buffalo, even though I was Irish. . . . And so it's a very unique community. And, you know it's really born, bred, and died out there.

One informant, a former elected official, is one of those persons who was born and bred in South Buffalo and who still resides there. I told this person about South Boston and how the people there perceived busing as the latest experiment used against their city by high status social planners, and I asked if this was the same perception in South Buffalo. The person denied that such was the case in South Buffalo:

I don't know how to phrase this, except to say that in some regards, maybe the Boston Irish are more Irish than they are American. Maybe, I don't know. Or maybe the people of South Buffalo are less identified with Irish-English issues. Although we do. You know, clearly, I don't think you'd find too many people sympathetic to the Irish Republican Army in South Buffalo. But I do think you'll find people in South Buffalo who'll blame the English for the problems. But not like the Irish in Boston, I suppose. Or even in New York. I just think it's different here. I couldn't tell you the history; I don't know why. I grew up in it, you know. Don't wear Irish on their sleeve the way other people do. I was very Irish; they're proud to be Irish.

Well we didn't really have the English here. We had the Germans. . . . I think the Irish there had another issue, the English issue, Yankee issue, whatever. And we didn't have that issue here. Seems to me we didn't have it. At least not to the degree they did there.

Another lifelong South Buffalonian I interviewed, one who had been very active in the South Buffalo Advisory Against Forced Busing, disagreed that the residents felt put upon when desegregation was implemented. When asked if the residents of South Buffalo felt as did those in South Boston, the informant responded as follows:

Not really because at that particular time, you've got to understand, in '77 Jim Griffin got elected mayor, which was the stronghold, I mean he lives in South Buffalo. So as far as that goes, no we didn't. We feel it now because we've got an Italian mayor (smiles). We're so used to having an Irish mayor.

One of the Italian-American informants also spoke of this Italian vs. Irish rivalry. This individual, a municipal official who was born and raised on the Italian West Side, said that the greatest amount of resistance to desegregation was in the South District. When asked why, the following response was given:

I think it's because it was pretty much a homogeneous community, comprised of Irish Americans, who may have had a different mindset than others had in the city.

I think it's a generational thing, okay. I mean I remember my grandmother telling me stories when I was a baby about the oppression they suffered when they came here and moved into certain [Irish] neighborhoods being Italians. . . .

So I mean, I think it was being the early settlers here, there was the turf issue. So it didn't really matter. If you were different, if you weren't Irish American it was a problem.

Another Italian-American informant, however, did not feel that there were ethnic tensions in Buffalo, neither between Catholics and Protestants, nor between the Irish and Italians. The following is what this native West Sider said in jest about ethnic relations:

> We always had a good relationship. We had heavy, heavy controversial divisive kind of battles, whether it was in sports. I remember when we played in South Buffalo, [they'd say] "those d--o b---ards," and we'd say, "those Irish son of a. . . ."

This informant made it clear that this was all in fun, and concerning ethnic tensions, said, "We didn't have those here." According to this person, there were neither tensions between the Catholic ethnic groups, nor between Protestants and Catholics. Another Italian-American informant, a retired former elected official, said, "I think Boston has a longer history of ethnic tension. In Buffalo it was easier to make the transition from being Italian, Polish, or Irish to being white."

One Polish-American informant from the "Polonia" section of the East Side expressed some feeling that the ethnic communities in Buffalo felt picked on. But like the individuals from the Irish and Italian communities, this informant did not identify whom the specific victimizers were, nor did this person express much resentment. When I asked if there was the perception in the communities that they were being picked on by social planners, the informant said, "I think all those influences are there." Then the informant went on to say much more about black and white parents' opposition to sending their children into unwelcoming communities. Though my question was answered in the affirmative, it did not generate the reaction that I received from the Boston informants. The respondent briefly acknowledged that my question had some validity, then went on to discuss the feelings of black parents. In Boston such questions evoked paragraphs of statements about how their communities were being trampled upon by elite outsiders.

A German-American respondent, however, denied that there was a perception among the ethnic communities that they were being picked on. This individual, who held elective office decades ago, said:

I don't think that was the case. I know my feelings. . . . Our feelings was the fact that we weren't against integration *per se*. What we were against at the time was the fact that little kids, regardless of black or white or who they are, had to get up at five, six o'clock in the morning and bused across town. We thought that was idiotic instead of going to the neighborhood. And I think that was our, at least it was my basic feeling. I just couldn't conceive of kids doing that. That's happening today.

One Catholic respondent in Buffalo made a comment that I would be hard-pressed to imagine Catholics in Boston making. While speaking of the strong influence of "old families" in the banking sector, this person said, "Of course, don't forget the Bluebloods helped build the country too. You've got to give 'em some credit."

The Boston respondents did indeed give the Bluebloods credit, but not for positive acts such as building the U.S. Rather they blamed the Brahmins and other persons of high social standing with using busing as a measure to punish their community. Such feelings were not expressed in Buffalo. They did not castigate busing as a part of some insidious plot. Though many opposed it, they did not describe it as some punishment, nor did they specifically name persons or groups of persons who were bent on punishing ethnic neighborhoods. In Buffalo busing was not identified with any hated group. None spoke of "liberals" or "suburbanites" who supported measures that they did not have to abide by.

### Comparing Perceptions of White Ethnics in Boston and Buffalo

The interview data clearly demonstrates that antibusing whites in Boston felt that the school desegregation plan was an insidious order used against their communities. The elites interviewed paired busing with measures imposed by social groups who had a long history of discriminating against ethnic communities. Some of the interviewees looked at it in terms of political ideology, and blamed the "liberals" for forcing busing on the city of Boston. They saw liberals as modern "reformers," the same group of persons whose progressive measures were used to strip the city of its autonomy and to prevent the Irish communities from having the political influence that their numbers dictated they should have had.

Others looked at it in spatial terms. They saw their tormentors as suburbanites who had little respect for the residents of the city of

Boston. This perception too is rooted in history, for during the reform era suburbanites used their power in the state legislature to restrict Boston's home rule. Underlying this blame of suburbanites is the class issue. Residents of the suburbs tend to be of a much higher income level than those of the ethnic communities affected by busing. A blame of suburbanites is a not so subtle attribution of class as the motivation for the actions of influential persons residing outside of the city limits of Boston. Some of the informants, however, were not subtle at all: they explicitly stated that their communities were being victimized because of the lower economic status of the residents.

Other informants saw ethnicity as the factor. Though there are no longer "Irish Need Not Apply" signs posted in Boston employment offices, Irish Americans in that city have a very keen sense of history and know how much of a reality ethnic and religious discrimination was in the Hub. The intensity of this discrimination in Boston has left bitter memories of the actual practice, or the lingering effects of it. Though some informants identified their victimizers as "suburbanites," "liberals," or wealthy people, none disagreed with me that ethnicity was thought to be a factor also. Moreover, the other groups mentioned (the liberals, suburbanites, etc.) are groups in which Irish Americans had historically been severely underrepresented, and Yankees overrepresented, while the white neighborhoods impacted by the desegregation order are communities where ethnics have been overrepresented. By the 1970s there were more Irish Americans in these high status groups, but their numbers were still small compared with their overall percentage in Eastern Massachusetts, while white Anglo-Saxon Protestants were still heavily represented.

The mental pairing of the court order with a group of persons who had long played the role of victimizer made the order more unpopular in Boston than it would be in cities without a similar history of ethnic tensions. For many it served as a bitter reminder that their group had not yet "made it," and that their age-old nemesis still had the power to force unwanted "reforms" upon them.

In Buffalo white Catholic ethnic groups did not experience as much oppression at the hands of Protestants, hence they did not associate Judge Curtin's decision with more than a century of discrimination. None of the interviewed Buffalo opponents of the order said that they believed busing was a measure being used to harm their community. Instead they saw it as a misguided opinion by an ill-informed federal judge. If there was anyone upon whom they placed the blame for the decision, it was Judge John Curtin. And unlike the Boston informants, they did not blame Curtin for being an outsider (he was born and raised in South Buffalo), or a suburbanite (he still resided within the city limits)[12], or for being an Irish traitor working on behalf of W.A.S.P.s. Their main criticism was that the judge was ill-informed and misguided. Some criticisms were much more powerfully worded, such as the following, which was made by a retired elective officeholder who resides in South Buffalo:

> That bum of a judge! And you know, I'll tell you that, and I told him that. So I'm not saying anything on tape here that I didn't tell him personally. Judge Curtin: he's the guy who ruined the city of Buffalo, in my opinion. The kids aren't educated any better now than they were before the court order. . . . He's the guy who ruined our city. Caused white flight. Not as much white flight as happened in other cities.

Other detractors of Curtin were less strident in their criticism. A retired elected official with a legal background criticized the legal merits of Curtin's finding of liability:

> I felt it was a very, very bad decision either by explicit statement or implicit in his decision. . . . I bleed for the poor people on the Board of Education after Curtin's decision came. . . .

Three of my informants from the South District, who were strongly against Curtin's orders when they were handed down, have given some praise of him. Each of the three held elected office, and each was a vociferous opponent of busing. Two had been raised in the old First Ward. The following are the comments made by these two individuals in regard to Judge John Curtin:

> Everybody's condemning Curtin, and 'Hang Curtin,' and all this kind of thing. That was just rhetoric. And I says, "There is the rule, now the next thing, the most important thing is—again, if you compare it with living in West Seneca, three miles away. Or Cheektowaga, or whatever. First thing that's going to happen is your kid's going to get on a bus." And I said, "What's so bad about that? They're not walking the street."

> Judge Curtin is very much disliked in a lot of those positions. I mean, I'm just talking about when a lot of people thought he was liberal: left or liberal in his views. But he was doing what he thought was right.

The third of these South Buffalonians was effusive in his praise of Curtin:

> The Irish community hates Judge Curtin. I don't. I love Judge Curtin. A great friend of mine, and I'm glad he did what he did. I'm different now. I've changed by years of exposure to the other world. And now I see all points of view. And I see what's good for the greater community.

The above three respondents were all very vocal opponents of busing while they held elected office. Their positions were well known. Nevertheless, they were able to give some praise to the Judge who rendered a decision they opposed. None of the opponents in Boston whom I interviewed made such positive statements about Judge Garrity. I believe that Curtin's ties to South Buffalo and his residence in the city limits insulated him from much of the criticism given to Judge Garrity, who had been born and raised in nearby Worcester and who resided in suburban Wellesley. Though Worcester is very close to Boston and is not suburban, it is not in Boston, and Garrity did not have the close personal ties with influential Bostonians that Curtin had with Buffalonians. Even though Garrity had Bostonians work as "masters" to help develop the plan, his residence in upscale Wellesley left him an open target of criticism for those who opposed busing. The higher level of respect that opponents in Buffalo had for their judge made it easier for them to accept his decision.

An interesting observation is that in neither city did the opponents place blame on the black community for the busing plan. In Boston many aspersions were cast, and the enemies were identified as the liberals, suburbanites, Yankees, etc., but none cast the blame on the black community in that city. They did not identify blacks among the list of persons trying to punish or victimize their communities. This may be due to the fact that I, a black man, conducted the interviews, and their hesitation to criticize black leaders may have been due to cordiality. However, several respondents did make other criticisms of the black community, criticisms that one could consider quite offensive. But never was there even subtle blaming of the black community for trying to punish white ethnic communities. The blame was placed on high status whites.

Though the public reacted by venting their anger at blacks, who served as the nearest target, the target of the leaders' opprobrium was a historical nemesis. The sensitivity of leaders in Boston's ethnic communities to this history of discrimination prevented them from assisting in the implementation of the order. Contrariwise, in Buffalo, where there was not the same history, and where the order was not seen as a punishment, the leaders were less reluctant to help to make the transition smooth.

## The Influence of Black Elected Officials

Throughout my interviews, several informants made note of the presence of black elected officials on the municipal level in Buffalo, and their absence in Boston, and the effect this may have had on the difference between the two cities. When the decision to desegregate was rendered in Buffalo there were three black members of the nine-member Board of Education, including the Board President, and four on the thirteen-member Common Council, including the Council President. In Boston there were no blacks on the School Committee, and none were on the City Council. This was a very significant difference between the two cities.

David J. Kirby sees this as a significant factor. Though he was not able to find the statistical evidence from regression equations that he ran, he did observe that in cities where blacks were more successful in politics, the superintendents were more responsive to the civil rights leadership.[13] If Kirby can assume that the chief executive officer of a school system is more receptive when there are black elected officials, then it can also be assumed that the chief executive officer of the municipal government (i.e. the mayor) is also more receptive when she/he has to work with black members in the municipality's legislative body.

In Boston the mayor's office avoided issues dealing with the public school system. And despite the receptivity of Mayor White to the black community during much of his first two terms, he did not address the demands of the civil rights community for more equity in the public schools. The following is a statement from a former official who was highly placed in the White Administration:

> The White Administration was guilty of washing its hands of the school system. Its support of the blacks was in federal programs and in jobs.

That statement reflects an individualistic or "jobs-oriented" political culture that avoids the politics of issues. The White Administration, despite its liberalism, did not involve itself in supporting such a moralistic aim as school desegregation, but was involved in providing employment opportunities for blacks. Perhaps had Mayor White had to deal with blacks on the City Council, he may have been pressed to address the educational concerns of the black community, just as he addressed the concerns of the white community after Garrity's decision.

Buffalo's Mayor Frank Sedita, who was in office until 1973, also opposed forced busing, but he was not thought to have washed his hands of the issue. Sedita's successor Stanley Makowski was viewed as sympathetic toward the black community, even on the issue of desegregation. This may have been due to the fact that he (and Sedita) had a collegial relationship with blacks on the city council. This was the opinion expressed by an informant who worked in the Sedita Administration. This informant spoke of Sedita's relationship with blacks such as Councilmen Delmar Mitchell and Horace Johnson, and future Councilman Herbert Bellamy:

> I think that [Sedita] was one very astute person, one way I would read it. Not overly naive as a politician. He relied on. He relied on, in those days, key people like Delmar Mitchell. . . . The one person who apparently had an influence on him was Herb Bellamy. The story Herb unravels is an interesting one, but apparently Sedita befriended him, and he worked very closely with Sedita, and Sedita counted on him for his insight and his perspective. He, along with councilman Billy Horace Johnson. . . .

Kirby believes that a mayor has some indirect influence on the smooth implementation of desegregation. Liberal racial attitudes of a mayor, and his willingness to express these attitudes, assist in the effort to desegregate schools.[14] These attitudes are more likely to be found when a mayor, such as Sedita, has close confidantes who are black, and a mayor is more likely to have such confidantes if there are blacks who hold elective office.

Kirby stated that another reason why having black elected officials helps the desegregation process is because the demands of these persons are perceived as legitimate, whereas those of civil rights leaders can be dismissed as belonging only to a vocal minority.[15] This was the case with several white informants in both cities, who claimed that desegregation was opposed by black parents. Black elected officials, on the other hand, can point to election results as evidence that they have a following, and that they truly speak for the communities they claim to represent. The Boston civil rights activist who spoke of Freedom House also spoke of the issue of legitimacy when I asked if having black elected officials would have made a difference:

> I think that could've shaped the debate in the early stages. And I just believe they would've been able to have the critical mass of people who would've heard a balanced kind of argument for, and it would've been a lot more sane and rational, and they would have— I'm not sure. I'm not suggesting that it would have been any different; I think it would have been. . . . I do think that it would have brought a balance to the table and shaped the debate a lot differently. Because you see, those days community leaders, vis-a-vis an elected official, were not particularly highly regarded. Certainly people are able to play off that and say, "Who does she or he represent? Maybe ten, fifteen people." They don't give it the regard that you give, naturally, to an elected official.

Black informants in Boston and Buffalo and some white informants in Buffalo agreed that the presence of black elected officials in Buffalo played a major role in keeping tensions at a minimum during desegregation in Buffalo. When the issue of school desegregation first surfaced in Buffalo in the early 1960s, there was one black person on the School Board, a pediatrician named Lydia Wright. Though Dr. Wright could only cast one vote, the consensus appears to be that this is far better than no representation at all. By having one representative from the black community, the concerns could be voiced to the rest of the Board's membership. This could not be done in Boston because there were no black members on the School Committee until 1978.

One informant, an official with the Buffalo NAACP, repeatedly stated the advantage of having Dr. Wright on the Board as a counter to Alfreda Slominski. The following are some of the statements made by this individual:

> One thing about Mrs. Slominski, we had Dr. Lydia Wright, a black woman physician, on the School Board. Who went right cheek-to-cheek with her. So whenever Mrs. Slominski said something, Dr. Lydia Wright, who's very smart and a pediatrician—So we had Dr. Lydia Wright there. . . .
>
> Dr. Lydia Wright on the School Board. That was a key, so that she could kinda fight Slominski. Because Slominski of course was

against school integration. So that was another key. So we had most
of our bases covered. . . .

We had not only blacks on the Council, but George K. Arthur, who
was a plaintiff in the case, which was a plus for us. And then the
fact that Dr. Lydia Wright on that School Board was fighting
Slominski, you know.

An activist from the Boston Branch of the NAACP regretted
that there was no black person on the Boston School Committee during the days of the desegregation battle. When I asked this individual what would have been the advantage of having black
representation on the School Committee during the 1960s, I received
the following response:

Well, they could keep the issue so in front. When you have an official position, you can keep the thing alive. And even though you
don't win it, it's very uncomfortable for the people who are on the
other side.

Another Boston activist, who later went to serve on the School
Committee, felt strongly that having blacks on the Committee in the
1960s and 1970s would have made a difference. This individual rem-
inisced about the days after a 1983 charter change, when there were
four blacks on the thirteen-member Committee:

Clearly we're the ones whose voices were heard as relates to what
is best for our people. And whenever it is that you have a decision-
making body that's not representative of the people who ought to
be served, then you're taking chances that there might be somebody
there who is just so wonderful, and out of the goodness of their
heart will then consider you in the decision-making. But you have
to have your own.

When I asked this former member if having had blacks on the School
Committee in the 1960s and 1970s would have prevented some of the
inciteful rhetoric that came out of the committee, I was given the following answer:

Yes, I think so. I mean you know that still you are outnumbered, but
it doesn't matter that as much as to the end results, whether you're
outnumbered as opposed to not being there at all.

In Buffalo the members of the elected Board of Education chose Florence Baugh, a black woman, as their President. Baugh was President during the implementation of desegregation. Two informants spoke of how beneficial this was to the process, particularly in light of Mrs. Baugh's commitment to desegregation and her community involvement prior to sitting on the School Board. One person who sat on the Board told the following anecdote concerning Mrs. Baugh's leadership:

> There were a couple of meetings that Florence chaired in the Council, a meeting in the Council chambers where the Board was closing a number of schools. And that always created a lot of emotional bitterness, you know, a lot of outpouring of anger. The councilpersons were there, and they were going to exploit that meeting to get across their own point of view, and also to gather them a gathering and a following. And Florence refused to allow them to talk. She ruled them out of order and told them that this was not that type of session. The Board was holding that session to hear from the people, from the parents. And that at another time the Board would gladly meet with them to hear their point of view.
>
> It was necessary to do that because they were going to exploit. The Council chambers were filled to the rafters, and it would've been time for them to be pompous and parade and do their bit. And they could've easily, because people were there from all across the city. And they could've easily exploited the emotions of those people and had nothing but complete chaos and a lot of divisiveness.

This informant spoke of the friendship that Mrs. Baugh cultivated with two very unlikely persons, Joe Murphy and Joe Hillary, two Irish-American Board members from South Buffalo, who were very much against busing:

> People think South Buffalo is the worst part for blacks, but Florence can go anywhere in South Buffalo because Joe Murphy and Joe Hillary became her strongest supporters as President.

Another informant, the former member of the South Buffalo Advisory Against Forced Busing, spoke highly of Mrs. Baugh and said, "Florence was like a sister out in South Buffalo." This informant also states that South Buffalonians have supported George Arthur in the three races where the people of Buffalo elected him as President of the Common Council:

We work on campaigns for George Arthur in South Buffalo. I mean, George has always carried South Buffalo. And he's black. And George is a plaintiff on the deseg. George is another wonderful person.

Since the charter change to an elected School Board, blacks have held one-third of the seats, and have become as potent a force on the Board as they had already been on the Common Council. The previously quoted School Board member gives credit to Delmar Mitchell, the first African American Council President, for the presence of a representative number of blacks on the School Board:

One of the persons also at the outset of the Board was Delmar Mitchell, who was then Council President in George Arthur's chair. And Delmar was, I guess I would hail him as being one of the most astute and capable elected officials I've ever seen. He was a Council President that was highly regarded and respected around the city. And could exert a lot of political pressure. And I think it was Delmar's position.

Now Delmar assisted in the drawing of the school [Board district] boundaries and getting that through the Council accepted as school boundaries. . . . They were boundaries so you could end up closer to a one-man-one-vote. Now Delmar did that, got that through the Council. But he also, I think, his whole perception of what a Board of Education should be was free of politics. And I think he conveyed that to his other councilpersons. I think his being there also did much to prevent the Board of Education from being politically manipulated. Because he saw the Board as being a Board of Education making decisions regarding the education of children, which was most important. And occupied a very strong position in the city hierarchy. So therefore I think his being there as Council President made a great difference in how much political meddling was done. And because he did not do so and did not allow Council, as President, to do much of that. And then George Arthur, pretty much, followed in that same vein of thinking. . . .

Common Council, because of the laws governing the financial support of the schools, had to approve the budget for the schools. . . . And the Council has always risen to the occasion. Most times they've added to the budget, especially when we were going through the days of integration and needed additional monies for what was going on. . . . Thank God through the leadership of Delmar Mitchell and also George K. Arthur there was always a majority of people there who they could gather together to get the budgets passed, without attaching any kind of addendum to the budget saying,

"We're giving you this money, but you must cease with your efforts
to . . . continue with the integration of the schools."

Several white interviewees have agreed that having blacks as
elected officials helped prevent a racial conflagration when the
schools were desegregated. They felt that, as a result of serving with
blacks in legislative bodies, white elected officials developed friendships that prevented them from making racially inflammatory
statements in public. One elected official from Little Italy contrasted
the district representation in Buffalo with the at-large representation in Boston:

> [In] Boston everybody was at-large, so there was no chance for an
> African American to be elected. The difference is we had the district
> make-up. Definitely helped. They were working with, I mean, their
> colleagues were different. So there was, you know, you were able to
> avoid that. And you may, if you were Caucasian and you wanted to
> speak out and make it an issue, or fan the racial fires, you had to go
> back into your chambers and deal with those people to get votes and
> legislation approved. Besides the camaraderie that developed when
> you're working with somebody everyday.

A former city councilman from South Buffalo spoke about the
friendships that developed on the Common Council between people
on different sides of the busing issue. He particularly spoke about
the friendship between Councilman George Arthur, the plaintiff in
the case, and Councilman Jerry "No Busing" Whalen from South
Buffalo. The informant believes that such friendships led influential
people to work hard to prevent racial tension. The following is an
excerpt of this informant's statements:

> I certainly don't want to dismiss the role Jerry Whalen played, and
> the tightness of this community, black and white. Genuine friends
> weren't going to allow this to happen. George and Jerry and Delmar
> and Jerry, they were great friends. And the Hillaries again, and
> Gene Reville. A big small town. These people were very close-knit
> friends. And they were not going to let this violence occur.

As stated in Chapter Four, there were two incidents where black
and white elected officials went together to high schools to prevent
racial violence. In Boston this would have been difficult to do because of the fact that on the municipal level there were no black
elected officials.

One black former member of the Buffalo Common Council did not specifically speak of forming friendships with white members, but did state that serving with them prevented them from going out in the streets and making racially offensive statements. The informant said, "You would never in the world have them say, 'Blacks gotta do this or that.' They were afraid of us sitting there in there." The Boston Branch NAACP member quoted earlier in this chapter agrees. This informant believes that the inflammatory rhetoric would not have been as freely espoused by School Committee members and City Councilors had they had black colleagues. This is what the informant said in this regard:

> They couldn't look at the person sitting beside them. That's what I mean when—I'm not silly when I'm saying one person makes a difference. But it does cancel the rhetoric. And I think if the rhetoric had been more temperate here, we might have been able to do, wouldn't have gone through all of that stuff we went through. How could they have people beating up black kids and throwing bottles at buses and everything, and their contemporary persons sitting right with them? They couldn't do it.

Another Boston informant, the black former member of the School Committee, stated that one advantage of having blacks on a school board about to undertake change is the fact that there may be several whites who can be convinced to come on board, and thus create a majority for a particular vote. This informant said, "When you have four members who are black out of thirteen, the likelihood is that you're going to have a few of those white members who will believe what you say and embrace what you say and support you. . . . It makes a difference." In Buffalo, Florence Baugh was able to find white members to support her, both as President and also in her work with Superintendent Reville to implement the desegregation plan. This could not have happened in Boston where there were no black members during Phase I or Phase II.

Though David Kirby was not able to prove this in his quantitative study, he is correct in holding fast to the belief that black elected officials is a variable that contributes to a smooth transition to a desegregated school system in northern cities. It is possible that he would have found data to support this had his research taken place in the early 1980s rather than the early 1970s, which was before the transitions in Boston and Buffalo.

# CHAPTER SEVEN

□

# Conclusions

The evidence presented in this study clearly demonstrates that local leaders have a strong influence over how a desegregation plan proceeds, but the manner in which the leaders react when faced with such a challenge depends on a number of factors. In the cases of Boston and Buffalo the major determinants of the behavior of the elites were local history, chronology and the presence of black elected officials. The refusal of the local leadership in Boston to cooperate with the courts was to be expected in light of how Irish Americans in that city perceive "reform" measures. The anger at the implementation of school desegregation was based upon a mental pairing of it with historical "reforms" used against the Irish community. The absence of black elected officials in Boston was due to an electoral structure that was created by reformers during the early part of the century. History plays a recurrent role in the diverse reactions of the two cities, and this study demonstrates the need to examine local history when studying the implementation of policies that bring about radical change.

Another contribution of this study is that it demonstrates the continued relevance of political culture. Daniel Elazar's writings on political culture are based upon the ethnic heritage of the residents of different parts of the U.S. But after many decades of cultural assimilation, as well as geographical mobility, some might question whether cultural distinctions remain sharp enough to use them to analyze political phenomena. This study, however, shows that some of the cultural distinctions persist. Massachusetts' Racial Imbalance Act, a moralistic measure, was supported by suburban legislators from heavily W.A.S.P. districts, yet opposed by white urban legislators from ethnic districts. The white informants from urban areas saw this Act and Garrity's enforcement of it as an inappropriate intrusion of the government. Likewise, in Buffalo Commissioner Allen's order to desegregate was seen by white urban informants as inappropriate, as was Curtin's order. In the latter case, however, some of the opposition was stifled when the superintendent of schools used the Order to create jobs and offer them to opponents. Here persons from an individualistic political culture were offered jobs to soften their opposition to a moralistic governmental action. Because of the ethnics' support of "job-oriented" politics, many abandoned their public opposition against busing in Buffalo.

While history influenced Bostonians not to cooperate with the courts, it was this lack of cooperation of the leaders that led to the reactions of the public. This study shows that the reactions of the public to the implementation of very controversial policies are reactions that can be either encouraged by or prevented by deliberate actions of the leaders. This is a top-down scenario in which the leaders shape the demands of their constituents, and have the ability to *prevent* these demands from manifesting themselves in an undesirable manner.

But the study also demonstrates the limitations of the leaders. While the leaders can often prevent violence from occurring, as they did in Buffalo, to do so they must intervene at an early stage, otherwise they will lose control over the public. In the High Wards and South Boston the intervention by white leaders was too late, hence they were limited in their ability to prevent many of the difficulties those communities encountered. While the leaders have a great deal of control over the priorities of the public, they do not have total control over how the public reacts on these priorities. This is particularly true if intervention comes too late during the mobilization of opposition.

## Lessons Learned from Boston

Buffalo and Boston shared a great deal of similarities, and these similarities were not lost on officials in Buffalo, including those who were strongly against busing. They saw the events happening in Boston as something that could also occur in Buffalo if preventive measures were not taken. Buffalo's officials had a nearby example to capitalize on, something not available to officials in Boston. Prior to 1974, the most prominent example of the dangers of refusal to cooperate with a federal order to desegregate was Little Rock, Arkansas in 1957. This, however, was not an example that officials in Boston saw as relevant to their situation. The temporal and spatial distance of Little Rock in 1957 made it inappropriate as a reference point. As Richard Rose states, in order for lessons to be drawn, there must be some *geographical propinquity*[1] between the two locales. Boston had no nearby example to capitalize upon. Even if the officials' aim was to avoid cooperation with the courts, they had no appropriate example to demonstrate that failure to cooperate would result in the violence and disruption that occurred.

The Charlestown section of Boston, in which busing was delayed for one year, and the city of Buffalo had the advantage of viewing the High Wards and South Boston, areas previously affected by the order to desegregate. Here they were able to draw upon the lessons of a locale that was nearby in both location and time. Leaders in Charlestown and Buffalo, including those who were strongly opposed to busing, intervened to prevent a reaction similar to that witnessed during Phase I of Boston's plan. From the 1974 experience in Boston they were able to learn two very important lessons: (1) neither peaceful or violent protests nor pronouncements would change the court order, and (2) without the intervention of community elites, there would be a very high level of violence.

## Legal Realities

Learning the first of the above mentioned lessons helped moderate the antibusing leadership. The South Boston experience proved that the court order would not be changed, and that efforts should instead be directed toward preventing violence. This sense of resignation was expressed by the following informant, a former elected official from South Buffalo:

> A federal court order is almost impossible to overturn. . . . And taking a kid that's in pre-kindergarten, kindergarten and putting them on a bus going across the city; I see no sense in it. But again it had to be done because the Court said it had to be done.

Such officials learned from the Boston Phase I experience that they could not avoid the inevitability of court-ordered busing. South Boston and other areas affected by Phase I of that city's decision were at a disadvantage in that there were no nearby examples to convince the leaders that busing was inevitable. While the interview data indicates that most antibusing leaders in Boston did not wish to see violence in their neighborhood, they believed that the way to prevent busing-related violence was to prevent or bring an end to busing itself. The belief that this could be done led many to direct their efforts towards overturning the order rather than towards accepting the decision and trying to convince angry residents to peacefully accept it. Many believed that this peace could be attained if an end was brought to court-ordered busing, and they worked to achieve that end.

One of the informants, a former official in a civil rights organization, expressed amazement that antibusing leaders believed they could triumph in the courts. The following is an excerpt from an interview with this informant:

> You saw intelligent legal lawyers in leadership positions telling people, "We're gonna get this overturned." It was just absolutely a travesty. . . . I mean, they were wasting money, resources, you know, appealing this thing to the Supreme Court, and all that kind of nonsense.

In his book *The Social Psychology of Social Movements,* Hans Toch states that some movements are sustained by the belief that the impossible will come to pass. This he calls "The occasion for miracles."[2] The belief in miracles keeps participants in a movement hopeful even when defeat is inevitable. This delays the painful recognition of defeat. Throughout Phase I, and during part of Phase II, many opponents of desegregation in Boston had the belief that the *Morgan vs. Hennigan* decision would be overturned. This hope was encouraged by public officials who vowed to fight the decision all the way to the Supreme Court.

By the time Phase II was implemented, many community leaders in Charlestown no longer believed that they would witness the miracle of the overturning of the decision. For this reason they worked for calm through acceptance of the decision, as opposed to working for calm through the cessation of forced busing. One year later, when Judge Curtin ordered the desegregation of the Buffalo Public Schools, opponents in Buffalo were even more aware of the futility of trying to overturn the decision.

Both Charlestown and Buffalo were able to draw lessons from those areas affected by Phase I in Boston, but Buffalo had an additional advantage. Charlestown was in the same municipality as the High Wards and South Boston, hence the Townies were required to submit to a desegregation plan that had limited grassroots input. Though many leaders in the Town resigned themselves to accepting the plan, they were under the jurisdiction of a School Committee that had refused to work to make the plan more palatable to Bostonians. In Buffalo, however, the new Board of Education that took office just before Phase I of Boston looked at Boston and decided to avoid such circumstances in Buffalo. One way in which this was done was by co-operating with the courts and trying to secure some concessions to prevent the initial phase of the plan from being as draconian as the initial phase in Boston. Though there was opposition to the Buffalo Plan, it was viewed as one in which local people had a great deal of input. Therefore it was accorded legitimacy by the public and was accepted without violence.

While leaders in Buffalo and in Charlestown accepted the legal reality that busing was inevitable, very few of the opponents in any of the communities addressed the legal merits of the case. Rather they framed it as an ill-advised measure used as an attempt to correct social ills. Several of the antibusing informants I spoke with were of the mindset that the actual purpose of busing was to accomplish more than an end to the dual school system. One informant said the following:

> I gotta keep asking you this: what did this accomplish? What did it accomplish? Still to this day, what did it accomplish?

Before I could answer the question, the informant said, "Nothing! Nothing!" Another informant questioned the value of civil rights measures by asking the following:

> How much has civil rights really helped? I have to question that. How much has it? Has it really helped? In the family concept, in the confines of the tradition of the morals and values of the two-parent family?

These informants seemed to believe that busing, like prohibition, was a social experiment designed to achieve a broad objective. This interpretation of the order is squarely at odds with the federal courts' reasoning behind ordering busing. The reason for busing is simply the enforcement of the Fourteenth Amendment as interpreted by the 1954 *Brown* decision. The Boston School Committee had been found guilty of deliberately segregating the public schools, a finding that warranted remedial action on the part of the federal courts. Judge Garrity was acting upon the authority granted him by a series of U.S. Supreme Court decisions. The first of these decisions was the *Brown* decision of 1954, which outlawed *de jure* segregation of public schools. This was followed by the *Brown II* decision the following year. *Brown II* instructs school boards to take deliberate action to eliminate dual school systems. In the *Green* decision of 1967, the Supreme Court ruled that "*Brown II* commands a board to achieve a 'racially non-discriminatory school system' in order to remedy a segregated system. . . . State-compelled dual systems were . . . clearly charged with the affirmative duty to take whatever steps might be necessary to convert to a unitary system in which racial discrimination would be eliminated root and branch."[3]

In the 1971 *Swann* decision, the Supreme Court opined that "If school authorities fail in their affirmative obligations under these holdings, judicial authority may be invoked. Once a right and a violation have been shown, the scope of a district court's equitable powers to remedy past wrongs is broad, for breadth and flexibility are inherent in equitable remedies. . . ."[4] In this decision the High Court ruled that cross-district busing is a means that a court can use to remedy segregation and discrimination in public schools. But the Court also ordered that such remedies were to be confined to the elimination of discrimination in schools, and nothing more. Within the opinion the justices stated that, "The elimination of racial discrimination in public schools is a large task and one that should not be retarded by efforts to achieve broader purposes lying beyond the jurisdiction of school authorities. . . . It would not serve the important objective of *Brown I* to seek to use school desegregation cases for purposes beyond their scope. . . ."[5]

In the 1973 case of *Keyes vs. School District No. 1, Denver Colorado,*[6] the Supreme Court ruled that even the elimination of *de facto* segregation is one of those "purposes beyond the scope" of the *Brown* decision. The court ruled that the purpose of Brown was to address *de jure* segregation, which was the result of intentional action on the part of public officials. Some informants opposed to Garrity's decision alleged that it led to the white flight that made *de facto* segregation inevitable, and thus did not provide a solution to the segregation of the Boston Public Schools. This argument was used to demonstrate that Garrity was in error when making the decision. Such an argument, however, ignores the proper role of the court in such matters. Garrity was restricted to addressing *de jure* segregation. Not a single informant denied that the decision eliminated *de jure* segregation in Boston.

Judicial researcher Donald Horowitz similarly observed that judicial remedies, though legally appropriate, often fail to address the social problems surrounding the cases. He cites a study by Leon H. Mayhew concerning housing segregation in Boston.[7] There the Massachusetts Commission Against Discrimination, a quasi-judicial body of the Commonwealth, adjudicated a number of cases alleging housing discrimination. Mayhew states that the findings in favor of black plaintiffs provided no assistance to the vast majority of blacks in Boston. This was because most of the cases were in suburban communities where middle-class blacks were discriminated against in their search for housing. The findings in favor of the black plaintiffs had no effect on the housing patterns of white communities whose homes were in the price range of the vast majority of Boston's black population.[8] This, Horowitz states, demonstrates the shortcomings of judicial remedies. They frequently do not address the broader social problems. The same could be said about decisions mandating the desegregation of schools. Nevertheless, Judge Garrity was acting within the confines of the judicial system. His role was to end official segregation; it was not to bring about more interracial interaction among Boston's public school students, as some interviewees believed.

The history of moralistic measures being forced upon Bostonians has shaped their perception of court-ordered school desegregation. Some opponents of desegregation are under the impression that the court ruling is tantamount to legislation passed to correct social ills. Very few saw the order as a judicially mandated remedy made necessary by the School Committee's disobedience of the Fourteenth Amendment. Some antibusing leaders believed that Judge Garrity was trying to punish their communities. Very few saw him as acting within the dictates imposed upon him by a higher court and by the U.S. Constitution. This view of desegregation is the result of years of similar measures being legislated by moralists upon unwilling individualists.

One informant, however, clearly understood the legal requirements imposed upon the judge. The following is an excerpt from the interview with this former elected official, who is also an attorney:

> It was a pretty tough order, Steve. And I don't fault the judge for that. It's very difficult for a judge to be particularly creative or imaginative when it comes to fashioning remedies for this kind of thing. I mean if the political system breaks down, and those of us who have been elected to positions of political leadership can't fashion creative and imaginative kinds of answers to these kinds of problems,

> we should not be surprised if, if the courts have to use what at times
> is a pretty clumsy tool. Because they don't have the flexibility. Judge
> Garrity is not the School Superintendent, he's not the School Com-
> mittee. He's the Judge. . . . The fact is that there are limits to what
> the judge can do. And he's got to use some pretty blunt instruments.
> But that I think is the result of the failure of the political leader-
> ship in the community and in the State to do the job that we might,
> under other circumstances, have been able to do.

The above assessment was not one that was expressed by other white
Boston informants. This individual, however, is not from the Irish-
Catholic community, nor was this person identified with the forces
strongly opposed to the Order. For the most part, informants from the
Irish-Catholic community could not separate busing from previous
"reforms" being forced upon them against their will.

Donald L. Horowitz shares the above interviewee's belief that
measures required by the adjudicative process are "clumsy." This is
due to the characteristics of the judicial branch, as opposed to the legislative branch, which is more accustomed to crafting policy. Unlike
legislation, adjudication does not invite compromise. Federal judges
and Supreme Court justices are required to respond to complaints,
and to focus solely on those complaints. Horowitz notes that their
role is restricted to addressing the *rights* of one party and the *duties*
of another. Remedies are required to redress the wrongs that violated
the rights of the aggrieved party.[9] Because of the requirement that
they focus on rights, duties, and legal remedies, and that they disre-
gard predictions of the social consequences of applying the constitutional law, judges are not always in a position to ascertain the
potential costs of their decisions.[10]

## De-racialization of the Conflict

The identification of the order as being a tool of the Establishment kept the antibusing leadership from viewing the black community as the enemy. In Boston they blamed those institutions that
have historically oppressed their community, and this excluded the
city's black populace. Likewise in Buffalo those who were opposed to
the desegregation order did not place blame upon the black community. Rather it was seen as the result of a misguided Judge John T.
Curtin. Nevertheless some of the masses in the affected communities
of Boston inflicted their wrath against black students being bused
into their neighborhoods. This was often to the consternation of the

leadership of the antibusing movement. The refusal of leaders to blame blacks as the enemy is what led some to force the white supremacist group out of South Boston, to hold a Southie Pride Rally to divert residents away from black demonstrators, and to plead with angry white students and adults to allow the departure of black students who were trapped inside South Boston High School.

Rather than view blacks as the enemy, some leaders of the antibusing movement saw them as fellow victims being used for a social experiment. Such sentiment was expressed by the informant who saw busing as a tool to disperse the black community and limit their political power. The leadership of the antibusing movement recognized the limited economic and political power of the black community. Therefore they did not see that community as having the wherewithal to inflict what they viewed as a punishment upon them. They were more inclined to believe that black leaders were the only members of their communities who supported busing. One informant expressed surprise that leaders within Boston's black community were disappointed with Mayor White for not supporting the decision. The following are the comments made by this individual, a current elected official:

> Can I tell you something? It's interesting that they say that. Because I don't think the average black mother or father in Roxbury wanted forced busing. I don't think they wanted their kids put on a bus and sent to East Boston or South Boston. It just, it accomplished nothing.

An elected official from the High Wards had the following to say:

> All over the city I meet minority people, and they say, "You know, you're so right." The minorities don't want it anymore. They want their children to go to the neighborhood schools. . . . I'll tell you, Steven, they want back now to the neighborhood schools. Two reasons: not only because the school is close. They're beautiful schools, gorgeous. But no, we've got to bus the kids out of Roxbury to Jamaica Plain, East Boston, Hyde Park, anywhere but where the nice schools are.

One informant blamed black community support for busing upon the black leadership, but not on the majority of the community. This individual, who held elective office on the state level, spoke of an antibusing demonstration attended by black women. He believes that their public opposition to busing ended after being spoken to by
*Copyrighted Material*

Paul Parks, a black leader who went on to serve as Secretary of Education for the Commonwealth under Governor Dukakis. The following is what the informant had to say about Parks' efforts to make it appear that the black community was united:

> The black community leaders stood shoulder-to-shoulder. There was one breach at one point in time, at which the mothers of the children who, when it first started. This is before the first child got on the bus. They participated in a demonstration at the State House. . . . Ninety percent of them, my recollection, were women. Mothers of the children. The fathers were not there. And I think fathers probably were not there because they were holding to the forces in the community saying, "Oh, no. We're gonna be a united front." And the mothers were saying, "Hey, my kid's not gonna get on a bus and go over to South Boston or over to Charlestown or into the North End of Boston. I want my son or daughter here, close to me in the community."
>
> And Paul . . . he spoke to them. He said, "You might not agree with what we're doing. But you now are the minority. If you turn around and you show that there's not total support in our community for this, then you're gonna give the so-called enemy, exactly what they want," saying blah, blah, blah.
>
> However he did it, his words I don't know. But that was enough at that point in time to squelch any community opposition about forced busing. . . . You never saw it from that point on until later on in years when the parents over there were fed up with the whole thing.

A former elected official in Buffalo, one who remains strongly opposed to busing, believes that both the leaders and the parents within the black community oppose busing. The following statement, quoted earlier, is what this individual says about the feelings in the black community:

> I've got to tell you. I've talked to a lot of black leaders, and the fact is that black mommies and daddies, just like white mommies and daddies, are not particularly (unintelligible word) about sending their kids into an unwelcoming community. In fact many black mothers are more concerned that they have to send their kids into a community that's hostile to them.

The interview data supports the fact that in neither Boston nor Buffalo do the antibusing leaders place the blame upon the black community for the imposition of busing. Just as some of the leaders in Boston have deracialized the conflict with the Establishment (no

longer naming their tormentors as "Yankees"), likewise *none* of the
leaders blamed the black community for forced busing. The leaders
have presented the conflict in non-racial terms, not as a conflict of
black versus white. When speaking with me, they tried to stress to
me that the black community, just like their community, was being
hurt by busing. And because of the poor conditions of the schools in
some white communities, the leaders there were unaware that, as
the courts stated, schools in the black community were in even worse
condition. The following are comments made by persons from South
Boston and Charlestown, who believed that the schools in their community were in no better shape than those in Roxbury:

> We didn't have it any better at South Boston High School. It was a
> class issue.
>
> You look at Charlestown High School, a dump. A real dump. The
> irony is, what were poor black children getting by going to
> Charlestown High? Not much, I can assure you. In addition to all
> this grief that they took. They didn't end up with that much.

Some white leaders, however, were aware of the disparities between the black schools and the white schools, but they did not see
busing as an appropriate remedy to these disparities. They were
more willing to support improving the black schools. As one South
Boston informant said, "You don't shuffle the cards; you shuffle the
resources." The informant, however, did not explain how the officials
could convince persons from more privileged and more politically
connected communities to accept some of their resources being shuf-
fled toward the minority schools. Nor did the informant explain how
the Judge could reconcile "shuffling resources" with the precedents
of the Supreme Court that outlawed *de jure* segregation and mandated remedies when a school board was found guilty of such, as was
the Boston School Committee.

While the antibusing leaders focused their anger against those
individuals whom they deemed responsible for implementing busing, the masses focused their anger against the black children who
were bused into their neighborhoods. Those spontaneous demonstrations not led by the elites had strong racial overtones. A prime
example is December 11, 1974 after the stabbing of Michael Faith at
South Boston High Students and adults surrounded the school,
yelled racial epithets in unison, and prevented the black students
from leaving. This was a demonstration of the masses, without the

organization of the leadership, and it demonstrated the difference of opinion as to who was responsible for busing. When Louise Day Hicks addressed the crowd and pleaded for them to disperse, she was ignored. Here was a prime example of the limits of the leaders' control over the masses.

### A Milder Response in Buffalo

One reason deracialization did not trickle down to the masses is that there was not a strong enough effort by the leaders to deracialize the conflict in Boston. Though many leaders of Boston's antibusing movement framed their struggle in non-racial terms, much of the public did not, as was evidenced by the reactions. Moreover, a small number of those leaders whose careers depended upon periodic support from the masses, i.e. the elected officials, gave deference to the racial attitudes of the public and occasionally made racially inflammatory comments in public. The "Declaration of Clarification," signed by three South Boston elected officials is one example of elected leaders playing to the racial fears of the masses. In the Declaration busing was presented as a black versus white issue, rather than in the populist terms that it was presented to me during the interviews. The sentiments in the Declaration were echoed by others seeking votes from the public. In Buffalo, however, there was no such Declaration from individuals seeking public office. Nor were any of the opponents seeking votes in Buffalo accused of referring to blacks as "pickaninnies," "jungle bunnies," or as being "one generation away from swinging in the trees," comments which were attributed to elected officials in Boston during the desegregation crisis.[11]

The major cause of the increased restraint on the part of Buffalo's antibusing leaders was the presence of black elected officials in Buffalo. Informants from both cities believe that this helped prevent much of the inflammatory rhetoric and also prevented antibusing leaders from exacerbating tensions in Buffalo.

Black informants from Boston bemoaned the fact that there were no black elected officials at the time the *Morgan vs. Hennigan* decision was rendered. They believed that even a small black minority on the School Committee or City Council could have helped stifle some of the rhetoric and would have led to the articulation of the concerns of the black community. One black informant from Boston believed that the votes received by a black official would have been evidence that he or she had a following in the community, and that his or her viewpoints were supported by others from the community. Had a pro-desegregation black person held office on the School Committee or the City Council, this individual could have used his/her electoral victory to refute claims that the black community was against desegregation. This would have made it more difficult for the previously quoted white informants to state that black parents were opposed to the measures used to desegregate the schools.

Black informants from Buffalo were grateful for the fact that their numbers were represented on the Common Council and Board of Education. One-third of Buffalo's population was black at that time, as was one-third of the members of the Common Council and School Board. Moreover, the presidents of both bodies were black. Most black and white interviewees from Buffalo saw this as an advantage. Opponents of desegregation who also served as elected officials were forced to develop working relationships with blacks, relationships which often led to friendships. One could not imagine elected officials talking publicly about "jungle-bunnies" "swinging from trees" and then returning to the chambers of the Council or the School Board to sit beside black friends and colleagues. Nor could persons making inflammatory statements expect black elected officials to provide help when votes are needed to pass legislation. The absence of peer sanction in Boston removed an incentive for elected officials to temper their rhetoric during the busing crisis.

Not only did the presence of black elected officials help put a check on the actions of desegregation opponents, but it was also advantageous during those racial outbreaks at Kensington High School and South Park High School. In both situations black and white officials went to the schools together and ended disturbances. When trouble occurred at Hyde Park, Roslindale, South Boston, and Charlestown High Schools, the elected officials from those areas were unable to travel to the schools with black officials and provide an example of interracial cooperation. These officials in Boston had no black colleagues with whom to appear.

### Other Possible Explanations for the Differences Between the Two Cities

Throughout the course of the interviews, many of the informants provided me with their own estimations as to why there was a difference between the two cities when desegregation was first implemented. Some explanations corresponded with those provided in this study, while there are others explanations that I did not research, but which are worth mentioning in this section.

One explanation is the different economic bases of the two cities. Buffalo, New York has been a city dominated by heavy industry. From the World War I years until the 1980s the mainstay of Western New York's economy was its industrial factories. The city was the home to major production centers of the steel industry, the auto industry, the food processing industry, and the grain industry. During World War I and the prosperous decade that followed it, there was a heavy demand for labor, and blacks migrating from the South (particularly from the state of Alabama) came to meet that demand. After immigration restrictions were passed in the 1920s, manufacturers depended more heavily upon the influx of Southern blacks. They came to these factories to work with white immigrants and descendants of immigrants. This led to a racially integrated workforce.

Concurrent with this industrial boom was the rise of the organized labor movement in Buffalo. Just as the workforce was integrated, so too were the ranks of the locals of the industrial unions in Buffalo. Some respondents are of the belief that the integration of the rank-and-file workforce of the factories and the integrated union locals set the tone for cooperation between blacks and whites in Western New York State, a cooperation that was also witnessed when desegregation was implemented. Working-class whites, whom some believe would demonstrate the most opposition to desegregation, may have been less resistant in Buffalo because they already had interaction with blacks in the factories and in the union locals affiliated with the factories. This interaction, however, was restricted to the factories. The neighborhoods in Buffalo are as segregated as they are in Boston; one study suggests that Buffalo is even more highly segregated than Boston.[12]

In Boston the economic situation was quite different. Much of the manufacturing associated with Massachusetts was in the textile industry, but these clothing factories had left the state at least a generation before desegregation. Many white working-class Bostonians were employed in the service sector, particularly in public service. Though working-class public service positions were unionized, this sector was so patronage-ridden that there were very few blacks on the municipal employment rolls. Consequently, white Bostonians had less interaction with blacks than white Buffalonians had. One Buffalo informant is a black former elected official who also had very close ties with the local labor movement. I asked the informant if race relations was an issue discussed among the local leadership of the AFL-CIO. The following is the answer I received:

> Oh, in union meetings you'd hear this all the time by people like Maloney and people like Ed Gray, who was his counterpart. Edward Gray was the Area Director for the United Autoworkers. Maloney was the Area Director for the Steelworkers. And so these area directors, and they would all come together in the Greater Buffalo Industrial Union Council. And Peter Ribka, who was on the Common Council, was the President of the Grain Millers Union, which is in South Buffalo.

The above interviewee brings up an issue that is certainly worth further investigation, and that is the relationship between the organized labor movement and progress in implementing civil rights policies. The impact of this factor would have been explored further in this study had more informants mentioned it as significant.

Another possible cause of the different outcomes is related to the greater ethnic diversity of Buffalo's white ethnic population, as opposed to the Irish numerical superiority in Boston. By the time of the Great Depression, the Irish were in the majority in Boston, and no candidate from any other ethnic group had a chance of becoming elected as mayor. Because of their superiority in numbers, leaders from Boston's Irish community had less of a need to coalesce with other communities in order to reap political success. Therefore Boston's Irish community did not develop as strong a tradition in the politics of compromise. In Buffalo, on the other hand, no ethnic group had such a strong domination over the political structure. Each ethnic group in that city had to build coalitions with other groups in order to survive politically. Developing a tradition of coalition politics was a necessity for each group, and it was this very tradition that allowed the Erie County Democratic machine to survive. The ethnic communities eventually had to coalesce with elected officials in the black community. This was noted by the following informant, who mentioned the names of black former members of the Buffalo Common Council:

> Trying to get their Irish candidates elected, they had to come to a Leeland Jones or a King Peterson who was in the Ellicott. Or to a Delmar Mitchell or Cora Molowney who was in the Masten. "Now look, we're seekin' your vote." Well in turn for this, you know, what are we getting? Quid pro quo, you know.

The above informant also stated that one of the terms of the deal was that the Machine leaders would try to keep elected officials from using racially inflammatory rhetoric during the desegregation saga in Buffalo. Three white informants from Buffalo, all having served as municipal elected officials at some point during the *Arthur vs. Nyquist* case, mentioned differences in local culture as a possible explanation of the difference. They assert that Buffalo has a small-town atmosphere that encourages the peaceful resolution of political conflicts. The following is the statement made by a respondent from South Buffalo:

> We didn't have the violence here, which surprised a lot of people. I think I know some of the reasons it didn't happen here, but I can't say why it happened in Boston. . . . The fact of the matter is Buffalo is a cozier city, I would think, than Boston. It's a pretty cozy town. And what I mean by that, people know each other here. . . .
>
> I think it goes back to Buffalo being a small big town. You know what I mean by that? Buffalo's accused of, when we're in big cities, wo're accused of being a hick town. And when we're in hick towns, we're accused of being too big. But I think Buffalo's kinda, it's a down-to-earth town. People are pretty close here for a big city. So that's what probably saved the day there.
>
> Boston's a big city. It's not the size of New York, but it's still a big city. I spent some time in Boston when I was in the service. It's a big city. . . . Buffalo's more like, more like Pittsburgh maybe. . . . Buffalo's a small-town home. I think of it more as a Toledo. I think that's why it was avoided. I hope that says something about Buffalo.

An elected official from Little Italy had the following to say about Buffalo's small-town atmosphere:

> Buffalo is a small large city. Everybody knows one another here. And people on the Council, and the Administration, even the School Board back in the '70s when this came to a head. Buffalo was a tighter knit city. Everybody knew one another.

A respondent from North Buffalo said the following:

> My own view is we're a smaller city than Boston. We're a smaller city, not just in population, but in attitude. And people in a smaller community have a sense that they have to get along and work together, even if they don't like each other, they still have to be civilized.

As a political scientist, not a sociologist, I cannot attempt to use this study to determine if the cultural factors mentioned above played a role. Verifying that this was a factor in resolving school segregation would necessitate a great deal of interdisciplinary research which would be beyond the scope of this study. Nevertheless it is definitely worth exploring.

## Contributions of this Study

This thesis has implications beyond academia; it is also relevant for practitioners in public policy. Though there are far fewer districts undergoing desegregation today than there were a generation ago, some districts are still faced with such changes. In those districts where desegregation is ordered, and where the school board is genuinely interested in facilitating a peaceful transition, the lessons learned from this study are quite important. One of the major lessons is the futility of trying to seek the reversal of a decision when the violations are blatant. In cases where the violations were gross it makes far more sense to cooperate with the courts than to risk contempt and give speeches against the order and promise the public that it will be overturned. Cooperating with the courts can help make the inevitable remedy of the violations less harsh.

Once a school board agrees to cooperate, the key to gaining acceptance is the involvement of parents. This study shows the example of Buffalo, where parental involvement in the plan made the public feel that they had something at stake in its success. Though it takes a great deal of work, time, and countless community meetings throughout the city, a school board is making a grave error if it refuses to solicit the most parental input possible, and to make use of this input when the plan is put into effect. Parents need to know that they have helped craft the plan. Persons are far less likely to oppose a plan that they have had a hand in developing. This involvement must not be confined to using parents' ideas, but a school board should hire as many opponents as possible in positions that help implement the plan. It was very difficult for opponents to stone buses in Buffalo when there are fellow opponents riding on those vehicles as "bus aides."

The data from the interviews and from the news articles also shows that the local media is influential in helping determine whether implementation will be successful or tumultuous. In Buffalo the media joined forces with the leaders in helping bring about a smooth transition. In Buffalo there was a concerted effort on the part of the print and broadcast media to avoid a tumultuous transition to a unitary school system. This effort appears to have paid off. Conversely in Boston the local media was at odds with leaders from both the black and white communities. They further antagonized the communities by inflating the perceived costs of desegregation through giving more coverage to the opponents and by giving primary focus on the schools where the most violence was expected. There was little mention of the smooth transition in the Boston elementary schools, or of the very low level of violence at predominately white Brighton High School, which received black students from the Mission-Hill neighborhood. The coverage in Boston helped contribute to much of the chaos and anger in those few trouble spots of the city.

The lessons learned from these two cities also extend to the implementation of policies outside the realm of public education. One very relevant example is public housing. In 1988 the federal department of Housing and Urban Development found that the City of Boston was guilty of illegally segregating its public housing developments and of preventing blacks from moving into projects in Southie and Charlestown. The city was ordered to allow blacks to move into these projects. Many residents of Boston worried that the desegregation of public housing would be as tumultuous as the desegregation of public schools. Fortunately their fears were not realized. This was because public officials capitalized on the lessons they had learned during school desegregation. The mayor at the time, Raymond Flynn of South Boston, who as a state representative strongly opposed the desegregation of the public schools, was unequivocal in his decision to obey the federal directive. This cost him the support of his neighborhood in his 1987 re-election, but it helped bring about a more peaceful change. Even the most vocal opponents of desegregating the projects, those who believed that persons from the immediate vicinity should be given priority in housing assignments, advocated calm. The result was that the public housing developments in South Boston and Charlestown were desegregated, and there were very few incidents in comparison to the desegregation of public schools.

Public housing desegregation is more likely than school desegregation to be an issue challenging urban areas. This study shows that such a transition should be approached with a willingness to obey the federal open housing laws, and it shows the need to solicit a great deal of community input when making the transition. In order to be successful, it is imperative that such input come from both the white and black communities, with priority on securing representation from those communities that are most resistant.

## Outlook for the Future

In addition to commitment from the municipal government, there must also be commitment from the federal government if a desegregation program is to receive community support from minority and majority communities. The decline of federal monetary support for urban public education is a current phenomenon that precludes a prediction of a happy ending for both Buffalo and Boston. A major reason why Buffalo was able to develop its popular magnet school program was because of assistance provided by funds from the U.S. Department of Health, Education, and Welfare (later the U.S. Department of Education). But in this era of budget balancing, one cannot expect a continuation of such assistance. In order for the magnet school programs to continue to offer the services and curricula they have throughout the past two decades, the municipal government must increase its commitment to offset the loss of federal funding. This too may be an unrealistic expectation. In the spring of 1995 one elected official in Buffalo, who has a strong concern about fiscal matters, had the following to say about the prospect of the city spending additional monies on the magnet schools:

> I'm concerned right now from a financial standpoint with what's going on with Judge Curtin, and the Board just submitting a budget for $55 million extra. And it's not that I don't think the money is needed. It's just a matter of affordability. We just, there's no way. If the Judge ordered an extra $50 million, I don't know where it would come from, Steven. And it would just further impact the City of Buffalo adversely, because to raise taxes to pay for it would just drive more middle income families out of the city, white, black, green, and yellow.

> And that's our problem right now. Middle income families are leaving. So we're left with a poor city getting poorer.

The last comment was particularly significant. This official was worried about the prospect of white flight. White flight from the Buffalo Public School System was arrested with the creation of the magnet school programs. This has made the public schools competitive with the diocesan schools and with the surrounding suburban school districts. A commitment from the federal government was partly responsible for providing the Buffalo Public Schools with the money to develop competitive programs. But with the decline in federal commitment, it will be contingent upon the city to tax middle income residents to continue the funding of the magnet schools. The choice Buffalo faces is either to scale back on the public school programs that have helped arrest white flight, or to increase taxes on the middle class, which will increase white flight. Either choice will adversely affect school desegregation.

The decline in governmental support for public education will also have an adverse impact upon urban school systems not under court orders. Many major urban centers are becoming less and less affluent as middle class residents flee the cities. The declining tax base deprives cities of the resources necessary to make the improvements that would encourage middle class parents to keep their children in urban schools. It also makes it difficult for schools to lure suburban parents back to the city, as happened in Buffalo during the late 1970s and 1980s. During the 1960s, 1970s, and 1980s, as the middle class abandoned the cities, urban school boards were able to make up for the shortfall in tax dollars through the use of federal funds. Without that source there is little hope for improvement of urban schools in the 21st century. Urban schools are becoming the domain of students whose parents are economically underprivileged and who are racial minorities. These groups have little political clout and are unlikely to command the public resources necessary to maintain the quality of the schools their children attend.

The challenges Buffalo is about to face with the decline in magnet school funding are challenges seen in Boston and other major cities throughout the U.S. These challenges will become increasingly difficult if states follow Congress' lead in advocating for the decrease in public school funding by providing vouchers to parents sending their children to non-public schools. If there is not a change in lawmakers' attitudes toward public education, the crises faced by urban school districts will become more severe in the coming years.

An added consequence of the reduction of support for public education is that it may lead to a rise in white parents' opposition to school desegregation and will reverse the support many have given in cities like Buffalo. Because of a decline in funding of magnet schools, there is less incentive for white parents to support sending their children on a bus into the inner city. A white member of the Board of Education said the following concerning the efforts to curtail white parents' opposition to busing:

I think we've been far, far less successful recently because the overall funding of Buffalo schools has been diminished to such a large
degree, or hasn't grown to the extent that it should grow to support
the activities that we're undertaking.

This lack of support was clearly obvious during one of my trips to
Buffalo. In December 1994 white parents in a middle class North
Buffalo community had just been informed that their neighborhood
school, School 81, would become a grades 3 to 8 academy, and that
the children from grades pre-K to 2 would be bused to the new Stanley Makowski Early Child Center, in the heart of the black community. Many members of the community were outraged that their
children would be sent to the Makowski ECC. At a December 7 Board
of Education meeting the scene was reminiscent of the early 1970s.
Irate white parents voiced their opposition to sending their children
to the new school.

One white informant, a resident of North Buffalo, had the following to say about the angry parents:

> Those folks didn't want their children to go into the African American
> community. They didn't want their children to go into that, "that ter-
> rible neighborhood," and it was that simple. They didn't want to
> know anything about the school.

The December 1994 meeting is evidence that after nearly two
decades of a successful desegregation program and very low levels of
racial violence, race is still a central issue in the minds of many parents. The actions of the angry parents in Boston in 1974 and the
words of some of the parents in North Buffalo in 1994 show the persistence of race and racial animosity as a salient issue among the
American public, even without the prompting of leaders. Due to the
continued salience of the race issue, local leaders must work care-
fully with their communities when they are forced to implement unpopular innovations. The actions taken by the local leaders will
determine whether the scenario will be one of conflict or cooperation.

# Notes

## Chapter One

1. W. E. B. DuBois, *The Souls of Black Folk,* (1903; report, New York: Penguin Books, 1989), p. 13.

2. "The '70 Census: How Many Americans and Where They Are," *U.S. News and World Report,* September 14, 1970, p. 24.

3. Technically speaking South Buffalo is only that part of the City that is south of the Buffalo River, but for the purposes of this study, I also include an area called the "First Ward" when I speak of South Buffalo. The First Ward, which adjoins South Buffalo, is also a working-class Irish community. The Ward and South Buffalo combined make up the South Councilmanic District.

4. *Morgan vs. Hennigan,* 379 F. Supp. 410, 424 (1974). *Arthur vs. Nyquist,* 415 F. Supp. 904, 914 (1976). The *Morgan vs. Hennigan* case was the Boston case, which presents data giving the percentages of each racial group. The *Arthur vs. Nyquist* case was the Buffalo case, which gives only the "white" and "non-white" percentages.

## Chapter Two

1. Daniel Elazar, *American Federalism: A View from the States,* (New York: Thomas Y. Crowell Company, 1971), p. 91.

2. Oscar Handlin, *Boston's Immigrants: 1790–1880,* (Cambridge, Mass.: Harvard University Press, 1941), p. 48.

3. Ibid., pp. 185–186.

4. J. Anthony Lukas, *Common Ground: A Turbulent Decade in the Lives of Three American Families* (New York: Alfred A. Knopf, 1985), p. 73.

5. Wallace Stegner, "Who Persecutes Boston?" *The Atlantic,* July 1944, p. 46.

6. Thomas H. O'Connor, *Fitzpatrick's Boston, 1846–1866: John Bernard Fitzpatrick, Third Bishop of Boston* (Boston: Northeastern University Press, 1984), p. 152.

7. Handlin, pp. 201–203.

8. O'Connor, pp. 95–96.

9. Elazar, p. 95.

10. Handlin, p. 210

11. Ibid. p. 229.

12. James Connolly, "Reconstituting Ethnic Politics: Boston, 1909–1925", p. 8.

13. John F. Stack, Jr., *International Conflict in an American City: Boston's Irish, Italians, and Jews, 1935–1944* (Westport, Connecticut: Greenwood Press, 1979), p. 33.

14. Thomas H. O'Connor, *The Boston Irish: A Political History* (Boston: Northeastern University Press, 1995), p. 235.

15. Stack., p. 33.

16. Ibid.

17. J. Clubb, William Flanigan, and Nancy Zingale, *Partisan Realignment: Voters, Parties, and Government in American History* (Boulder, Colorado: Westview Press, 1990), p. 112.

18. Ibid., p. 35

19. V. O. Key, "A Theory of Critical Elections," *The Journal of Politics,* vol. 17, no. 1, February 1955, pp. 3–18.

20. Stack, p. 24.

21. Stegner, p. 45.

22. James Michael Curley, *I'd Do it Again: A Record of All My Uproarious Years* (Englewood Cliffs, N.J.: Prentice-Hall, 1957), p. 296.

23. Stegner, p. 46

24. John Daniels, *In Freedom's Birthplace* (New York: Houghton Mifflin Company, 1914), p. 8.

25. Ibid., p. 102.

26. Ibid., p. 270.

27. Ibid., p. 272.

28. *Bay State Banner,* November 11, 1977.

29. James Jennings and Mel King, eds., *From Access to Power: Black Politics in Boston* (Cambridge, Mass.: Schenkman Books, Inc., 1986), p. 17.

30. David A. Gerber, *The Making of an American Pluralism: Buffalo, New York, 1825–60* (Urbana, Illinois: University of Illinois Press, 1989), p. 24.

31. Mark Goldman, *High Hopes: The Rise and Decline of Buffalo, New York* (Albany: State University of New York Press, 1983), p. 72. Hereinafter referred to as "Goldman, 1983."

32. Ibid., pp. 81–82.

33. Gerber, p. 371.

34. Ibid., p. 372.

35. Ibid., p. 385.

36. Ibid., p. 402.

37. Ibid., p. 384

38. Clubb, Flanigan, and Zingale, p. 101.

39. Gerber, p. 396.

40. Walter Borowiec, "The Prototypical Ethnic Politician: a Study of the Political Leadership of an Ethnic Sub-community," (Ph.D. Diss., State University of New York at Buffalo, 1972), p. 1.

41. Goldman, 1983, p., 167.

42. Ibid., p. 170.

43. Brenda K. Shelton, *Reformers in Search of Yesterday: Buffalo in the 1890s,* (Albany: State University of New York Press, 1976), p. 55.

44. Ibid., p. 18.

45. Ibid., pp. 28–29.

46. Ibid., p. 63.

47. Clubb, Flanigan, and Zingale, p. 52.

48. Shelton, p. 63.

49. Ibid., p. 49.

50. Ibid.

51. Virginia Yans-McLaughlin, *Family and Community: Italian Immigrants in Buffalo, 1880–1930* (Ithaca, N.Y.: Cornell University Press, 1977), pp. 12–13.

52. Ibid., pp. 38–39.

53. Ibid., p. 43.

54. Ibid., p. 116.

55. Ibid., pp. 112–114.

56. Borowiec, p. 72.

57. Ibid., p. 69.

58. Ibid., p. 80–81.

59. Ibid., p. 86.

60. Ibid., p. 87

61. Goldman, 1983, p. 215.

62. Ibid., p. 91.

63. Arthur O. White, "The Black Movement Against Jim Crow Education in Buffalo, New York, 1800–1900," *Phylon,* vol. 30, no. 4, 1969, p. 393.

64. Ibid.

65. Goldman, 1983, p. 92.

66. Niles Carpenter, "Nationality, Color, and Economic Opportunity in the City of Buffalo," *The University of Buffalo Studies,* vol. 5, no. 4, June 1927, p. 155.

67. Mark Goldman, *City On The Lake: The Challenge of Change in Buffalo, New York* (Buffalo: Prometheus Books, 1990), p. 97. Hereinafter referred to as "Goldman, 1990."

68. Carpenter, p. 158.

## Chapter Three

1. In 1966 the School Committee voted 4–1 against funding Operation Exodus. (U.S. Civil Rights Commission, *Hearing before the United States Commission on Civil Rights: Hearing Held in Boston, Massachusetts,* October 4–5, 1966), page 131.

2. *Morgan vs. Hennigan* at 450.

3. United States Commission on Civil Rights, Hearing Held on October 4–5, 1966, pp. 129–130.

4. *Morgan vs. Hennigan,* at 451.

5. Ibid., at 452.

6. Ibid., at 454

7. Ibid, at 455.

8. Ibid.

9. Ibid.

10. Ibid., p. 429.

11. Ibid., p. 438.

12. Ibid., p. 426.

13. Ibid., p. 428.

14. Ibid., p. 447.

15. Ibid., p. 448.

16. Ibid.

17. Ibid., p. 447.

18. Ibid., p. 448.

19. *Morgan vs. Kerrigan,* 509 F. 2d, 580 (1974).

20. *Morgan vs. Hennigan,* at 473.

21. Massachusetts State Advisory Committee to the U.S. Commission on Civil Rights, *Report on Racial Imbalance in the Boston Public Schools,* Washington, D.C.: U.S. Government Printing Office, January 1965, pp. 8–9.

22. Ibid., p. 10.

23. *Morgan vs. Hennigan,* at 473.

24. *Arthur vs. Nyquist,* 415 F. Supp. 904, 961 (1976).

25. *Morgan vs. Hennigan,* at 471.

25. Ibid.

27. Ibid.

28. *Morgan vs. Kerrigan,* at 591.

29. U.S. Civil Rights Commission, Hearing Held on October 4–5, 1966, p. 94.

30. *Morgan vs. Hennigan,* at 466.

31. Ibid., at 469.

32. Ibid., at 459

33. Ibid.

34. *Morgan vs. Kerrigan,* at 596.

35. *Morgan vs. Hennigan,* at 463.

36. Ibid., at 463–464.

37. George J. Alexander, *Civil Rights U.S.A.: Public Schools; Cities in the North and West, 1963, Buffalo,* Staff Report Submitted to the United States Commission on Civil Rights, Washington, D.C.: U.S. Government Printing Office, 1963, p. 13.

38. *Arthur vs. Nyquist,* at 952.

39. Ibid., at 953.

40. Ibid., at 959.

41. Alexander, p. 41.

42. *Arthur vs. Nyquist,* at 934.

43. Ibid.

44. Ibid., at 937.

45. Ibid.

46. Ibid., at 939.

47. Ibid., at 938.

48. Ibid., at 939.

49. Ibid., at 928.

50. Ibid., at 924.

51. Ibid., at 928.

52. *Arthur vs. Nyquist,* 573 F. Supp. 2d 134 (1978), at 144. Hereinafter referred to as "Arthur vs. Nyquist, 1978."

53. *Arthur vs. Nyquist,* 1976, at 929.

54. Ibid., at 928–929.

55. Ibid., at 941.

56. Ibid., at 942.

57. Ibid., at 954–955.

58. Ibid., at 961–962.

59. Ibid., at 963.

60. Ibid.

61. Ibid., at 964.

62. Ibid., at 966.

63. Ibid., at 967.

64. Ibid., at 944–945.

## Chapter Four

1. *School Committee of Boston vs. Board of Education,* Mass., 302 N.E. 2d 916.

2. Ibid., at 924.

3. *Morgan vs. Kerrigan,* 401 F. Supp. 216 (1975), p. 253. Hereinafter referred to as "*Morgan vs. Kerrigan, 1975.*"

4. Ibid., at 246.

5. Lukas, p. 134, 136-137.

6. Jon Hillson, *The Battle of Boston* (New York: Pathfinder Press, 1977), p. 29.

7. *Boston Globe,* September 8, 1974.

8. David J. Kirby, T. Robert Harris, Robert L. Crain, and Christine Rossell, *Political Strategies in Northern School Desegregation* (Lexington, Mass.: D. C. Heath and Company, 1973), p. 96.

9. Morton Inger and Robert T. Stout, "School Segregation: the Need to Govern," *The Urban Review,* vol. 3., no. 2., November 1968 p. 35.

10. Ibid., p. 34.

11. Ibid., p. 38.

12. Lukas, pp. 223–227.

13. Hillson, pp. 165–166.

14. Ibid., p. 186.

15. Ibid., p. 215.

16. D. Garth Taylor, *Public Opinion and Collective Action,* p. 140.

17. Lukas, p. 609.

18. J. Michael Ross and William M. Berg, *"I Respectfully Disagree With the Judge's Order": The Boston School Desegregation Controversy* (Washington, D.C.: University Press of America date), p. 219.

19. Ibid., p. 362.

20. Hillson, pp. 207, 213, and 253.

21. Taylor, *Public Opinion and Collective Action*, p. 127.

22. Ibid., p. 128.

23. Christine Rossell, "The Mayor's Role in School Desegregation Implementation," *Urban Education*, vol. 12, no. 3, October 1977, p. 254.

24. Kirby, et al. p. 129.

25. Lukas, p. 621.

26. Susan L. Greenblatt and Charles L. Willie, "School Desegregation in the Management of Social Change," in Charles V. Willie and Susan L. Greenblatt's, eds., *Community Politics and Educational Change: Ten School Systems Under Court Order* (New York: Longman, 1981), p. 325.

27. Christine H. Rossell, "The Effect of Community Leadership and Media on Public Behavior," *Theory Into Practice*, vol. 17, February, 1978, p. 134.

28. Hillson, p. 255.

29. Ibid., p. 137.

30. Jennifer L. Hochschild, *The New American Dilemma: Liberal Democracy and School Desegregation* (New Haven, Conn.: Yale University Press, 1984), p. 111.

31. Ibid., p. 195.

32. Jonathan Kelley, "The Politics of School Busing," *Public Opinion Quarterly*, vol. 38, no. 1, spring 1974, p. 26.

33. Ibid., pp. 25–27.

34. Ibid., p. 39.

35. Taylor, *Public Opinion and Collective Action*, pp. 47–49.

36. Hillson, pp. 214–215.

37. Ibid., pp. 111, 114.

38. Mel King, *Chain of Change: Struggles for Black Community Development* (Boston: South End Press, 1981), p. 30.

39. Ibid., p. 32.

40. Ibid., p. 38.

41. U.S. Commission on Civil Rights, *Hearing Held Before the United States Commission on Civil Rights: Hearing Held in Boston, Massachusetts,* June 16–20, 1975 (Washington, D.C.: U.S. Government Printing Office, 1978), p. 395.

42. J. Brian Sheehan, *The Boston School Integration Dispute: Social Change and Legal Maneuvers* (New York: Columbia University Press, 1984), p. 247.

43. *Bay State Banner,* September 18, 1974.

44. Goldman, 1990, p. 76.

45. Ibid.

46. Bill Kovach, "Republicans Divided and Democrats Face Negro Defections." *The New York Times,* July 15, 1969, p. 34, Column 1.

47. Goldman, 1990, p. 115

48. Ibid., p. 190

49. Ibid., p. 191.

50. Harrell R. Rodgers, Jr. and Charles S. Bullock, III, *Coercion to Compliance* (Lexington, Mass.: D. C. Heath and Company, 1976), p. 39.

51. Goldman, 1990, p. 147.

52. Mark A. Chesler, Bunyan I. Bryant, and James E. Crowfoot, *Making Desegregation Work: A Professional's Guide to Effecting Change* (Beverly Hills, Cal.: Sage Publications, 1981), p. 36.

53. Hochschild, p. 101.

54. Ernest R. House, *The Politics of Educational Innovation* (Berkeley, Cal.: McCutchan Publishing Corporation, 1974), p. 45.

55. Daniel U. Levine and Connie Campbell, "Developing and Implementing Big-City Magnet School Programs," in Daniel U. Levine and Robert J. Havighurst, eds., *The Future of Big City Schools: Desegregation Policies and Magnet Alternatives* (Berkeley, Cal.: McCutchan Publishing Corporation, 1977), p. 251.

56. *Courier Express,* May 19, 1976.

57. In 1976 school opened on September 8, but closed one day later when the Buffalo Teachers Federation went out on strike. They did not return to work until September 27, which was another "first day of school."

58. *Courier Express,* September 26, 1976.

59. Hillson, p. 250.

60. Goldman, 1990, p. 148.

61. Ibid., p. 189.

62. *Courier Express,* April 1, 1981.

63. *Courier Express,* May 20, 1981.

64. Robert A. Dahl, *A Preface to Democratic Theory* (Chicago: University of Chicago Press, 1956), pp. 463–469.

65. *Courier Express,* February 22, 1972.

66. Goldman, 1990, p. 200.

67. Ibid., p. 146.

68. Ibid., pp. 146–147.

69. Hochschild, p. 114.

70. Goldman, 1990, p. 189.

71. Ibid., p. 205.

72. Everett M. Rogers, *Diffusion of Innovations* (New York: The Free Press, 1962), p. 13.

73. Sheehan, pp. 67, 82–83.

74. Fred W. Grupp and Alan R. Richards, "Variations in Elite Perceptions of American States as Referents for Public Policy Making," *The American Political Science Review,* vol. 69, no. 3, September 1975, p. 851.

75. Richard Rose, *Lesson-Drawing in Public Policy: A Guide to Learning Across Time and Space* (Chatham, New Jersey: Chatham House Publishers, Inc., 1993), p. 22.

76. Ibid., p. 5.

77. Ibid., p. 96.

## Chapter Five

1. Ross and Berg, p. 210, 233–234.

2. Boston Globe, October 8, 1974.

3. U.S. Civil Rights Commission, Hearing Held on June 16–20, 1975, p. 263.

4. Ibid., p. 272.

5. Ibid., pp. 360–361.

6. Hillson, p. 145.

7. Ibid., p. 151.

8. Ross and Berg, p. 225.

9. Ibid., p. 312.

10. Ibid., p. 212.

11. Ibid., p. 227.

12. Hillson, pp. 16–18.

13. Ross and Berg, pp. 274–275.

14. Ibid., p. 145.

15. Ibid., pp. 149–150.

16. Hillson, pp. 156–157.

17. Ibid., p. 107.

18. Ross and Berg, p. 350.

19. Sheehan, p. 248.

20. Hillson, pp. 175–176.

21. Lukas, pp. 293–294.

22. Ibid., pp. 299–300.

23. Hillson, p. 202.

24. Lukas, p. 314.

25. Ibid., p. 257.

26. Ibid., pp. 455–456 and Hillson, p. 212.

27. Hillson, p. 200.

28. Ross and Berg, p. 502.

29. Hillson, pp. 145–146.

30. Ross and Berg, p. 502.

31. Ibid., p. 168.

32. Ibid., p. 212.

33. Ibid., p. 208.

34. Ibid., p. 245.

35. Ibid., p. 250.

36. Ibid., pp. 246–247.

37. Hillson, p. 159.

38. Taylor, *Public Opinion and Collective Action,* p. 65.

39. Ibid., p. 66.

40. Ibid., p. 69.

41. Ibid., p. 64.

42. Ibid., p. 67.

43. Norman Frohlich, Joe A. Oppenheimer, and Oran R. Young, *Political Leadership and Collective Goods* (Princeton, N.J.: Princeton University Press, 1971), p. 6.

44. Taylor, *Public Opinion and Collective Action,* pp. 82–85.

45. Ibid., p. 66.

46. Ibid., p. 86.

47. Sheehan, p. 255.

48. United States Civil Rights Commission, *School Desegregation in Boston* (Washington, D.C.: U.S. Government Printing Office, 1975), pp. 131–132.

49. Ibid., p. 133.

50. Ibid., pp. 136–137.

51. Ibid., p. 141.

52. Ibid., p. 146.

53. *Boston Globe,* May 4, 1976.

54. United States Bureau of the Census. *Population and Housing Characteristics for Census Tracts and Block Numbering Areas,* 1950–1990 censuses.

55. Boston Public School System, "BPS Historical Enrollment Data," Boston Public Schools, 1994.

56. U.S. Census Bureau, *Population and Housing Characteristics for Census Tracts and Block Numbering Areas,* 1960–1990 censuses.

57. U.S. Census Bureau, 1970 and 1980 decennial censuses.

58. *Courier Express,* September 28, 1976.

59. Christine Rossell, "The Buffalo Controlled Choice Plan," *Urban Education,* vol. 22, no. 3, October 1987, p. 341. Hereinafter referred to as "Rossell, 1987."

60. *Courier Express*, September 10, 1981.

61. Ibid.

62. Goldman 1990, p. 205.

63. Ibid.

64. Christine H. Rossell, *The Carrot or the Stick for School Desegregation Policy: Magnet Schools or Forced Busing* (Philadelphia: Temple University Press, 1990), p. 91.

65. Ibid.

66. *Boston Globe*, September 12, 1974.

67. Rossell, 1987, p. 341.

68. United States Census Bureau. "Population and Housing Characteristics for Census Tracts and Block Numbering Areas," 1950–1990 Censuses.

69. Rossell, 1987, p. 335, and Boston Public School System, "BPS Historical Enrollment Data," 1994.

70. Goldman, 1990, p. 206.

71. Ibid., p. 209.

72. U.S. Census Bureau, "Population and Housing Characteristics for Census Tracts and Block Numbering Areas," 1960–1990 censuses.

73. Rossell, 1987, p. 348.

74. U.S. Census Bureau, 1970 and 1990 censuses.

75. Data on Buffalo is from Christine Rossell's article "The Buffalo Controlled Choice Plan," while data on Boston comes from a one-page document entitled "BPS Historical Enrollment Data," printed by the Boston Public School System in 1994.

76. Rossell, 1987, p. 348.

77. Ibid.

78. Ibid.

79. Goldman, 1990, p. 209.

## Chapter Six

1. Doris Kearns Goodwin, foreward to James Carroll's *Mortal Friends* (Boston: Beacon Press, 1992), p. viii.

2. Taylor, *Public Opinion,* p. 69.

3. Paula Kane, *Separatism and Subculture: Boston Catholicism, 1900–1920* (Chapel Hill: The University of North Carolina Press, 1994), pp. 26–27.

4. Lukas, p. 135.

5. Hunter S. Thompson, *Fear and Loathing: On the Campaign Trail '72* (New York: Quick Fox Inc., 1973), p. 487.

6. Thomas H. O'Connor, *South Boston, My Hometown: The History of an Ethnic Neighborhood* (Boston: Northeastern University Press, 1994), p. 125.

7. Lukas, p. 223.

8. David Gelman, "Backlash in Boston—And Across the U.S.," *Newsweek,* November 6, 1967, p. 29.

9. Richard Hofstadter, *The Paranoid Style in American Politics, and Other Essays* (New York: Alfred A. Knopf, 1965), p. 4.

10. Ibid., p. 32.

11. Thomas R. Dye and L. Harmon Zeigler, *The Irony of Democracy: An Uncommon Introduction to American Politics* (Belmont, Cal.: Duxbury Press, 1972), p. 138.

12. Goldman, 1990, p. 12.

13. Kirby, et al., p. 83.

14. Ibid., p. 113.

15. Ibid., p. 163.

## Chapter Seven

1. Rose, p. 96.

2. Hans Toch, *The Social Psychology of Social Movements* (Indianapolis: Bobbs-Merrill, 1965), p. 42.

3. *Green et al. vs. County School Board of New Kent County et al.,* 391 U.S., 430 at 437 (1967).

4. *Swann et al. vs. Charlotte-Mecklenburg Board of Education et al.,* U.S. 402, at 15 (1971).

5. Ibid., at 22.

6. *Keyes vs. School District No. 1, Denver, Colorado,* 413 U.S. 189 (1973).

7. Donald L. Horowitz, *The Courts and Social Policy* (Washington, D.C.: The Brookings Institution, 1977), p. 43.

8. Leon H. Mayhew, *Law and Equal Opportunity: A Study of the Massachusetts Commission Against Discrimination* (Cambridge, Mass.: Harvard University Press, 1968), p. 167.

9. Horowitz, pp. 34–35.

10. Ibid., p. 51.

11. Lukas, pp. 137–138.

12. Douglas S. Massey and Nancy A. Denton, "Hypersegregation in U.S. Metropolitan Areas: Black and Hispanic Segregation Along Five Dimensions," *Demography*, vol. 26, no. 3, August 1989, p. 378.

# Bibiography

## Books and Excerpts from Books

Brady, David W. *Critical Elections and Congressional Policy Making.* Stanford, Calif.: Stanford University Press, 1988.

Browne, Millard C. "Buffalo." *Encyclopedia Americana,* 1992 ed.

Carmines, E. G. and J. A. Stimson. *Issue Evolution: Race and the Transformation of American Politics.* Princeton, N.J.: Princeton University Press, 1989.

Caroll, James. *Mortal Friends.* Boston: Beacon Press, 1978.

Chesler, Mark A., Bunyan I. Bryant, and James E. Crowfoot. *Making Desegregation Work: A Professional's Guide to Effecting Change.* Beverly Hills, Calif.: Sage Publications, 1981.

Clubb, Jerome, William H. Flanigan, and Nancy Zingale. *Partisan Realignment: Voters, Parties, and Government in American History.* Boulder, Colo.: Westview Press, 1990.

Crain, Robert L. *The Politics of School Desegregation.* Chicago: Aldine Publishing Company, 1968.

Cromwell, Adelaide M. *The Other Brahmins: Boston's Black Upper Class 1750–1950.* Fayetteville, Ark.: University of Arkansas Press, 1994.

Crowfoot, James E. and Mark A. Chesler. "Implementing 'Attractive Ideas': Problems and Prospects." In *Effective School Desegregation: Equity, Quality, and Feasibility,* edited by Willis D. Hawley. Beverly Hills, Calif.: Sage Publications, Inc., 1981.

Curley, James Michael. *I'd Do it Again: A Record of All My Uproarious Years.* Englewood Cliffs, N.J.: Prentice-Hall, 1957.

Cutler, John Henry. *"Honey Fitz": Three Steps to the White House; the Life and Times of John F. Fitzgerald.* Indianapolis: Bobbs-Merrill, 1962.

Dahl, Robert A. *A Preface to Democratic Theory.* Chicago: University of Chicago Press, 1956.

Dalton, R. J., P. A. Beck, and Scott Flanagan. *Electoral Change in Advanced Industrial Democracies: Realignment or Dealignment?* Princeton: Princeton University Press, 1984.

Daniels, J. *In Freedom's Birthplace.* New York: Houghton Mifflin Company, 1914.

Dexter, Lewis A. *Elite and Specialized Interviewing.* Evanston, Ill.: Northwestern University Press, 1970.

Dooley, Roger B. *Days Beyond Recall.* Milwaukee: Bruce Publishing Company, 1949.

———. *The House of Shanahan.* Garden City, N.Y.: Doubleday, 1952.

Du Bois, W. E. B. *The Souls of Black Folk.* 1903. Reprint, New York: Penguin Books, 1989.

Dye, Thomas R. and L. Harmon Zeigler. *The Irony of Democracy. An Uncommon Introduction to American Politics.* Belmont, Calif.: Duxbury Press, 1972.

Edelman, Murray. *The Symbolic Uses of Politics.* Urbana, Ill.: University of Illinois Press, 1964.

Eisinger, P. K. *The Politics of Displacement: Racial and Ethnic Tension in Three American Cities.* New York: Academic Press, 1980.

Elazar, Daniel J. *American Federalism: A View from the States.* New York: Thomas Y. Crowell Company, 1972.

Fenton, John H. *Midwest Politics.* New York: Holt, Rinehart, and Winston, 1966.

Formisano, R. P. *Boston Against Busing: Race, Class, and Ethnicity in the 1960s and 1970s.* Chapel Hill: University of North Carolina Press, 1991.

———, and K. Burns, eds. *Boston 1700–1980: The Evolution of Urban Politics.* Westport, Conn.: Greenwood Press, 1984.

Frey, Frederick W. "Cross-Cultural Research in Political Science." In *The Methodology of Comparative Research,* edited by Robert T. Holt and John E. Turner. New York: The Free Press, 1970.

Friedman, D. J. *White Militancy in Boston: A Reconsideration of Marx and Weber.* Lexington, Mass.: D.C. Heath and Company, 1973.

Frohlich, Norman, Joe A. Oppenheimer, and Oran R. Young. *Political Leadership and Collective Goods.* Princeton, N.J.: Princeton University Press, 1971.

Gamson, William A., Bruce Fireman, and Steven Rytina. *Encounters with Unjust Authority.* Homewood, Ill.: The Dorsey Press, 1982.

Gerber, David A. *The Making of an American Pluralism: Buffalo, New York, 1825–60.* Urbana, Ill.: University of Illinois Press, 1989.

Ginsberg, Yona. *Jews in a Changing Neighborhood: The Study of Mattapan.* New York: Free Press, 1975.

Goldman, Mark. *City on the Lake: The Challenge of Change in Buffalo, New York.* Buffalo: Prometheus Books, 1990.

———. *High Hopes: The Rise and Decline of Buffalo, New York.* Albany: State University of New York Press, 1983.

Goodwin, Doris Kearns. Foreword to *Mortal Friends,* by James Carroll. Boston: Beacon Press, 1992.

Greenblatt, Susan L. and Charles V. Willie. "School Desegregation and the Management of Social Change." In *Community Politics and Educational Change: Ten School Systems Under Court Order,* edited by Charles V. Willie and Susan L. Greenblatt. New York: Longman, 1981.

Handlin, Oscar. *Boston's Immigrants: 1790–1880.* Cambridge, Mass.: Harvard University Press, 1941.

Hapgood, Norman and Henry Moskowitz. *Up from the City Streets: Alfred E. Smith.* New York: Grossett and Dunlap Publishers, 1927.

Hentoff, Nat. *Boston Boy.* New York: Alfred A. Knopf, 1986.

Hillson, Jon. *The Battle of Boston.* New York: Pathfinder Press, 1977.

Hochschild, Jennifer L. *The New American Dilemma: Liberal Democracy and School Desegregation.* New Haven, Conn.: Yale University Press, 1984.

Hofstadter, Richard. *The Paranoid Style in American Politics, and Other Essays.* New York: Alfred A. Knopf, 1965.

Holt, Robert T. and John E. Turner. *The Methodology of Comparative Research.* New York: The Free Press, 1970.

Horowitz, Donald L. *The Courts and Social Policy.* Washington, D.C.: The Brookings Institution, 1977.

House, Ernest R. *The Politics of Educational Innovation.* Berkeley, Cal.: McCutchan Publishing Corporation, 1974.

Huckfeldt, Robert and Carol Weitzel Kohfeld. *Race and the Decline of Class in American Politics.* Urbana, Ill.: University of Illinois Press, 1989.

Janda, Kenneth, Jeffrey M. Berry and Gerry Goldman. *The Challenge of Democracy.* 2d. ed. Boston: Houghton Mifflin Company, 1989.

Jennings, James and Mel King, eds. *From Access to Power: Black Politics in Boston.* Cambridge, Mass.: Schenkman Books, Inc., 1986.

Kane, Paula M. *Separatism and Subculture: Boston Catholicism, 1900–1920.* Chapel Hill, N.C.: University of North Carolina Press, 1994.

Key, V. O. *Southern Politics in State and Nation.* New York: Vintage Books, 1949.

King, Melvin. *Chain of Change:* Struggles for Black Community Development. Boston: South End Press, 1981.

Kirby, David J., T. Robert Harris, Robert L. Crain, and Christine H. Rossell. *Political Strategies in Northern School Desegregation.* Lexington, Mass.: D.C. Heath and Company, 1973.

Kornhauser, William. *The Politics of Mass Society.* Glencoe, Ill.: Free Press, 1959.

Kotler, Milton. *Neighborhood Government; the Local Foundations of Political Life.* Indianapolis: Bobbs-Merrill Co., 1969.

Kozol, J. *Death at an Early Age: The Destruction of the Hearts and Minds of Negro Children in the Boston Public Schools.* Boston: Houghton Mifflin Company, 1967.

Lane, Robert E. *Political Life: Why People Get Involved in Politics.* Glencoe, Ill.: Free Press, 1959.

Levesque, George A. *Black Boston: African American Life and Culture in Urban America, 1750–1860.* New York: Garland Publishing, Inc., 1994.

Levine, Daniel U. and Connie Campbell. "Developing and Implementing Big-City Magnet School Programs." In *The Future of Big City Schools,* edited by Daniel U. Levine and Robert J. Havighurst. Berkeley: McCutchan Publishing Corporation, 1977, pp. 247–266.

Levine, Hillel and Lawrence Harmon. *The Death of an American Jewish Community: a Tragedy of Good Intentions.* New York: The Free Press, 1992.

Levinsohn, Florence Hamlish. "TV's Deadly Inadvertent Bias." In *School Desegregation: Shadow and Substance,* edited by Florence Hamlish Levinsohn and Benjamin Drake Wright. Chicago: University of Chicago Press, 1976.

Litt, Edgar. *The Political Cultures of Massachusetts.* Cambridge, Mass.: M.I.T. Press, 1965.

Little, Alan N. "Compensatory Education and Race Relations: What Lessons for Europe?" In *Lessons from America: An Exploration,* edited by Richard Rose. London: Macmillan Press Ltd., 1974.

Lockard, Duane. *New England State Politics.* Princeton, N.J.: Princeton University Press, 1959.

Lubbell, Samuel. *The Future of American Politics.* New York: Harper and Brothers, 1952.

Lukas, J. Anthony. *Common Ground: A Turbulent Decade in the Lives Three American Families.* New York: Alfred A. Knopf, 1985.

Lupo, Alan. *Liberty's Chosen Home: The Politics of Violence in Boston.* Boston: Beacon Press, 1988.

Manheim, Jarol B. and Richard C. Rich. *Empirical Political Analysis: Research Methods in Political Science.* Englewood Cliffs, N.J.: Prentice-Hall, Inc., 1981.

Mann, Arthur. *Yankee Reformers in the Urban Age.* Cambridge, Mass.: Belknap Press of Harvard University Press, 1954.

Massey, Douglas S. and Nancy A. Denton. *American Apartheid: Segregation and the Making of the Underclass.* Cambridge, Mass.: Harvard University Press, 1993.

Mayhew, Leon H. *Law and Equal Opportunity: A Study of the Massachusetts Commission Against Discrimination.* Cambridge, Mass.: Harvard University Press, 1968.

McCracken, Grant. *The Long Interview.* Newbury Park, CA: Sage Publications, 1988.

McFarland, Andrew S. "Interviewing Interest Group Personnel: The Little Village in the World." In *Representing Interests and Interest Group Representation,* edited by William Crotty, Mildred A. Schwartz, and John C. Greene. Lanham, Md.: University Press of America, 1994.

O'Connor, Thomas H. *The Boston Irish: A Political History.* Boston: Northeastern University Press, 1995.

———. *Building a New Boston: Politics and Urban Renewal 1950–1970.* Boston: Northeastern University Press, 1993.

———. *Fitzpatrick's Boston, 1846–1866: John Bernard Fitzpatrick, Third Bishop of Boston.* Boston: Northeastern University Press, 1984.

———. *South Boston, My Home Town: The History of an Ethnic Neighborhood.* Boston: Northeastern University Press, 1994.

Orfield, Gary. *Must We Bus? Segregated Schools and National Policy.* Washington: The Brookings Institution, 1978.

———. "Why it Worked in Dixie: Southern School Desegregation and Its Implications for the North." In *Race and Schooling in the City,* edited by Adam Yarmolinsky, Lance Liebman, and Connie S. Shelling. Cambridge, Mass.: Harvard University Press, 1981.

Punch, Maurice. "Politics and Ethics in Qualitative Research." In *Handbook of Qualitative Research,* edited by N. Denzin and Yvonna Lincoln, 80–87. Thousand Oaks, Cal.: Sage Publications, 1994.

Reville, Eugene. "Desegregation as a Tool for Establishing Quality Education." In *Brown Plus Thirty: Perspectives on Desegregation,* edited by LaMar P. Miller, 63–64. New York: Metropolitan Center for Educational Research, 1986.

Rodgers, Jr., Harrell R. and Charles S. Bullock, III. *Coercion to Compliance.* Lexington, Mass.: D.C. Heath and Company, 1976.

Rogers, Everett M. *Diffusion of Innovations.* New York: The Free Press, 1962.

Rubin, Lester, and William Smith. *Negro Employment in the Maritime Industries: A Study of Racial Policies in the Shipbuilding, Longshore, and Offshore Maritime Industries.* 3 vols. Philadelphia: The University of Pennsylvania, 1974.

Rose, Richard. *Lesson-Drawing in Public Policy: A Guide to Learning Across Time and Space.* Chatham, N.J.: Chatham House Publishers, Inc., 1993.

Ross, J. Michael and William M. Berg. *"I Respectfully Disagree with the Judge's Order": The Boston School Desegregation Controversy.* Washington, D.C.: University Press of America, 1981.

Rossell, Christine H. *The Carrot or the Stick for School Desegregation Policy: Magnet Schools or Forced Busing.* Philadelphia: Temple University Press, 1990.

Rubin, Lillian B. *Busing and Backlash: White Against White in a California School District.* Berkeley, Calif.: University of California Press, 1972.

Ryan, Dennis P. *Beyond the Ballot Box: A Social History of the Boston Irish, 1845–1917.* Rutherford, N.J.: Fairleigh Dickinson University Press, 1983.

Schrag, Peter. *Village School Downtown: Boston Schools, Boston Politics.* Boston: Beacon Press, 1967.

Sheehan, J. Brian. *The Boston School Integration Dispute: Social Change and Legal Maneuvers.* New York: Columbia University Press, 1984.

Sheehy, Gail. *Pathfinders.* Toronto: Bantam Books, 1982.

Shelton, Brenda K. *Reformers in Search of Yesterday: Buffalo in the 1890s.* Albany: State University of New York Press, 1976.

Spradley, James P. *The Ethnographic Interview,* New York: Holt, Rhinehart, and Winston, 1979.

Stack, John F. *International Conflict in an American City: Boston's Irish, Italians, and Jews: 1935–1944.* Westport, Conn.: Greenwood Press, 1979.

Stinchcombe, Arthur L. and D. Garth Taylor. "On Democracy and Integration." In *School Desegregation: Past, Present, and Future,* edited by Walter G. Stephan and Joe R. Feagin, 157–186. New York: Plenum Press, 1980.

Taylor, D. Garth. *Public Opinion and Collective Action: The Boston School Desegregation Conflict.* Chicago: The University of Chicago Press, 1986.

Taylor, Jr., Henry Louis. *African Americans and the Rise of Buffalo's Post-Industrial City, 1940 to Present.* Buffalo: Buffalo Urban League, Inc., 1990.

Teele, James E. *Evaluating School Busing: Case Study of Boston's Operation Exodus.* New York: Praeger Publishers, 1973.

Thompson, Hunter S. *Fear and Loathing: On the Campaign Trail '72.* New York: Quick Fox Inc., 1973.

Toch, Hans. *The Social Psychology of Social Movements.* Indianapolis: Bobbs-Merrill, 1965.

Trout, Charles H. *Boston, the Great Depression, and the New Deal.* New York: Oxford University Press, 1977.

Walker, Jack L. "Innovation in State Politics." In *Politics in the American States: A Comparative Analysis,* edited by Herbert Jacob and Kenneth N. Vines. Boston: Little, Brown and Company, 1971.

Whyte, William Foote. *Street Corner Society: the Social Structure of an Italian Slum.* Chicago: University of Chicago Press, 1943.

Woods, Robert A. ed. *Americans in Process: A Settlement Study.* New York: Arno Press and the New York Times, 1970.

Yans-McLaughlin, Virginia. *Family and Community: Italian Immigrants in Buffalo, 1880–1930.* Ithaca, New York: Cornell University Press, 1977.

## Articles from Journals, Magazines, and Nationally Circulating Newspapers

Aberbach, Joel D., James D. Chesney, and Bert A. Rockam. "Exploring Elite Political Attitudes. Some Methodological Lessons." *Political Methodology* (1975): p. 3.

"Boston: An Old City Looks Ahead." *Life,* vol. 18, no. 3 (January 14, 1945): pp. 65–73.

Bruner, Jerome S. and Sheldon S. Korchin. "The Boss and the Vote: Case Study in City Politics." *Public Opinion Quarterly* (spring 1946): pp. 1–23.

Carmines, E. G. and J. A. Stimson. "The Two Faces of Issue Voting." *American Political Science Review,* vol. 74 (1980) p. 78–91.

Carpenter, Niles. "Nationality, Color, and Economic Opportunity in the City of Buffalo." *The University of Buffalo Studies,* vol. 5, no. 4 (June 1927).

Coleman, James S. "Recent Trends in School Integration." *Educational Researcher,* vol. 38, no. 1 (spring 1974): pp. 3–12.

Cornwell, Jr., Elmer E. "Bosses, Machines and Ethnic Politics." *Annals,* 353 (May 1964): pp. 28–39.

———. "Party Absorption of Ethnic Groups: The Case of Providence, Rhode Island." *Social Forces,* vol. 38, no. 3 (March 1960): pp. 205–210.

Crain, Robert L. "Fluoridation: The Diffusion of an Innovation Among Cities." *Social Forces,* vol. 44, no. 4, pp. 466–476, June 1966.

"Freedom-Proud Boston." *Ebony,* vol. 2., no. 5, (March 1947): pp. 9–15.

Gamson, William A. "Rancorous Conflict in Community Politics." *American Sociological Review,* vol. 31 (January 1966): pp. 77–81.

Gatlin, Douglas A., Michael W. Giles, and Everett F. Cataldo. "Policy Support Within a Target Group: The Case of School Desegregation." *The American Political Science Review,* vol. 72, no. 3 (September 1978): pp. 985–995.

Gelman, David. "Backlash in Boston—And Across the U.S." *Newsweek* (November 6, 1967): pp. 29–34.

Gordon, Daniel N. "Immigrants and Urban Governmental Form in American Cities, 1933–60." *The American Journal of Sociology,* vol. 74, no. 2 (September 1968): pp. 158–171.

Grupp, Fred W. and Alan R. Richards. "Variations in Elite Perceptions of American States as Referents for Public Policy Making." *The American Political Science Review,* vol. 69, no. 3 (September 1975): pp. 850–858.

Inger, Morton, and Robert T. Stout. "School Desegregation: The Need to Govern." *The Urban Review,* vol. 3, no. 2 (November 1968): pp. 34–39.

Kelley, Jonathan. "The Politics of School Busing." *The Public Opinion Quarterly,* vol. 38, no. 1 (spring 1974): pp. 23–39.

Key, V. O. "A Theory of Critical Elections." *The Journal of Politics*, vol. 17, no. 1 (February 1955): pp. 3–18.

Kinder, D. R. and D. R. Kiewiet. "Sociotropic Politics: the American Case." *British Journal of Political Science*, vol. 11 (1981): pp. 129–61.

Kovach, Bill. "Republicans Divided and Democrats Face Negro Defections." *The New York Times*, July 15, 1969, p. 34, Column 1.

Longshore, Douglass. "Race Composition and White Hostility: A Research Note on the Problem of Control in Desegregated Schools." *Social Forces*, vol. 61, no. 1 (September 1982): pp. 73–78.

Lubbell, Samuel. "Post Mortem: Who Elected Roosevelt?" *The Saturday Evening Post*, vol. 213, no. 30 (January 25, 1941): pp. 9–11.

Massey, Douglas S. and Nancy A. Denton. "Hypersegregation in U.S. Metropolitan Areas: Black and Hispanic Segregation Along Five Dimensions." *Demography*, vol. 26, no. 3 (August 1989): pp. 373–391.

Merelman, Richard M. "On the Neo-Elitist Critique of Community Power." *The American Political Science Review*, vol. 62, no. 2. (June 1968): pp. 451–460.

"Night at the Pops." *Ebony*, vol. 4, no. 9 (July 1949): pp. 42–44.

Parenti, Michael. "Ethnic Politics and the Persistence of Ethnic Identification." *The American Political Science Review*, vol. 61, no. 3 (September 1967): pp. 717–726.

Pettigrew, Thomas F. and Robert L. Green. "School Desegregation in Large Cities: A Critique of the Coleman 'White Flight' Thesis." *Harvard Educational Review*, vol. 46, no. 1 (February 1976): pp. 1–53.

Rossell, Christine H. "The Buffalo Controlled Choice Plan." *Urban Education*, vol. 22, no. 3 (October 1987): pp. 341–348.

———. "The Carrot or the Stick for School Desegregation Policy?" *Urban Affairs Quarterly*, vol. 25, no. 3 (March 1990): pp. 474–499.

———. "The Effect of Community Leadership and Media on Public Behavior." *Theory into Practice*, vol. 17, no. 2. (February 1978): pp. 131–139.

———. "The Mayor's Role in School Desegregation Implementation." *Urban Education*, vol. 12, no. 3 (October 1977): pp. 247–270.

———. "School Desegregation and White Flight." *Political Science Quarterly*, vol. 90, no. 4 (winter 1975–1976): pp. 675–693.

———. "What is Attractive About Magnet Schools?" *Urban Education*, vol. 20, no. 1 (April 1985): pp. 1–22.

———. and Robert L. Crain. "The Importance of Political Factors in Explaining Northern School Desegregation." *American Journal of Political Science,* vol. 26, no. 4, (1982), pp. 772–796.

Scales-Trent, Judy. "A Judge Shapes and Manages Institutional Reform: School Desegregation in Buffalo." *New York University Review of Law & Social Change,* vol. 17, no. 1 (1989–1990): pp. 130–169.

———. "School Desegregation in Buffalo: The Hold of History." *Harvard BlackLetter Journal,* vol. 7 (spring 1990), pp. 115–118.

Sears, David O., Richard R. Lau, Tom R. Tyler, and Harris M. Allen, Jr. "Self-Interest vs. Symbolic Politics in Policy Attitudes and Presidential Voting." *American Political Science Review,* vol. 74, no. 3 (September 1980): pp. 670–684.

"The '70 Census: How Many Americans and Where They Are." *U.S. News and World Report* (September 14, 1970): pp. 22–25.

Stegner, Wallace. "Who Persecutes Boston?" *The Atlantic* (July 1944): pp. 45–52.

Weinberg, Meyer. "A Critique of Coleman." *Integrated Education,* vol. 13, no. 4 (September-October 1975): pp. 3–7.

White, Arthur O. "The Black Movement Against Jim Crow Education in Buffalo, New York, 1800–1900." *Phylon,* vol. 30, no. 4 (1969): pp. 375–393.

Whyte, William Foote. "Race Conflicts in the North End of Boston." *The New England Quarterly,* vol. 12, no. 4 (December 1939): pp. 623–642.

Wilson, James Q. and Edward Banfield. "Public-Regardingness as a Value Premise in Voting Behavior." *American Political Science Review.* vol. 58. (December 1964): pp. 876–887.

Wolfinger, Raymond E. "The Development and Persistence of Ethnic Voting." *The American Political Science Review,* vol. 59, no. 4 (December, 1965): pp. 908–986.

Wood, Robert. "Professionals at Bay: Managing Boston's Public Schools." *Journal of Policy Analysis and Management,* vol. 1, no. 4. (1982): pp. 454–468.

## Government Documents and Reports of Governmental Proceedings

Alexander, George J. *Civil Rights U.S.A.: Public Schools; Cities in the North and West, 1963, Buffalo.* Staff report submitted to the United States

Commission on Civil Rights. Washington: U.S. Government Printing Office, 1963.

Boston Public School System. "BPS Historical Enrollment Data," 1994.

Congressional Quarterly. *Congressional Quarterly Almanac, 95th Congress, 2nd Session, 1978,* vol. 34. Washington, D.C.: Congressional Quarterly, Inc., 1979.

———. *Congressional Quarterly Almanac, 97th Congress, 1st Session. . . . 1981,* vol. 37. Washington, D.C.: Congressional Quarterly, Inc., 1982.

Massachusetts State Advisory Committee to the United States Commission on Civil Rights. *Report on Racial Imbalance in the Boston Public Schools.* Washington, D.C.: U.S. Government Printing Office, January 1965.

United States Bureau of the Census. Decennial Census Reports: 1940, 1950, 1960, 1970, 1980, and 1990.

United States Commission on Civil Rights. *Desegregating the Boston Public Schools: A Crisis in Civic Responsibility.* Washington, D.C.: Government Printing Office, 1975.

———. *Fulfilling the Letter and Spirit of the Law: Desegregating the Nation's Public Schools.* Washington, D.C.: Government Printing Office, 1976.

———. *Hearing before the United States Commission on Civil Rights: Hearing Held in Boston, Massachusetts,* October 4–5, 1966. Washington, D.C.: Government Printing Office, 1967.

———. *Hearing Before the United States Commission on Civil Rights: Hearing Held in Boston, Massachusetts,* June 16–20, 1975. Washington, D.C.: Government Printing Office, 1978.

———. *School Desegregation in Boston.* Washington, D.C.: Government Printing Office, 1975.

## Newspapers

*Bay State Banner,* 1974–1977, September 18, 1974, November 11, 1977.

*Boston Globe,* 1972–1977, September 8, 1974, September 12, 1974, October 8, 1974, May 4, 1976, March 5, 1995.

*Boston Herald,* December 15, 1994.

*Courier Express,* 1972–1977, 1981, November 12, 1958, November 13, 1958, February 22, 1972, May 10, 1976, September 26, 1976, September 20, 1976, April 1, 1981, May 20, 1981, September 10, 1981.

## Videotape

*Eyes on the Prize II. Program 7, The Keys to the Kingdom, 1974–1980.* Blackside Productions, Inc., 1990, 60 minutes.

## Court Cases

*Arthur vs. Nyquist.* 415 F. Supp. 904 (1976).

———. 429 F. Supp. 206 (1977).

———. 573 F. Supp. 2d 134 (1978).

———. 473 F. Supp. 830 (1979).

———. 636 F. 2d 905 (1981).

———. 514 F. Supp. 1133 (1981).

———. 547 F. Supp. 468 (1982).

———. 566 F. Supp. 511 (1983).

*Brown vs. Board of Education of Topeka.* 347 U.S. 483 (1954).

———. 349 U.S. 249 (1955).

*Green vs. County School Board of New Kent County.* 391 U.S. 430 (1967).

*Keyes vs. School District No. 1, Denver, Colorado.* 413 U.S. 189 (1973).

*Milliken vs. Bradley.* 418 U.S. 717 (1974).

*Morgan vs. Hennigan.* 379 F. Supp. 410 (1974).

*Morgan vs. Kerrigan.* 509 F. 2d 580 (1974).

———. 401 F. Supp. 216 (1975).

———. 530 F. 2d 401 (1976).

*Morgan vs. McDonough.* 548 F. 2d 28 (1977).

*Morgan vs. Nucci.* 617 F. Supp 1316 (D.C. Mass., 1985).

*School Committee of Boston vs. Board of Education et al.* Mass., 227 N.E. 2d 729 (1967).

———. Mass., 292 N.E. 2d 338 (1973).

———. Mass., 292 N.E. 2d 870 (1973).

———. Mass., 302 N.E. 2d 916 (1973).

*Spangler vs. Pasadena City Board of Education.* 311 F. Supp. 501 (C.C. Calif., 1970).

*Swann vs. Charlotte-Mecklenburg Board of Education.* U.S. 402, 1971.

## Unpublished Works

Borowiec, Walter A. "The Prototypical Ethnic Politician: a Study of the Political Leadership of an Ethnic Sub-community." Ph.D. diss., State University of New York at Buffalo, 1972.

Connolly, James. *Reconstituting Ethnic Politics: Boston, 1909–1925,* 1995.

Orfield, Gary. Interview conducted by author on December 1, 1993, Cambridge, Massachusetts.

Rossell, Christine. Interview conducted by author on April 29, 1994, Boston, Massachusetts

## Community Interviews

*Boston*

There were 30 informants interviewed who were affiliated with the Boston school desegregation case, 12 of whom were black, while 18 were white. Of the 12 black informants, four were current or past elected officials, one was a former appointed government official, five were civil rights activists, and two were church officials. Of the 18 white informants, ten were current or former elected officials, three were antibusing activists, one was a former appointed government official, one was a tenant activist, one was a civil rights activist, one was a court official, and one was a church official.

Three of the informants were interviewed through telephone calls in March, April, and May of 1995, while the other 27 were interviewed during the five trips taken to Boston and New York City. The following are the months when the trips were taken to Boston and New York: December 1993, April 1994, October 1994, December 1994, and April 1995.

*Buffalo*

There were 35 informants interviewed who were affiliated with the Buffalo school desegregation case, 14 of whom were black, while 21 were white. Of the 14 blacks, seven were current or former elected officials, two were current or former appointed government officials, and five were civil rights activists. Of the 21 whites, 16 were past or current elected officials, one was an appointed government official, one was associated with the civil rights community, one was an antibusing activist, and two were affiliated with the federal courts.

Three of the informants were interviewed during telephone calls made in January, February, and March of 1995. The 32 in-person interviews were made during five trips to Buffalo. The following are the months the trips were taken to Buffalo: December 1993, April 1994, October 1994, November through December 1994, and May 1995.

# Index

Printed in Great Britain
by Amazon

80723033R20163